Learning In and O

In the World Library of Educationalists series, international experts them-selves compile career-long collections of what they judge to be their finest pieces – extracts from books, key articles, salient research findings, major theoretical and practical contributions – so the world can read them in a single manageable volume.

John MacBeath has spent the past 30 years researching, thinking and writing about some of the key enduring issues in education. He has been involved in advising on policy both nationally and internationally, and has contributed books and articles across topics as diverse as the curriculum, the nature of schooling, homework, self-evaluation and leadership. In this book, John MacBeath brings together many of his most influential writings including chapters from his best-selling books, articles from leading journals, and excerpts from his contributions to the press. Also included are examples of press responses to research reports and to controversial issues.

Starting with a specially written introduction, which gives an overview of John MacBeath's career and contextualises his selection, the chapters cover topics such as:

- Developing skills for life after school
- The talent enigma
- Schools on the edge: responding to challenging circumstances
- Leadership as a subversive activity
- Do schools have a future?

Through this book, readers can follow the themes and strands that John MacBeath has researched and written about over the past three decades, and see his important contribution to the field of education.

John MacBeath is Professor Emeritus at the University of Cambridge, UK.

World Library of Educationalists series

Other books in the series:

Lessons from History of Education
The selected works of Richard Aldrich
Richard Aldrich

Education Policy and Social Class
The selected works of Stephen J. Ball
Stephen J. Ball

In Search of Pedagogy Volume I
The selected works of Jerome Bruner, 1957–1978
Jerome S. Bruner

In Search of Pedagogy Volume II
The selected works of Jerome Bruner, 1979–2006
Jerome S. Bruner

Reimagining Schools
The selected works of Elliot W. Eisner
Elliot W. Eisner

Reflecting Where the Action Is
The selected works of John Elliot
John Elliot

Constructing Worlds through Science Education
The selected works of John K. Gilbert
John K. Gilbert

Learning, Curriculum and Life Politics
The selected works of Ivor F. Goodson
Ivor F. Goodson

Teaching, Learning and Education in Late Modernity
The selected works of Peter Jarvis
Peter Jarvis

Learning In and Out of School

The selected works of John MacBeath

John MacBeath

Routledge
Taylor & Francis Group

LONDON AND NEW YORK

First published 2012
by Routledge
2 Park Square, Milton Park, Abingdon, Oxon OX14 4RN

Simultaneously published in the USA and Canada
by Routledge
711 Third Avenue, New York, NY 10017

Routledge is an imprint of the Taylor & Francis Group, an informa business

British Library Cataloguing in Publication Data
A catalogue record for this book is available
from the British Library

Library of Congress Cataloging in Publication Data
MacBeath, John E. C.
  [Selections. 2012]
  Learning in and out of school : the selected works of
  John MacBeath / John MacBeath.
    p. cm.
  1. Education—Great Britain.   I. Title.
  LA632.M235 2012
  370.941—dc23

                                  2011022574

ISBN: 978–0–415–69295–3 (hbk)
ISBN: 978–0–415–69296–0 (pbk)
ISBN: 978–0–203–15461–8 (ebk)

Typeset in Sabon
by RefineCatch Limited, Bungay, Suffolk

Printed and bound in Great Britain by
CPI Antony Rowe, Chippenham, Wiltshire

CONTENTS

ACKNOWLEDGEMENTS

The publishers would like to thank the following for permission to reprint their material:

The *TES* for permission to reprint *Reflection's Leading Light*, originally published in the *TES*, 15 August, 2008

Forum of Education for permission to reprint *Developing Skills for Life after School*, originally published in *Forum of Education*, Vol. 51, No. 1, April 1996

ISEA for permission to reprint *New Relationships for Old: inspection and self-evaluation in England and Hong Kong*, originally published in *ISEA*, Vol. 34, No. 2, 2006

The *TES* for permission to reprint *Revived by Post Mortems; Briefing; Research Focus*, originally published in *TES Magazine*, 16 April, 1999

The *TES* for permission to reprint Geraldine Hackett, *Inspectors Worthy of Kafka*, originally published in the *TES*, 4 December, 1998

Routledge for permission to reprint John MacBeath and Archie McGlynn, *Should We Sugar Coat the Pill, Miss?*, originally published in John MacBeath and Archie McGlynn, *Self Evaluation, What's in it for Schools?* (London: Routledge, 2002), pp. 110–111

Routledge Journals for permission to reprint *The Talent Enigma*, originally published in the *International Journal of Leadership in Education*, July–September 2006, Vol. 9, No. 3, 183–204

The *TESS* for permission to reprint Neil Munro, *School Leadership Crisis*, originally published in the *TESS*, 6 November, 2009

Scotsman.com for permission to reprint 'Vacancy. Headteacher required 7/24/365 . . .' Originally published on www.scotsman.com, 8 November, 2009, entitled *Heads Need Hearts to Survive in Scottish Schools*

Emerald Group Publishing for permission to reprint *Leadership as a Subversive Activity*, originally published in the *Journal of Educational Administration*, Vol. 45, No. 3, 2007, 242–264

The *TESS* for permission to reprint Neil Munro, *Shame Tactics Don't Work*, originally published in the *TESS*, 6 November, 1998

SAGE publications for permission to reprint *Stories of Compliance and Subversion in a Prescriptive Policy Environment*, originally published in *Educational Management Administration and Leadership*, BELMAS 2008, Vol. 36, No. 1, 123–148

The *TES* for permission to reprint David Marley, *Magic Moments have Disappeared, Experts Believe*, originally published in the *TES*, 17 October, 2008

The *TES* for permission to reprint Josephine Gardner, *Mathematics for All: the way it spozed to be?* Originally published in the *TES*, 27 February, 1998

The *TES* for permission to reprint *TES* editorial, *Chief Inspector Targets Professors*, originally published in the *TES*, 27 February, 1998

Edinburgh University Press for permission to reprint *Do Schools have a Future?* Originally published in T. G. K. Bryce and W. M. Humes (eds), *Scottish Education: Beyond Devolution*, 2008, (Edinburgh: Edinburgh University Press, 2008)

The *TES* for permission to reprint *Hell-Bent on Reform, but who Cared about Teacher Morale?* Originally published in the *TES*, 17 September, 2010

The *TESS* for permission to reprint *Learning from the Learning School*, originally published in the *TESS*, 17 January, 2003

The *TESS* for permission to reprint *Inside the Thinking Brain*, originally published in the *TESS*, 20 June, 1997

The *TESS* for permission to reprint *In the Very Thick of Things*, originally published in the *TESS*, 9 May, 1997

Disclaimer

INTRODUCTION
A life in education

The first sentence counts. Its purpose is to draw you in, to promise something that will repay the investment of time. That is the genius of good storytelling. You expect to be effortlessly engaged and, hopefully, surprised. Academic storytelling, however, generally works to a different convention. Before you get to the first sentence the plot is revealed and the ending given away even before you begin.

So, it is with trepidation that this storyline begins with something as uninspiring as homework, something so familiar to any reader that it inevitably brings back unhappy memories, captured by one prescient teenager as 'a lonely and tedious activity'. Yet, when I embarked on research into homework over two decades ago the story was to end with surprise, with political intrigue, a hint of scandal and a cast of characters which included a once and a future king.

I have to credit homework with putting me on the trail of something far more encompassing and significant than that lonely and tedious activity. The report we produced for the Scottish Education Department we entitled *Learning out of School*, signalling that 'home work' deserved much deeper probing and more intelligent and nuanced understanding than as reported by too narrowly framed research studies. For example, an effect size of .43 for homework, reported by John Hattie's much quoted meta analysis of differential effects on attainment, conceals considerably more than it reveals.[1]

We came to that homework study with the profoundly unsettling experience of previous research commissioned by the Scottish Education Department. Entitled *Home from School*,[2] that 1986 study took us into homes and families, places where we could observe at first hand the contexts in which homework was nested. These visits were sometimes attended with considerable apprehension on our part as to what might lie behind the heavily fortified and graffiti adorned tenement door, not to mention the statutory Alsatian waiting to greet us. Over the course of anything up to three and a half hours of observation and conversation in the home, the focus on homework receded progressively as the reality of children's lives, learning and familial relationships was laid bare.

These indelible experiences shaped how we approached the follow-up study *Learning out of School*,[3] commissioned to offer some practical advice to policy makers on what could be done to make more coherent links between learning in and out of school. Following its publication I was introduced to a Scot in exile, Jock Barr, employed by Prince Charles under the auspices of the Prince's Trust to look for ground breaking educational initiatives in unlikely places. I was to write somewhat lyrically later about the experience of being chauffeured with Jock, very nervously, through dark and mean streets in the Ardoyne in Belfast at the height of the Troubles, suddenly emerging into a pool of light which spilled from St Gemma's School. Inside, over a hundred children and young people were engaged in reading, sharing, playing, talking with teachers, with student mentors or other adults, motivated to return to school for up to three hours of an evening to enjoy a vitally different quality of learning in a relaxed, friendly and stimulating environment.

This visit was the catalyst for a three-year study funded by the Prince's Trust,[4] exploring after-school, weekend and residential approaches to 'out of hours' learning, under the unfortunate umbrella term 'study support'. These initiatives were very much about support in the widest conception of that term but not about 'study' in the narrow sense in which we have come to know it. In the course of working with schools, as their numbers increased and as interest grew exponentially, we identified over 50 different kinds of activities that came under the study support umbrella, from film making to gourmet cooking, spacecraft design to African drumming. These were activities that brought disaffected children and young people back into the main-stream of school life, re-invigorated them and re-ignited an interest in learning. The connection between African drumming and achievement in Maths may seem tenuous but it was one we pursued with interest.

Prince Charles attended a number of the conferences and workshops at which schools celebrated their achievements. These were moving occasions on which chil-dren spoke evangelically about life changing experiences, and in a workshop in Glasgow's then notorious Easterhouse he was presented with evidence of just how much study support meant to these young people living with deprivation and violence on a daily basis. Yet, there was a more strident voice in the wings. It was that of Chief Inspector Woodhead, a confidant of the Prince whose counsel HRH was apparently willing to accept ahead of all the research evidence and the strong steer given to him by his own Prince's Trust advisors. To great dismay within the Trust, the University's research money was withdrawn and an embarrassed DfE took over the funding to allow the study to finish its contracted term.

Less learning and more teaching, extra schooling after hours, more of the same was the proposed remedy, this counsel from someone apparently unable to distin-guish between teaching and learning, as immortalised in his own words, 'Teachers teach and children learn. It's as simple as that.'[5]

There is a definition of insanity as 'doing the same thing over again and expecting different results'. The consistent message of study support over two decades has been the need to distinguish between direct and indirect effects. Direct effects argue for intensification – teaching more to raise attainment. Indirect effects focus on building up self confidence, resilience and learning strategies through activities and relation-ships which may have little obvious connection to the subject in question but affect, and effect, deep learning. African drumming can, by however circuitous a route, increase engagement and achievement in Maths. The evidence consistently shows that indirect effects perhaps take a little longer to get there but pay off in the longer term, whereas force feeding can, at best, lead to surface learning, short term gains and even disaffection with learning itself.

'The only true education comes through the stimulation of the child's powers by the demands of the social situation in which he finds himself.' So wrote John Dewey[6] more than a century ago, a recognition that context matters and that a seat at a wooden desk is not always the most conducive way to engage the mind or the emotions. We were able to show that study support did indeed raise attainment even in the narrowest of terms, the report to the DfE launched by David Blunkett himself in his own Sheffield constituency.

Fast forward to 2011 and the Children's University (CU). Out of school activities offered by 67 centres encompassing 85,000 children provide the most recent expression of what can be achieved by indirect effects when children find themselves in contexts which stimulate thinking, provoke questioning and discussion and celebrate achievement, however embryonic. These 'construction sites' may be museums, art galleries, theatres, science centres, airports, football stadia, places in which there is a structured programme of inquiry with 'outcomes' validated by a stamp in the holder's learning passport. My most recent evaluation, published in 2011, provides further confirmation of raised achievement for children who attend CU and also testimony to the power of the indirect effect. The evaluation contains the following letter from a parent[7]:

> Children's University has been a fantastic experience for all three of our children. They are, as you know, three very different characters and Children's University has inspired and challenged them all.
>
> The experience of Children's University has been, for us, a wonderful learning experience, it has made learning a reality beyond the academic studies and given the children a positive outlook to learning and how '... boring ...' skills can be used in real life.
>
> The children have enjoyed team work and friendship during the exploration of different modules. They have tackled subjects they thought they wouldn't be able to do and faced challenges that took them beyond the comfort zone. But we believe that having taken these challenges in safety and with all the fun of Children's University partner events the children have grown in confidence....
>
> Children's University has helped support our children's learning and widen their world. I wish you all the best for the future and hope that you will be able to support many more children through the experience that is Children's University.

Coincident with my ongoing evaluation of the Children's University is a remarkably similar initiative in Hong Kong. OLE (Other Learning Experiences) are now a mandatory aspect of the curriculum, requiring schools to devote 15 per cent of a secondary student's time to learning in the community, in residential contexts or in focused visits to other countries – to mainland China, Singapore, Australia or beyond. The interim evaluation of OLE[8] contains these words:

> Ultimately it is about learning, inextricable from whole person development and intrinsic to a whole school approach, creating the optimum conditions for young people to be effective communicators, responsible citizens and equipped as lifelong learners.
>
> It is striking the degree to which when asked to record the high points of their school life young people consistently single out experiences beyond the classroom and often beyond the school. There were examples of organisational and leadership skills, implicit in organising an event such as a fair, a competition, a school trip, leading a team, and taking responsibility on behalf of your peers.
>
> As a vehicle for English and Putonghua, for example, it makes the active use of the subject in context much more effective than desk bound study. It also makes an effective bridge between OLE and a core curriculum subject. Not only had English language markedly improved but also grades in exams.

Self evaluation: schools speaking for themselves

In 1986 the publication of *Home from School* had caught the attention of Tory Minister Michael Forsyth who contacted HMCI Archie McGlynn at the Scottish Office and asked him to get in touch with the author with a brief to update the report. While the resulting publication, *Home from School: its current relevance*[9] was not to become a major best seller, it laid the foundations for deeper inquiry into the school effect, addressing the perennial questions – 'What makes a good school?', 'Who knows?' and 'How do they know?' These were the framing questions for a national survey of parental expectations, emanating in a series of four publications in 1990 entitled *Talking about Schools*.[10]

These publications, which identified perceptions and expectations of 'good schools', illustrated just how much could be learned from tuning in to the voices of the key investors – parents – with a right to expect schools to repay their trust and goodwill. Documenting the range of expectations as well as a common core of concerns was the catalyst for further exploration and policy implication. To what extent could criteria for school self evaluation be built from the bottom up, from the perspectives of the key stakeholders?

Commissioned by the Scottish Office to explore the potential of schools to evaluate themselves, my premise was that those best positioned to judge the quality of the school were not only the parents, and not only those who spent their daily lives in classrooms – the teachers, but even more tellingly perhaps those at the sharp end of teaching – the pupils. Pupil 'voice' was becoming a fashionable notion, in part stimulated by the seminal work of Gow and Macpherson in Scotland. Their book *Tell from Me*,[11] published in 1980, was a moving account of what school could mean to those who described themselves in the Gow Macpherson book as 'flung aside, forgotten children'. There were echoes here of the book *Letter to a Teacher*,[12] written by Italian children at the School of Barbiana, describing school as 'a hospital, which tends to the healthy and rejects the sick'.

Yet, 'voice', however compelling, can too easily be ignored, and indeed continues to be silenced by impatient policies which have little time to be distracted from the pursuit of unforgiving targets. Embedding voice within policy, however, was to give it a status and power, to bring to the foreground what pupils, parents and teachers wanted from their schools, what they deemed to be key 'indicators' of good schools, and by which criteria schools should, and could, be 'measured'.

The suite of indicators which developed from exploratory work with 25 Scottish primary, secondary and special schools in the late 1980s was entirely the product of those three stakeholder groups. Many of the indicators were couched in the fresh spontaneous language of the children. For example, 'teachers help you when you're stuck', 'teachers don't give up on you' and 'teachers make you feel clever', criteria with both directness and powerful insight. These children hadn't read about the self fulfilling prophesy or the Pygmalion effect. They invented it all by themselves.

As part of the piloting of questionnaires we provided space for pupils to write in comments, furnishing a wonderful portfolio of observations and anecdotes that would on their own have made a wonderful book. Despite employing a cartoonist whose line drawings were a sharp and humorous complement to the pupil quotes, this was a book that regrettably never saw the light of day. Stored in a cardboard box (in an age when paper was still the primary medium of communication), the cartoons and quotes alike proved to be irresistably tasty morsels for a renegade herd of mice.

Putting 'voice' to the service of school self evaluation and school improvement was to give it a finer cutting edge. While a triangulation of perspectives from pupils, parents and teachers may not provide definitive 'evidence', the congruences and divergences of view from differing standpoints offered a 'tin opener' for further exploration, discussion, development planning and school improvement. So powerful is the potential of those data that when examined openly, sensitively and constructively they can be put to the service of changing the culture, or 'ethos', of a school and its relations with parents and community. And so it was to prove when the process was replicated in over 30 countries over the following two decades.

'Ethos indicators' was the title of guidance documents published by the Scottish Office in 1992.[13] These indicators, developed entirely from expectations of the three groups of stakeholders, were circulated in colourfully produced ring binders to every school in the country with the exhortation not simply to use these criteria and accompanying tools off the shelf but to either adapt them or 'grow your own'. Guidance was given as to how schools themselves could engage children, teachers and parents in creating and taking ownership of measures by which they could judge the quality of school experience. The value and impact of developing indicators from the bottom up was persuasive enough for the National Union of Teachers to suggest an English and Welsh replication of the Scottish study.

The resulting publication *Schools Must Speak for Themselves*[14] in 1999 was to be the first of five books on school self evaluation to be published by Routledge. Later translated into Danish, Greek and Thai, the potential of stakeholder-led self evaluation generated unstoppable momentum with progressively increasing global application.

The origin and dissemination of *Schools Must Speak for Themselves* was largely due to the initiative of John Bangs, then Equal Opportunities Secretary at the National Union of Teachers. Working with him on that publication and in subsequent skirmishes at the Tory Party conferences with then Junior Minister Eric Forth, and on numerous platforms with Chris Woodhead, was primarily owed to John's keen sense of mischief. More importantly, his entrepreneurship was to extend to six further N.U.T. publications, four of these co-authored with my Cambridge colleague Maurice Galton, focusing on the lives of teachers in primary, secondary and special schools and, most controversially, on inclusion policies. *The Costs of Inclusion*[15] was to receive wide endorsement internationally although it met with much less favourable a reception closer to home from our special education colleagues. The thaw in Faculty relations was to take a few months.

The publication of *Self Evaluation in European Schools*[16] extended the protocols of stakeholder expectations to 101 schools in 18 countries. Described by the European Head of Section, Anders Hinkel, as 'the beautiful project', its genius lay in the highly creative team of Denis Meuret from France, Michael Schratz from Austria, Lars Bo Jakobsen from the Commission and myself. Numerous meals and bottles of wine in Brussels bistros were the lubricant for a story which would be told from the perspectives of Serena, a 15-year-old student, her mother, her teacher, the principal of her school and the critical friend to the project.

In Luxembourg, at the first conference at which the beautiful project was presented, a student from Sarah Bonnell school in Newham found herself on a question-and-answer panel facing questions (not all friendly) from the European Association of Teachers. She described how students rallied round before the Ofsted inspection to help 'bury the bodies'. Echoing the words of a teacher, she described the contribution of self-evaluation as 'leading you to where the bodies are buried'.

Bridges across boundaries

'The beautiful project' was picked up by an Italian policy advisor, Francesca Brotto, giving birth to a further European Commission project, 'Bridges Across Boundaries', and resulting in the translation of the book into Italian, Greek, Polish, Slovakian, Czech, Hungarian and Portuguese together with the previously published German version. Its scope and long term benefits received a particular accolade from the European Union.

> The project worked with schools, and other 'end users', whereby these were testing and piloting the approach amongst themselves. Potential exploiters were engaged in the project. In terms of exploitation, there is evidence of continued use of the methodology as well as enquiries from new territories. There is ample evidence of a multiplier effect in terms of take-up by schools. There is also evidence of exploitation in terms of the project promoting policy debates in the partner countries. Interest in the project results continues, suggesting a longer term impact in terms of exploitation.
>
> (Cost-effectiveness Analysis of Dissemination and Exploitation Actions, European Commission, 2008)

The sustainability and continuing impact long after 'Bridges' had been put to bed is owed to Gzregorz Mazurkiewicz in Poland and to Milan Pol in the Czech Republic for whom the project and the EU endorsement gave impetus to major policy thrusts in those countries, while in Slovenia Andrej Koren continues to play a leading role in advocacy and implementation of self evaluation. Self evaluation in that country continues to be a growing movement, widely welcomed by teachers and by policy makers eager to find a quality assurance mechanism with impact and cost-benefit.

Self-evaluation in the Global Classroom,[17] which followed in 2003, extended the compass of stakeholder agency still further to schools in Sweden, Japan, Germany, South Africa and South Korea. This book, the one of which I am most proud, was written entirely by school pupils with the lightest of editing by myself and my Japanese colleague Hidenori Sugumine. The testimony from students as to its deep imprint on their lives and learning was a timely reminder of how the experience of challenging construction sites can change hearts and minds.

> My eyes are now opened to the world I live in … My confidence as a person has grown. My confidence in English has also grown. To speak English has become part of my daily communication and is no longer a problem. The bigger presentation to the Scottish Office and to BP have been great challenges and how well the performances went has increased my self confidence. The year of the Learning School has made me a better person. At least I hope so.
>
> (Jimmy Kartunnen)

The project is briefly described in the final chapter of this volume.

The celebration of student voice and leadership in this global enterprise was convincing enough for HMCI McGlynn to send a policy missive to the Scottish Inspectorate arguing for school pupils to be part of inspection teams. Not long afterwards he was to co-author the third Routledge book (now also in Slovenian and Swedish) *Self evaluation: what's in it for schools?*[18] in which we included a wonderful anecdote from a teacher whose class conducted their own evaluation of the Ofsted team. A short excerpt from that chapter is included under the title 'Should we sugar coat the pill, Miss?', a fine sensitivity to the impact of too critical, and too honest, a report.

The collaborative relationship with HMCI McGlynn set in train a policy thrust which has continued to grow over the subsequent two decades, international in its reach and impact. Appointed by the OECD to chair one of four networks on international indicators, Archie brought me in as a consultant to draw on what we had learned from developments in Scotland and to test their applications on a global scale. We spent three challenging years with delegates from six OECD countries developing, and eventually publishing, *Public Expectations of the Final Stage of Compulsory Education*[19] in 1995, later included in the OECD publication *Education at a Glance* as a complement to international comparative attainment data.

That the choice of venue for our final network meeting was Washington, DC at the time of the World Cup was, of course, purely serendipitous. There are always lessons to be learned as to how decisions are made within policy forums!

Inspection and self evaluation: are they by any chance related?

Working closely with the Scottish inspectorate, with external review in other countries and a somewhat fraught relationship with Ofsted in England, was one source for the publication of *School Inspection and Self evaluation*.[20] Its primary impetus, however, came from a series of national seminars sponsored by the National College of School Leadership which included over 300 headteachers. Chapter 2 of that book is a conversation with David Bell HMCI, a successor to Woodhead. David Bell's views on inspection and self evaluation were refreshingly thoughtful and open to dialogue. As Director of Education in Newcastle, one of the first local authorities to embrace *Schools Must Speak for Themselves* and its policy implications, he was, in conversation, tentative as to the influence and reach of inspection in improving schools, and he is quoted as saying 'I have always been cautious in saying inspection causes improvement because frankly we do not', then quick to add the caveat as to the importance of the collegial conversation around data and classroom observation.

Published in 2006 (and now being translated into Czech) the final chapter of *School Inspection and Self Evaluation* addresses the question 'What can we learn from other countries?', drawing lessons from collaborative initiatives in New Jersey, Quebec, Australia and Hong Kong as well as from countries of Eastern Europe where self evaluation has been particularly influential.

It is in Hong Kong that a decade of evaluation and development of self evaluation has had the greatest impact. It is here that the relationship between self evaluation and external review has probably advanced further and been more receptive to research and critique than in any other country. It is sobering, singular and salutary when policy makers adopt all the recommendations of the researcher. Progressively publication of school results on the web has been withdrawn, requests for documentation drastically slimmed down, greater flexibility introduced for schools' own protocols, review teams sensitised to contextual issues, and continuing workshops held for school leaders and self evaluation co-ordinators.

Considerable investment has been made by the Hong Kong Education Bureau in an Online Interactive Resource (OIR)[21] designed to share good practice territory-wide and to engage school principals, teachers and School Improvement Teams (SITS) in exploring quality, sharing tools of inquiry and speaking for themselves. The making of the OIR stretched over nearly two years involving filming in classrooms, conducting interviews with children, teachers, principals, policy makers and international experts. The editing of 50 plus hours of footage was designed to create short focused excerpts, interactive activities and feedback from a range of international commentators. This was a collaborative venture between myself and the Scottish Interactive Technology Centre at the University of Edinburgh.

The longitudinal evaluation of self evaluation and external review which began formally in 2001 has now been extended to 2014. The second paper in this volume, written in 2006, compares the Hong Kong experience with the New Relationship with Schools in England.

Another country in which the relationship between inspection and self evaluation has matured, and in which policy has been receptive to external review, is New Zealand. In August 2010, I was a member of an OECD review team which visited schools and held over 30 focus groups with young people, parents, teachers, school principals, professional associations and unions, Pacifika and Maori stakeholders. The role of students in self evaluation is explicitly commented on in the report.[22]

> Students have a part to play in evaluating the quality of their school as well as contributing to external review. Including them requires that they are party to the language of assessment, evaluation and review and that they have the confidence to articulate their views as well as their concerns. There is exemplary evidence from schools visited by the OECD team that school leaders and teachers have taken this issue seriously and have equipped their students with the skills and vocabulary to talk to external visitors on achievement and quality issues.

Improving school effectiveness

The power of student voice in self evaluation and in influencing policy at both school and national level was further exemplified in a major three year study in Scotland.[23] In 1997 the Scottish Office put out to tender three research projects, one on ethos, one on development planning and a third on leadership. A telephone call from Peter Mortimore, then Director at the London Institute of Education, suggesting a collaborative bid, persuaded us to go for all three projects in collaboration with a team from the Institute. Described as the first study to bring effectiveness and improvement seamlessly together, the project was also the most ambitious research ever mounted in Scotland. It was in this project with a meticulously drawn sample of 80 schools across the country that the perspectives of pupils, parents and teachers came to assume a critical central space.

While the quantitative data on attainment and value added were *de rigueur*, it was the perceptions and expectations data from the three key stakeholder groups that proved most fascinating, controversial and challenging. One headteacher phoned our Strathclyde office to tell us that we had got the teacher attitudinal data all wrong as she had interrogated every member of staff as to whether they had made such a negative comment and 'hand on heart' they all denied such perfidy!

The employment of a critical friend to work with schools proved to be important in cases where data came as a shock to head teachers, met in in some cases by denial, by rationalisation, or projection of blame on to others. Beyond those first instinctive responses, with support from the critical friend, many of the schools were enabled to move on to address data that were almost always challenging of the status quo.

The power of attitudinal data as tin openers had been brought home to us vividly in the earlier piloting of questionnaires in the 25 schools. As part of the protocol, questionnaire data are fed back to schools which then set up groups of teachers, parents and pupils to discuss the aggregated, and disaggregated, data. So illuminating were these discussions that we made a series of videos to be sent to all schools to demonstrate what could be done to excavate the bald statistics. In one video excerpt an 11-year-old boy is seen leading a group of five other children in exploration of the data. So intelligent and insightful was the conversation and so astute the chairing that when shown to teachers in other schools it drew comments such as, 'It's all right in a school like that but it couldn't happen in an area like this'. In fact the video was shot in the most deprived primary school in Edinburgh and indeed one of the most challenging in the whole of Scotland.

Schools on the edge

The continuous thread of attitudinal data as powerful in its impact came to fruition in another context. In 2001 we tendered for a research project which came to be known simply as SFECC, standing for Schools Facing Exceptionally Challenging Circumstances.[24] This was a high profile DfE initiative designed to show that with adequate resourcing, strong leadership and continuing professional development, even schools in the most dire of circumstances could improve to the point of competing with schools in more privileged circumstances.

The eight schools of the SFECC research were chosen primarily by virtue of their low levels of attainment, the disadvantaged neighbourhoods in which they were sited and what was deemed to be strong leadership, resilient in the face of adversity. In each of these schools there were headteachers seen as capable of turning their schools around. Over a period of three years a Cambridge team followed these eight schools, collecting both attainment and attitudinal data, in the case of young people primarily from focus group interviews. Their voice played an important part in evaluation which is described in the third paper in this volume.

William Atkinson, now Sir William, perhaps symbolises best the heroic turn-around head, appointed to Phoenix School in Hammersmith and Fulham to build something from the ashes of its ill fated predecessor. When appointed as a member of the Government Task Force on Standards in 1997 following Labour's ascendancy to power, William was not there to toe the line, to simply assent to policy dictate. He enjoyed a large measure of idiosyncracy credit with government, leaving him considerable latitude to fly below the radar. Thirteen years later his testimony for our latest Routledge books (*Re-inventing Schools*)[25] brings subversive leadership up to date.

Leadership

Half a lifetime of research into homework, out of school learning, pupil voice and school self evaluation was not the obvious path into my appointment as Chair of Educational Leadership at the University of Cambridge in 2000. On the other hand it could be argued that all of these themes pointed towards the need for inspiration and inspirational people who could breathe life into what in many cases was simply ritual compliance to external mandate.

Most studies of leadership tend to proceed from the top down, from studies of highly influential figureheads, the kind of larger than life individuals studied by Howard Gardner, Napoleon Hill and by the myriad collection of volumes to be found on shelves in the leadership section of bookstores. Approaching leadership from the bottom up, or at least from alternative entry points, allowed a more distributive notion of leadership from the outset.

- The example of leadership cited above by an 11-year-old, evidencing all the skills of which a chair of governors would be envious – listening, probing, clarifying, negotiating, intervening, supporting and challenging and shepherding the group towards a final decision.

- The outstanding example in the Improving School Effectiveness research of Matthew Boyle, the youngest, newly appointed teacher in the school inspiring his senior colleagues in the drive for school improvement, the Head of the English Department and the Deputy Headteacher frequent visitors to his classroom to learn from him.
- The young people from Anderson High School in the Shetland Islands who have led for eight successive years the international project referred to above – the Learning School – travelling the world, researching classrooms, feeding back to school senior management and to policy makers, giving presentations to government bodies and to universities. After one such presentation in Cambridge Jean Rudduck wrote, 'A good example of just what young people can achieve when trusted with a task that is "for real".'[26]

Theirs is also testimony to the vision and leadership of one Stewart Hay, an assistant headteacher in Anderson High School in the Shetlands, who created a network called the Global Classroom in which, through video networking, lessons were shared between schools in different parts of the world. Wanting to push the boat out further, he contacted me with what I deemed to be a venture too far – to take young people from six countries out of their schools for a year, to train them in self evaluation techniques and then to send them round the world on their own to evaluate schools from Sweden to Japan via four other countries. While my first instinct was that he should probably be locked up, eight years later his vision had not only exceeded expectation but had grown to encompass schools and young people from Australia, the United States and England.

I had the opportunity to proselytise about this project to a more receptive king three years ago. At the invitation of Peder Wallenberg, the Swedish philanthropist and funder of much of our Cambridge work, I was a facilitator at two half-day workshops in Stockholm. King Gustaf, Queen Silvia and their grown-up children constituted one of the working groups seated in the carousel arrangement of tables in the library of the Royal Palace. I was able to call on their table for feedback from time to time on the assumption that they would have something to say about leadership. My faith in royalty was at least partially restored by the ease with which a royal family could participate on an even playing field and allow themselves to be directed and advised to stay on task from a commoner such as myself.

Understanding of leadership also comes from probing the dark side, the monumental destruction of lives by world leaders willing to sacrifice their people for the gratification of their own ego. The 15 incompetences identified in Dixon's book *On the Psychology of Military Incompetence*[27] have served me well in workshops with headteachers, teachers and students for whom resonances with their own experience are all too real. Paper II in this volume, presented to the Australian Council of Educational Leaders in 2006, discusses the Dixon book and illustrates some of the parallels with school leadership. It contains the sentence 'leadership is made visible by its explicit failings as well as by its transparent successes' (p. 5).

Those incompetences resonate particularly forcibly with my own experience as a pupil and as a teacher. In both capacities I witnessed the hugely destructive leadership of two rectors' reign of fear, not uncommon in Scotland during the 1950s to 1970s. Despite attaining 100 per cent in Latin in my first year, taught by the rector with belt in hand, any mistake earning on the spot retribution, I was to drop Latin as soon as I could due to its unhappy associations. Discovering years later that I needed a classical language before I could go to university, I taught myself Greek rather than revisit those painful memories. A decade later as a teacher I was not prepared to accept the bullying of another rector, an uncompromising stance which did nothing at the time to further my teaching career.

The brutality of those dark years is almost incomprehensible in the current climate where headteachers' licence has been severely and, mostly justifiably, curtailed. If headship was a sought after job then, that is no longer true. In two studies, one international in compass, the other in Scotland, we identified some of the push and pull factors which underlie what has come to be described as a 'recruitment and retention crisis'.

My 2006 contribution to the *International Journal of Leadership in Education (IJLE)*, reproduced in this volume,[28] was a desk study, a prelude to a Hay-McBer study of headteacher recruitment in England. Entitled 'The Talent Enigma', it calls into question some of the inert ideas as to the nature and creation of 'talent'. It identified 'satisfiers' and 'dissatisfiers' such as stress, workload, accountability, bureaucracy, intensification and lifestyle factors, which account for much of the reluctance of deputies and teachers to apply for the job.

The *IJLE* piece was the catalyst for a recruitment and retention study in Scotland in 2008–9, a major policy study in collaboration between Cambridge, Edinburgh and Glasgow Universities.[29] As with parents who were too busy to give us more than an hour, then two hours later still wished to continue the dialogue, so it was with headteachers who promised no more than an hour, yet would still be deep in conversation two and a half hours later. In both cases, parents and headteachers, the subtext was the loneliness and lack of opportunity to speak frankly and emotionally about the struggles and dilemmas they faced.

How heads coped with pressures from below – pupils and teachers – and pressures from above – insistent policy demands – varied widely according to a number of factors: the socio-economic context of the school, length of experience, marital and domestic status, sources of peer support, the competence of senior colleagues as well as personal strength and resilience. We identified five categories of response to those pressures:

- dutiful compliance
- cautious pragmatism
- quiet self-confidence
- bullish self-assertion
- defiant risk-taking.

In an interview for our most recent Routledge book, *Re-inventing School, Reforming Teaching* David Hargreaves describes creative leaders as 'flying below the radar'. If these heads are subversive they tend to be discreet rather than overt in their resistance. They are closer to the Scottish heads' quiet self confidence than to those we described as defiant risk takers.

How headteachers respond to policy mandate is the theme of Paper 13 in this volume which draws on in-depth interviews with headteachers in the three year ESRC funded study 'Learning how to learn'. The paper's title, written two years before the Scottish study, is 'Stories of compliance and subversion in a prescriptive policy environment'.[30] It has echoes yet again of the struggle between determined resistance and reluctant implementation of government policy. The final few paragraphs of the paper contain this quote from Lejf Moos, 'School leaders can easily find themselves blindsided unless they are able to bring a more critical "reading" to the larger policy context of the leadership activities.'

The way it spozed to be?

There are two papers in this volume – 'The way it spozed to be?' and 'Do schools have a future?' – which may be attributed in part to my own biography but equally to the work of educational heretics, conscientious dissenters and non-conformists. As a prelude to those two papers it is important to establish my own credentials as a heretic and to describe the shaping of my beliefs. The origins of my disaffection are owed primarily to my miseducation as a pupil at the High School of Glasgow in the 1950s and the obliviousness of my fellow pupils to the dire nature of the experiences to which they were subject. It was, for them, simply 'the way it spozed to be'.

That I was unceremoniously released from school and not allowed to attend the final prizegiving or to receive my French and German prize was a result of my constant challenge to the way it spozed to be, to institutionalised bullying, the punitive powers of prefects, the silencing of dissent and the stultifying nature of classroom teaching.

A decade or so on as a Visiting Professor at the State University of New York, I chose as one of my set texts *Selected Educational Heresies*[31], containing excerpts from Socrates to A.S. Neill. I was privileged only to correspond with the latter, up until his death, but I was to visit Summerhill on a number of occasions and to visit many of its American imitators in the heady flower power days of the 1970s. One outcome of those visits was the founding of Scotland's first and only free school – Barrowfield Community School – in the east end of Glasgow, a neighbourhood which taxi drivers and delivery vans refused to enter. Such was the threat of a 'free school' to the educational establishment that I found myself not only banned from any Glasgow Council School but my lectures being proceeded by the disclaimer that 'John MacBeath's views are entirely his own and do not represent the views of Jordanhill College'. I was later to discover that the Scottish Inspectorate kept a voluminous file on the school and, to my surprise, offered a very favourable appraisal.

Inexplicably, I was appointed as one of two independent researchers in the case against Summerhill at the Royal Courts of Justice. I was to peruse a veritable mountain of documents – inspection reports, government guidelines and legalisation, responses from the school, letters to and from parents, newspaper reports, etc. I was also required to attend for the week at the Royal Courts and give testimony. A high ranking Queen's Counsel (QC) Geoffrey Robinson, representing the school, had before him on the podium the book *Schools Must Speak for Themselves*.

Despite being called as 'independent' researchers, the two of us shared the room with the government side and were party to their discussions and alarm calls to the Department and to the Chief Inspector, by day two admitting that 'we' were losing the case. When asked what I was going to say late on day three when I was due to be called there were sudden alarm bells on the part of the government team who famously observed 'But you're not on our side'. It was a further lesson on what possible 'independence' can mean in a high stakes policy arena.

As the government side realised they were not going to win they asked Anna Neill (A.S. Neill's daughter) to accept the verdict of the Tribunal that the government demands be dropped. She could not make that decision, she said, as she was not 'the school' but the caretaker. The court was therefore cleared and the Tribunal bench taken over by three Summerhill pupils with their colleagues – all pupils of the school in the hall – asked to vote on the final decision. This process lasted for one hour until finally the pupils agreed to accept the government climb down. Celebrations followed outside the court while the government team (without me) disappeared hurriedly and without a backward glance.

Why learn maths?

My contribution to the Bramall and White book *Why Learn Maths?*[32] might have passed unnoticed had I not written an article for the *Sunday Times* which was published just prior to HMCI Woodhead's annual Ofsted lecture. Entitled 'Blood on the Tracks', he used the occasion to pillory three academics 'at the heart of the darkness in British education' – myself in the honourable company of Robin Alexander and Ted Wragg.

I continue still to pose the question to anyone who cares to listen and have yet to receive an answer that I find persuasive. The argument is not about numeracy and not about choice but about a compulsory 'core' curriculum and the justifications for its construction. 'The way it spozed to be' seems to be the prevailing rationale. David Hargreaves' response, when I posed the question to the Government Task Force on Standards, was that knowing the square on the hypotenuse etc. helped him to calculate whether or not his ladder would fit into his new garage diagonally. The paper included here posits a situation in which, had you to start from square one in the world as we know it, what would you put in to the curriculum to stimulate, engage and inform young people on their journey to self confident and self directing adulthood?

The larger question 'Why School?', a proposition contained in the volume *Scottish Education*,[33] might be seen as a reaction to my own miserable experience but it is also owed to a lifetime of work with schools, families and communities and with closely observed policy making. Having visited Parkway in Philadelphia, the first 'school without walls' and later its counterparts in Boston and Rochester, New York, and been hugely impressed by the young people I met, I was challenged by Kenneth Richmond of Glasgow University to test the idea in Scotland. Chapter 17 briefly describes the very powerful impact of releasing bored and alienated 14- and 15-year-olds from their schools to learn in 'construction sites' such as hospitals, shops, zoos, museums, orchestras, observatories, Naval bases, farms, the Ambulance Service, the AA, an 'experiment' that could not be repeated in today's risk averse society. Less adventurous perhaps, but the Children's University, OLE in Hong Kong, and other forms of out-of-hours learning owe something to those pioneering explorations of learning beyond schooling.

Finally, Chapter 18, a short article by me, John Bangs and Maurice Galton, revisits many of the recurring themes that cross the decades. It is a postscript to the latest Routledge publication, 'a ripping good read', as Sir William Atkinson declares on the front cover. Taking the lid off policy making, it confirms so much of our darkest suspicions, revealed in the title of Chapter 2, 'There's nothing rational about decision making'.

Notes and references

1 Hattie, J. (2007). 'Developing Potentials for Learning: Evidence, assessment, and progress', EARLI Biennial Conference, Budapest, Hungary. http://www.education. auckland.ac.nz/uoa/education/staff/j.hattie/j.hattie_home.cfm

2 MacBeath, J. (1986) *Home from School*, Glasgow, Jordanhill College.

3 MacBeath, J. (1991) *Learning out of School*, Glasgow, Jordanhill College.

4 MacBeath, J, Kirwan, T., Myers, K, McCall, J., Smith, I. and Mckay, E. with Sharp, C., Bhabra, S., Weindling, D. and Pocklington, K. (2001). *The Impact of Study Support: A Report of a Longitudinal Study into the Impact of Participation in Out-of-school Hours Learning on the Academic Attainment, Attitudes and School Attendance of Secondary School Students* (DfES Research Report 273). London: DfES.

5 Woodhead, C. (2002) *Class Wars*, London: Little, Brown.

6 Dewey, J. (1902) *The Child and the Curriculum*, Chicago, The University of Chicago Press.
7 MacBeath, J. (2010) *Evaluation of the Children's University*, Cambridge, Cambridge University.
8 MacBeath, J. (2007) *Living OLE, 'Other' learning experiences or vital learning for all?* Cambridge, University of Cambridge.
9 MacBeath, J. (1990) *Home from School: its current relevance*, Edinburgh, Scottish Office Education Department.
10 MacBeath, J. and MVA Consultancy (1990) *Talking about Schools*, Edinburgh, HMSO.
11 Gow, L. and Macpherson, A. (1980) *Tell Them from Me*, Aberdeen, Aberdeen University Press.
12 School of Barbiana (1987), *Letter to a Teacher*, Harmondsworth, Penguin Education.
13 Scottish Office Education Department (1992) *Using Ethos Indicators in Secondary School Self-evaluation: Taking Account of the View of Pupils, Parents and Teachers* (School Development Planning Support Materials), Edinburgh, HMSO.
14 MacBeath, J. (1999) *Schools Must Speak for Themselves: The Case for School Self-evaluation*, London, Routledge.
15 MacBeath, J. and Galton, M. with Steward, S., MacBeath, A. and Page, C. (2006) *The Costs of Inclusion*, London: University of Cambridge, National Union of Teachers.
16 MacBeath, J., Jakobsen, L., Meuret, D. and Schratz, M. (2000) *Self-Evaluation in European Schools: A Story of Change*, London, Routledge.
17 MacBeath, J. and Sugumine, H. with Gregor Sutherland and Miki Nishimura and students of the Learning School (2003) *Self-evaluation in the Global Classroom*, London, Routledge, p. 48.
18 MacBeath, J. and McGlynn, A. (2003) *Self-evaluation: What's in it for Schools?*, London, Falmer.
19 McGlynn, A. and MacBeath J. (1995) *Public Expectations of the Final Stage of Compulsory Education*, Paris, OECD.
20 MacBeath, J. (2006) *School Inspection and Self-evaluation: Working with the New Relationship*, London, Routledge.
21 OIR http://hk.sitc.co.uk/2009/E.html
22 Nusche, D., Laveault, D., MacBeath, J. and Santiago, P. (2011) *OECD Reviews of Evaluation and Assessment in Education: New Zealand*, Paris, OECD.
23 MacBeath, J. and Mortimore, P. (2001) *Improving School Effectiveness*, Buckingham, Open University Press.
24 MacBeath, J., Gray, J., Cullen, J., Frost, D., Steward, S., and Swaffield, S. (2007) *Schools on the Edge: Responding to Challenging Circumstances*, London, Sage.
25 Bangs, J., Galton, M. and MacBeath, J. (2010). *Re-inventing Schools, Reforming Teaching: From Political Vision to Classroom Reality*, London: Routledge.
26 MacBeath, J. and Sugimine, H. with Gregor Sutherland and Miki Nishimura and students of the Learning School (2003) *Self-evaluation in the Global Classroom*, London, Routledge, p. 65.
27 Dixon, N. (1994) *On the Psychology of Military Incompetence*, Pimlico, Amazon.
28 MacBeath, J. (2006) The Talent Enigma, *International Journal of Leadership in Education*, July–September 2006 Vol. 9, No. 3, pp. 183–204.
29 MacBeath, J, Gronn, P., Opfer, D., Lowden, K., Forde, C., Cowie, M., O'Brien, J. (2009) *The Recruitment and Retention of Headteachers in Scotland*, Edinburgh, Scottish Government.
30 MacBeath J. (2008) Stories of compliance and subversion in a prescriptive policy environment, *Educational Management, Administration and Leadership*, 35 No. 1, 123–148.
31 Neill, W.F. (1969) *Selected Educational Heresies*, Glenview, IL: Scott, Forsemman and Co.
32 Bramall, S. and White, J. (2000) *Why Learn Maths?* London, Institute of Education, Bedford Way Papers, pp. 120–130.
33 MacBeath, J. (2008) Do Schools Have A Future? in T. Bryce and W. Humes, *Scottish Education: Third edition Post-devolution*, Edinburgh, Edinburgh University Press.

CHAPTER 1

REFLECTION'S LEADING LIGHT

Originally published in the *TES*, 15 August, 2008

All heads and teachers know about self-evaluation. It runs through school life, encompassing not only Ofsted's statutory requirements, but also ideas about departmental self-review, pupils as independent learners, positive engagement with parents and, of course, pupil voice.

But how many know the extent to which its growth, and the movement away from confrontational top-down inspection, can be largely credited to one professor of education and his team?

John MacBeath, chair of educational leadership at Cambridge University since 2000, was formerly director of the University of Strathclyde's Quality in Education Centre. It was there in the late 1980s that he and his colleagues developed a framework for school self-evaluation acceptable both to schools and to those responsible for them.

Professor MacBeath's evangelical belief in self-evaluation is of a piece with his broader conviction that children and teachers learn best when they have freedom to shape their learning together in the classroom. It is a philosophy that harks back to his roots: first as a pupil in Glasgow ('We had so much to say about the quality of our school and never had a chance to say it') and later as a teacher at Paisley Grammar School.

These experiences led him, as a lecturer at the then Jordanhill College in the early 1970s, to set up the Barrowfield Community School, a democratically organised haven and learning centre for 25 disaffected and excluded children in Glasgow.

'It was very influential for me,' he says. 'I saw how much even the lowest achieving children could contribute, and how passionately interested they were in their education when given the freedom to pursue their own interests.'

Over the years, that conviction became the driver for producing, at Strathclyde, a workable and effective set of tools for school self-evaluation. In the early 1990s, it was taken up by the Scottish inspectorate and became the nationwide system of self-evaluation known as 'How Good is Our School?' – today familiar to all Scottish teachers as HGIOS.

In England, however, government through the early 1990s remained ideologically and explicitly committed to the need to tackle failing schools from the outside. Preferring the 'big stick and little carrot' approach, they went for Ofsted and 'naming and shaming'.

But change was afoot. The early Ofsted model was expensive and unwieldy, and evidence from Scotland and around the world showed that self-evaluation really did work as a way to improve teaching and learning. Arguably, though, the drive to convert English national and local government to self-evaluation only really took off when the National Union of Teachers (NUT) committed its political experience and negotiating skills to the cause. Seeking a positive, practical and academically credible alternative to the Ofsted way, NUT education secretary John Bangs commissioned Professor MacBeath to replicate his Scottish work in a 1995 report: Schools Speak for Themselves.

Presented to the main party conferences in 1996, the document was treated with contempt by Conservative junior education minister Eric Forth, who threw away a prepared speech in order to castigate it. But by then local authorities were already adopting Schools Speak for Themselves as the developmental framework for schools that they were looking for. Newcastle's director of education David Bell, later to become chief inspector of schools and now permanent secretary at the Department for Children, Schools and Families, became an active enthusiast, seeing the framework introduced across Newcastle schools.

Then Labour came to power in 1997 and committed Ofsted at least to the beginnings of a form of self-evaluation, starting the journey that has brought school inspection to the present 'light touch' system based on the Self Evaluation Form (SEF). For Professor MacBeath, though, it is all a very long way from 'job done'. Today's self-evaluation is, for him, still 'top-down'. What he would like, clearly, is for schools to look beyond making periodic checks on their performance, and instead to ask themselves constantly: how good is our learning?

'If that becomes a way of thinking, then you don't need this ritual approach of questionnaires and interviews,' he says.

All of that, far-reaching though it is, tells only part of the John MacBeath story, because his expertise in – and desire to learn about – self-evaluation has led to his ideas and writings being sought by dozens of schools and governments across Europe and the rest of the world. Of all those projects, he singles out as particularly satisfying his work on developing self-evaluation in the traditionally authoritarian Hong Kong school system. He points to the development of a government website showing how various schools have put their own approaches to self-evaluation into practice. His favourite bit of video shows a 10-year-old girl describing with clarity and insight – and in English – the importance of 'learning how to learn'.

Deep down, Professor MacBeath is undoubtedly a radical. 'I believe that we are failing schools, failing teachers and failing children by too much prescription, too much pressure, stunting the capacity for growth and creativity,' he says.

Others have said that, too, over the years. But Professor MacBeath, rather than preach the revolution, has focused on producing a way to improve schools that both respects his philosophy and actually works within the system as we have it.

'I've seen self-evaluation's transformational power in 30 countries where I have worked with teachers and young people,' he says. 'I've seen them responding to the trust invested in them, almost always surpassing expectation, relishing the freedom to craft their own approaches to what they see as worth evaluating and worth improving.'

It is a common characteristic of the thinkers in this TES series that, working always with the evidence, they have turned theory that was some-times unconventional, sometimes politically risky, into solid and acceptable practice. Professor MacBeath is firmly in that mould.

John Bangs sums it up: 'He has provided a very rigorous but teacher-sympathetic balance to the top-down, data-driven school improvement approach. But at the same time, he has retained massive respect from the Government. John really has, in a very quiet and strong way, made a massive difference and knocked off many of the rough edges of government policy.'

Further reading

School Inspection and Self-Evaluation: Working with the New Relationship by John MacBeath (Routledge, 2006)

Self-evaluation in the Global Classroom by John MacBeath and Hidenori Sugimine (Routledge, 2003)

Self-Evaluation in European Schools: A Story of Change by John MacBeath, Michael Schratz, Lars Jakobsen and Denis Meuret (Routledge, 2000, now published in 16 European languages)

CHAPTER 2

DEVELOPING SKILLS FOR LIFE AFTER SCHOOL

Originally published in *Forum of Education*, Vol. 51, No. 1, April 1996

Homework has traditionally been defined in very narrow terms and surrounded by ambivalence about its purpose and effects. Research and development work carried out in Scotland in the early 1990s suggested that bridging the hiatus between learning in the classroom and at home could make learning more meaningful not only to children but to their parents. When the profile of homework was raised a number of national initiatives followed, the most promising of which has been 'supported study', a vehicle for addressing the needs of the most disenfranchised group. One of the unexpected benefits of supported study has been to offer a 'laboratory' for teachers to learn about how children learn and how they might be taught more effectively in and out of school.

When we embarked on research into homework in the late 1980s we came to it with some of the assumptions that we are now quick to challenge when expressed by teachers. We were ambivalent about the value and purposes of homework, and dubious about its significance in terms of school effectiveness. Indeed 'school effects research' was itself ambivalent on the subject with some researchers finding homework an important factor (Bosker, 1995) and others less convinced (Borger, 1984). However, when we began to probe a little more deeply into the subject we began to raise questions which we had previously given little thought to.

The most forceful challenge to our thinking came when the focus of our research moved from the school and classroom into home and community. Carrying out interviews, usually during the evening, in someone's living room, over the course of two or three hours provided more than just a set of parental views on the subject. The interviews were set in the context of ongoing family life, its patterns and rhythms, often with comings and goings of children and their occasional interjections into the conversation. It gave us an insight into the nature of relationships, the ethos within which children did their homework and how work home from school was embedded in a wider approach to life and learning.

Those experiences with children and families made it less easy for us to separate out 'homework' as a discrete phenomenon and explains why we entitled our research report 'Learning out of School' (1992).

Homework can, of course, be quite simply defined as the pieces of work which teachers prescribe for children to do in their own time, but it became increasingly obvious to us that the meaning and context of that work is the crucially significant factor. When we looked more closely at those contextual influences we could see the connections between micro and macro, between homework and the 'non-school effects' which have preoccupied researchers since Coleman (1966) and Jencks (1972).

The contextual home effect can be seen most clearly at the age of 5 or 6 when children bring their first homework home, their tin with its five or six selected words, the three pages of the first reader or three sums. The time given to that by adults or older siblings, the quality of the interaction, the expectations which encompass it are the factors which begin to stretch the difference between those who are going to succeed and those who are not. These are by no means the only factors which ultimately separate success and failure but there are few who would now dispute the growing body of evidence on the power of the parent as educator (Epstein and Dauber, 1991).

The debate has been conducted for the last three or more decades in terms of social class. School effectiveness researchers took up the issue where the sociologists and ethnographers left off, seeking to demonstrate that 'good' schools could indeed compensate for social and economic disadvantage, and intent on disproving the Coleman/Jencks thesis that schools can have no more than a marginal influence in comparison with the birthright of social class. Despite the catchy titles—*Schools Can Make a Difference* (Brookover, 1979), *School Matters* (1986)—there is a continuous thread running that work that has socio-economic status remains by far the most powerful correlate of achievement.

Assumptions about social class effects have, however, been held up to question by work such as that of Feuerstein (1990). Successful learners, according to Feuerstein, are successful because of the way in which their learning is mediated by effective adults—adults who have the time and the relationship in which to support the individuality of the learning process. He cites the example of children brought up in conditions of extreme poverty, without formal teaching and virtually written off by the school system. A child's ability to make rapid progress when given the opportunity he puts down to a background of adult mediation between child and environment, helping the child to make sense of the world and so to be in the appropriate 'frame of mind' to make equal sense of school learning. In Vygotsky's terms (1981) this would be described as the meeting point of 'spontaneous' and 'scientific' learning.

Peter Hannon (1993) has argued that parents can be, in some important respects, more effective teachers of reading than school teachers. He concludes from his own research that:

- pre-school teachers seriously underestimated the value of parental support for children's reading;
- the quality of children's experiences reading to their parents were in some respects superior to what happened in school;
- home readings were longer and had fewer interruptions than reading sessions in the classroom;
- parents' relationship with children allowed them to relate what they were reading to children's experience;
- teachers used praise more but it was often a mechanism of control and a reflection of their more distant relationship with the child.

There is an irony in the announcement by the British Shadow Education Minister in October 1993 of a new Labour policy for homework which would start at the age of 7. Perhaps there is, underlying that view, a confusion between homework and home work, what children do for their teachers as against what parents do for their children.

We found, in our study, children who taught their younger pre-school siblings so that they came to school not only able to read but confident self-assured learners. We did not conduct a longitudinal study to follow young people as they moved up the school but cross-sectional slices of children's and families' experiences at different ages and stages suggested that the parental relationship and the home learning context continued to exert a powerful but changing form of influence (MacBeath and Turner, 1992).

We asked young people at different stages to keep a detailed log for one week documenting what they did, who with, and how long they spent on it. We also asked them to record their feelings, their completion or incompletion of the task and their level of frustration or satisfaction. At one extreme there were young people who had private tutors in a range of secondary school subjects and at the other extreme young people who, left entirely to their own devices, invested huge amounts of time on ineffective unfocused copying or reading, struggling to make their own sense of the printed page or giving up at the first hurdle. Some had the physical and psychological space, encouragement and support from parents or peers who knew little about the subject matter but had a lot of good sense about timing and pacing and strategies for finding out. Some lived in conditions which crowded out all possibilities for school-related learning.

We also found that schools tended to know very little about the context for children's learning out of school and learned a great deal from the log-keeping exercise. Reading those logs some teachers were sceptical of pupils' claims to have spent four to five hours on a Sunday especially when they then matched this evidence with the name of the pupil on the log. Their scepticism arose from their knowledge of the pupil in the classroom. Or they tried to match that evidence of time spent with a commensurate pay-off in achievement. Yet in interviews with parents and pupils there was usually strong confirmation of the accuracy of the logs and explanations of why the benefits of independent study were often minimal in relation to the costs.

There were three main kinds of explanation at the in-school end and three at the out-of-school end:

In school

- unclear formulation and communication of the task by the teacher;
- unhelpful patterns, timing and distribution of work within the school as a whole;
- failure to use homework as an effective bridge between learning in and out of school.

Out of school

- lack of clarity of purpose and continuity of the task;
- lack of support, reinforcement and feedback at critical points;
- lack of strategies for effective learning.

Some issues could be addressed relatively easily. Homework could be communicated more effectively, not as an afterthought while the bell was ringing and pupils were exiting the classroom both mentally and physically. It could be planned and integrated into courses in advance rather than as a finishing-off of class work, a still common practice not only iniquitous but suggestive of bad planning and lack of differentiation. Primary schools could build some progression up through the school and secondary schools could ensure some horizontal co-ordination across different departments.

Most fundamentally, though, the evidence pointed to a hiatus between class work and homework, and an underlying failure on the part of the school to think through what that relationship might be. While learning *in* school had apparently become more varied, more differentiated and more imaginative, learning *out* of school seemed to be stuck in a time warp. Classroom learning was often stimulating and inventive; pupils worked in pairs and groups and discussed and shared what they were doing. In the evening work at home was, as one boy put it, 'a lonely and tedious activity'. Homework tasks were not given the same thought as to the needs and context of the learner nor to coherence and progression of learning.

Advice to young people and their parents often betrayed a lack of under-standing of the character of children's learning out of school. Advice to pupils and parents typically advocated a quiet place to work, a desk and a desk light, an upright chair, a place free from interruptions. Young people were encouraged to plan their time over the week, a timetable beforehand, a routine of work in the early evening or after school. These admonitions failed to reflect the reality of young people's lives. Like adults, young people worked in a variety of ways and places and at times which suited their domestic routines or personal biorhythms, or fitted the geography and social composition of the home.

Something like half the sample of pupils worked to a background of loud music. They eventually persuaded initially sceptical researchers that it actually helped them to concentrate. It created a sound barrier between them and the outside distractions of half-heard conversations, television, phones and doorbells ringing, parents and siblings arguing. Parents' graphic descriptions of opening the bedroom door to find their child 'sitting behind a wall of noise' was a piece of convincing imagery. Some described how distracting the utter silence of a library could be when each shuffle and drop of a pencil became resounding events.

The response from schools to the publication of the study demonstrated clearly that homework was seen both as important but also a contentious and complex issue for teachers and school management. Many of the issues raised seemed to touch the very heart of learning and teaching and could only be addressed through long-term development and a change of expectations on the part of teachers, parents and pupils.

The commissioning by the Scottish Office Education Department (SOED) of a further study came as a response to that widely expressed view. How could schools address the differing expectations of those three key constituencies? How could they be brought into the process of policy development? How could schools monitor something which was outside their jurisdiction and to which they could not by law apply sanctions?

For a period of two years we worked with ten schools in very different rural and urban contexts in different parts of Scotland. The object of the exercise was to support them in developing policy, addressing the thorny questions and documenting for the benefit of other schools the process involved. Two examples, one from a primary school and one from a secondary, illustrate how two of the most difficult of issues were dealt with.

A primary school

In Aberdour Primary School in a region of Scotland still bearing the name 'the Kingdom of Fife' a parent evening was planned to address the issue of continuity in the quality of what pupils did at home and what they did in school. Aberdour parents, like parents all over Scotland, supported the practice of homework but had spent little, if any, time in thinking through the criteria by which the quality of homework might be judged. Homework was self evidently, a good thing.

A meeting was arranged for parents with a three line whip to attend together with the inducement of wine, cheese and other goodies at the end of the evening. The invitation to the meeting also promised feedback on the homework questionnaires which parents had filled out a few weeks before. As they entered the school hall parents were given a sheet of paper and asked to study the large sheets on the wall and write their response to the items and questions there. One contained various descriptors of homework—'exciting, really fun, mundane, horrible, tiring, nice when Mum helped'. The parents' task was to guess the source of the adjectives—parent or pupil. Another had lists of tasks (also drawn from pupil and parent questionnaires) describing examples of homework, again asking them to say whether they came from a parent or child. Examples included 'We made puppets at home and then made up plays about them', 'We had to go home and with our parents to make a list of spices in the cupboard', 'Finding out how many inches there were in the Forth River'.

After some discussion of the issues arising from that exercise parents circulated in groups around a series of tables, trying out a range of different classroom activities set out on each. The tasks had been selected carefully to be enjoyable and challenging and were all patently about learning. Before leaving the activity and moving on to the next table the group was asked to record their rating for the interest and value of the activity and to write a few key words on the skills they had used in undertaking the task set.

This was followed by a discussion which attempted to tease out from the activities some of the principles of learning, considering how these could be applied to homework. Parents were then referred back to their own descriptions of homework and the things they had enjoyed and benefited from as children. This gave the basis for arriving at a shared understanding of purposes and principles and offered a useful base on which to construct a programme of monitoring and evaluation. The term homework was ditched in favour of School Home Activity Research Exercises, or SHARE.

For us as researchers this provided an interesting contrast with another primary school. In this school parents were invited in for the same kind of purpose but the evening started with a brainstorming session in which the headteacher asked for, and wrote down on a flip chart, all the things that parents expected of the school in terms of homework. It provided her with a list of all the things she did not want—two pages of reading, five spelling words, ten sums. Perhaps it should have been foreseen that parents, without a stimulating menu, would reach back into their own experiences of home-work. Having consulted parents on their wishes this headteacher effectively painted herself into a corner from which she could not easily escape without some material damage.

A secondary school

The secondary school, situated just to the south of Scotland's capital city, also came to the issue through an audit of parents', teachers' and pupils' views, conducted by sampling each of those three constituencies and carrying out individual and group interviews. One of the main issues for parents was the drop off in the quantity of homework between the end of primary and the first year of secondary. They also worried about the variability from teacher to teacher and class to class. The complaint that 'my eleven-year-old works two hours a night while her older brother does little or no homework' was a fairly common one. Interviews with pupils confirmed their parents' accounts.

The summary and analysis of the interviews were fed back to the learning effectiveness working party of teachers who came to the conclusion that, although for them there were bigger issues than those raised by parents, the big issues would be arrived at through addressing the immediate concerns of parents. It was agreed by the working party that a coherent effective whole school approach was an ambitious and long-term aim, and that the starting point should be with the new intake of pupils and parents at Secondary 1. Entitlements of pupils, parents and teachers could then be made part of a 'compact' from day one setting expectations that would, hopefully, be sustained as that cohort moved up through the school.

The school succeeded in getting 90% of the parent body to attend an evening meeting at which the issues were discussed. Parents were divided into small working groups and given a number of tasks, addressing the three issues of time, continuity and equity, but at the same time opening up other problems such as monitoring, supervision and support. Each group included one or two teachers who contributed as other members but discouraged the group to turn to them as experts. After feedback from the small groups and discussion of their findings in plenary each group was asked to draw up, on large poster paper, a three column set of entitlements—for pupils, parents and teachers.

This formed the basis for the working out of a charter and a commitment to try and respect its principles. It was agreed, for example, that pupils were entitled to homework that was engaging, challenging, at their level of ability and which fed into and enhanced what they learned in the classroom. They deserved to know well in advance what they had to do, and why, and they were entitled to feedback and help on completed work. Parents were entitled to similar kinds of information, as well as to advice on what they could do to support their children, where and how they could get help and what redress they had when entitlements were not being met. Teachers were entitled to some specific forms of communication and support from parents, co-operation from pupils in completing and preparing work and taking responsibility for supporting and informing their classmates.

As well as the *entente cordiale* and a basis for effective learning and teaching, the initiative had more far-reaching benefits. It opened up a dialogue, a channel of communication and a relationship on which to build for the future. For all concerned it sharpened awareness of the relationship between learning in, and out of, school and brought a new focus to the quality of learning and teaching in the classroom.

Taking the issues further

This development work was followed by a number of significant national and local initiatives. The profile of homework, home study and out-of-school learning was raised at national and local authority level. Policies were developed, and homework became more firmly established and embedded in development planning and quality assurance procedures. The Scottish Office Education Department (SOED) financed the production and national distribution to all schools of *The Homework File*—a set of support materials with guidelines on developing policy, auditing, evaluating quality, supporting independent learning, communicating with and involving parents. The reception for the File from schools suggested it had met a real need at school and classroom level and was widely regarded as one of the most successful ever productions by the SOED.

Perhaps the most far-reaching initiative, whose potential is yet to be fully grasped, came from Scotland's largest local authority—Strathclyde—and went under the name of 'supported study'. Its purpose was to provide support for the most disadvantaged and disenfranchised young people in the city of Glasgow and surrounding rural and island areas where poverty took different forms but resulted in the same kind of educational failure.

In a time of severe cutbacks the Regional Council's Anti-poverty Strategy Group set aside half a million pounds to be spent on a pilot initiative in a dozen or so schools. Schools were encouraged to devise their own ways of reaching the most disadvantaged of their pupils for whom studying at home was made impossible by physical conditions or a large number of younger siblings. The most common form of provision was opening classrooms and resource centres during the late afternoon or evening. Some schools ran residential weekends, weeks, or summer schools. Most employed selected teachers as tutors. Some involved parents, community volunteers, university students or senior school students as supervisors or mentors.

Nearly five years on from that pilot scheme 150 schools in the Region are running supported study schemes, costing Strathclyde one and a half million pounds a year. Depending on the approach taken by the individual school, they have reached anything from 10% to 50% of the school population or, when aimed at a specific cohort (11-year-olds or 16-year-olds, for example), anything up to 100%. The evaluation of the scheme after its first year of operation (MacBeath, 1992) pinpointed some of the benefits from the point of view of young people involved:

It is free from distractions
For some young people it was an oasis of peace which they could not find at home. Just to be free from distractions and counter attractions was a big plus:

> It's wonderful, it's so peaceful and calm. Nobody shouts. It's not like school or home.

> You cannae get distracted. The phone always goes at home.

> You don't get the disruptive elements.

It is a place for work
Some pupils emphasised that it encouraged them to work. It supplied not just a place but a set of attitudes to go with it. It was a working environment. It 'makes you work':

> I need something to make me work. It is just the place, the way it is.

> You get in the mood for working. It just feels like that. Everyone else is working and there's no one pressuring you but you just do it because you're there.

There are books and stuff
Some young people placed most emphasis on the fact that this was a place where you get books, materials or computers which made school work easier or more rewarding:

> You can get things you don't have at home and that makes you feel a wee bit more secure in what you are doing.

> Having computers and stuff makes it less of a drag. You enjoy it more because you can do it on the Apple Mac and see it nicely printed an' that.

There are teachers there to help you
Some pupils, often who normally did homework without the existence of after school classes, particularly appreciated the quality of help from teachers:

> I don't mind working at home, but the thing I like most is that teachers here seem to understand more and help you more than in the classroom. They are more sympathetic to you if you canny understand anything.

> If you get stuck you can talk it out with them. At home you'd be just be getting stuck and all frustrated.

You can work with your pals
One of the biggest differences between supported study and normal home work was the social context in which it took place. Young people tended to come to sessions with their friends, in twos or threes. They sat together and sometimes helped each other with work but sometimes just enjoyed the company. The fact that someone else was working away alongside you, in a sense validated what you were doing:

> I always come with my pals. We chat away sometimes but most of the time we just do our own work because it's sort of a club and the members of the club are all doing the same thing, so it's O.K.

From a young person's perspective there were some clearly identifiable benefits of supported study. A warm comfortable place free from distractions, a pleasant social environment and—the icing on the cake—teachers there to help you when you were stuck. In most respects it did no more than replicate the ideal conditions of a supportive family.

Developing the concept

In the early days targeting of supported study tended to be aimed at the 16- to 17-year-olds about to sit exams. It was an important and useful support for them at a difficult time and resulted in some marked improvements in examination attainment. In a context where exam results are published nationally this is an important gain for individual schools; nonetheless supported study schemes have, from often quite conservative beginnings—homework classes, subject tutoring—become more adventurous. They are now tackling issues closer to their roots, trying to help young people to develop more effective learning styles and strategies, helping them to revise more economically and become more creative and proactive in their approach to learning.

Innovation and development for new ideas has received strong support from The Prince's Trust. Prince Charles himself has taken a personal interest, visiting some of the schools and attending seminars and conferences on the subject. In 1993 the Trust produced a set of resource materials for schools and community organisations on how to initiate, organise and evaluate supported study (Prince's Trust, 1993). It is currently asking for imaginative bids from schools and other community or business agencies on how to push the concept still further.

Supported study as staff development

Supported study has typically offered a dynamic form of staff development for teachers involved, demonstrating an alternative view of teacher–learner relationships and helping teachers to develop a more learner-centred perspective. By discussing with young people their homework tasks and approaches to learning secondary teachers became aware, usually for the first time, of what their colleagues expected by way of homework. Having to take a learner's perspective on the tasks set was, in itself, a salutary lesson. A tutor's brief was set out in the Strathclyde Region report at the end of the first year's pilot (MacBeath, 1993):

- free young people from distractions
- ensure a comfortable motivating environment
- identify, or create useful books/study guides
- set boundaries for behaviour
- be alert to when help is needed
- have patience
- offer encouragement
- structure learning and help to set targets
- encourage self-assessment
- reward progress and achievement
- get to know the young person as an individual
- share something of yourself as a person
- be available
- be willing to listen
- suspend judgement.

This list describes perhaps no more than what good teachers do as a matter of course, or indeed how good parents support their children's learning. In a sense supported study offered a laboratory in which teachers had the time and space to reflect on and evaluate these behaviours. The acid test is how much of this feeds back into school policy and into daily classroom practice. This is the challenge currently facing schemes which are growing at an accelerating pace across the country. Their potential will be limited to the degree that they develop, or fail to develop, an approach which genuinely empowers young people to become effective learners, not just up until examination day, but for life.

Supported study and learning

In Entwistle's epistemology (1987) young people need to become both 'strategic' and 'deep' learners, able to have at their fingertips a range of tricks and techniques for passing examinations, a conceptual facility with ideas, and a meta-cognition which guides them when to use one, the other, or both, strategies.

Study support for young people in the year before they embark on their exams is likely to be guided by pragmatism. It is likely to encourage the adoption of a strategic approach to acquiring the necessary bank of information and an efficient withdrawal system for short-term memory. Study support at a much younger age, at primary school level even, can afford a longer-term view. It can take a learner-centred view and build bridges into, and out of, the classroom. There are those who argue that ultimately study support should wither away as schools become more effective learning organisations and outgrow the need for the prop, or compensatory function, that study support currently serves.

Supported study has, in a number of schools, offered a strong and direct challenge to mainstream practice and caused teachers to take a longer, harder look at how they teach and what they expect of young people after the teaching is over. Yet, however much schools improve their pedagogy, there will probably be a growing need to focus on how young people learn outside school. Ivan Illich's 'convivial networks' for learning (1971) are becoming a reality in the 1990s in the shape of Internet and other instant information systems. They will offer as yet unimaginable opportunities for learning exchange which will inevitably increase the power of those who master the medium, and further open the gap between them and the disenfranchised. Study support with an emphasis on learning and information skills may come to play an even more significant role in that future, but in what form will depend on how prescient teachers, researchers and other policy visionaries are. If we are not that forward-looking, schools may suddenly be overtaken by the future.

References

Borger, J. B. *et al.* (1984). Effective schools: A quantitative synthesis of constructs. *Journal of Classroom Interaction*.

Bosker, R. *et al.* (1995, January). *Foundational studies in school effectiveness.* International Congress for School Effectiveness and Improvement, Leeuwarden.

Brookover, W. *et al.* (1979). *School social systems and student achievement; Schools can make a difference.* New York: Praeger.

Coleman, J. *et al.* (1966). *Equality of educational opportunity.* Washington D.C.: US Government Printing Office.

Epstein, J. & Dauber, S. L. (1991). School programs and teacher practices of parent involvement in inner-city elementary and middle schools. *The Elementary School Journal, 91*(3), 289–305.

Entwistle, N. (1987). *Understanding classroom learning*. London: Hodder and Stoughton.

Feuerstein, R. *et al.* (1990). *Instrumental enrichment: An intervention programme for cognitive modificability*. Baltimore: University Park Press.

Hannon, P. (1993). Conditions of Learning at Home and in School. In *Ruling the margins*. University of North London Institute of Education.

Illich, I. (1991). *Deschooling society*. New York: Random House.

Jencks, C. *et al.* (1972). *Inequality; A reassessment of the effect of family and schooling in America*. New York: Basic Books.

MacBeath J. (1993). *Learning for yourself*. Strathclyde Region QIE Centre, University of Strathclyde.

MacBeath, J. (1993). *A place for success*. Quality in Education Centre, London: The Prince's Trust.

MacBeath, J. & Turner M. (1989). *Learning out of school*. Scottish Office Education Department, Glasgow: Jordanhill College.

Mortimore, P., Sammons, P., Stoll, L., Ecob, R. (1988). *School matters: The junior years*. Salisbury: Open Books.

The Prince's Trust (1993). *Study support resources pack.*

The Quality in Education Centre (1994). *The homework file.* SOED The University of Strathclyde.

Vygotsky, L. (1981) *Thought and language.* Cambridge: MIT Press.

CHAPTER 3

SCHOOLS ON THE EDGE
Responding to challenging circumstances

John MacBeath, Jane Cullen, David Frost and Sue Swaffield

Originally published as a paper within the symposium
Leadership for Learning: The Cambridge Network,
20th International Congress for School Effectiveness and
Improvement (ICSEI), Portoroz, Slovenia, 3–6 January 2007

This paper draws on the evaluation of a three year project into schools in 'exceptionally challenging circumstances'. This comprised eight schools in English towns and cities seen to be seriously underachieving. The government intervention was designed to raise achievement and close the gap between this 'Octet' of schools and their more privileged counterparts. The project and the evaluation of it were financed by the Department for Education and Skills (the DfES) in England. This emanated in a report to the Department and a book *Schools on the Edge*, by the evaluation team – John MacBeath, John Gray, Jane Cullen, David Frost, Susan Steward and Sue Swaffield.

On the edge

The history of school education, wherever and whenever it has been written, provides accounts of schools in the centre of a social mainstream with much less attention to the stories of schools perpetually on the periphery. What brings these schools together is a common policy framework despite the fact that their social and economic circumstances are worlds apart. Schools on the edge face a constant struggle to forge a closer alignment between home and school, parents and teachers, and between the formal world of school and the informal world of neighbourhood and peer group.

These schools serve families and communities that have been cut adrift of the mainstream. The decline of traditional industries in the hinterland of cities has stranded adults and young people on the periphery of economic life and the schools they attend often sit amid the rubble of run down neighbourhoods, distanced from their surroundings by their values, traditions and inflexible structures. Sometimes they are also physically distanced, on the edge of town, drawing young people literally and symbolically to a different place.

Education may be the route out of challenging circumstances if the will and skill can be found to navigate a path through the rigid conventions of schooling. For some young people, however poor the financial status of their families, they are able to draw on a social capital in the home which provides momentum and support. There are others who, with no such legacy, still manage to surmount the obstacles of both school and social conventions to achieve beyond expectation. Others follow the line of least resistance into the twilight economy. Their uncelebrated intelligence is put to use on the margins of the law, lured over the edge into the twilight economy and criminality, what Manuel Castells (2000) has described as 'perverse integration', the back door entry to becoming accepted and achieving success.

Those who teach these young people also come from a different place. The neighbourhoods these teachers visit on a daily basis are rarely the ones they would choose to live in or whose lifestyle they would choose to emulate. It is that very ability to choose that separates these teachers from those they teach. And it is the freedom to choose that distinguishes them from parents to whom governments proffer a choice of schools, as if choosing well might make all the difference between life on the edge and life in the social mainstream.

Yet choice *is* exercised. It is often a rejection of the local school and the immediacy of its problems and the children who litter gardens and pavements with disused wrappers and Coke cans and inscribe their personal slogans on shop fronts and bus shelters. As these families choose schools in better neighbourhoods, with 'nicer' children, they leave behind schools with a critical mass of parents and pupils who have less resilience or capacity to choose. They leave behind them schools which struggle to survive, year on year on the edge of viable numbers and attempting to meet the demand for public evidence that they are able to perform just as well as any other school despite the unevenness of the playing field.

Yet, however bleak the picture. there are schools in all countries which succeed in defying the odds, sometimes by statistical sleight of hand, sometimes by a concentrated and strategic focus on those students most likely to reach the bar and, in some instances, by inspirational commitment to deep learning across boundaries of language and culture. These schools are, in every sense, exceptional.

The effectiveness and improvement story

The effectiveness and improvement story has been a generally upbeat one, optimistic about what schools could achieve with a combination of the right factors. It was spurred into life by the pessimism of Coleman's (1966) conclusions that the spectrum of young people's needs could not be met within the single institution of schooling and that it was unreasonable to expect schools to equalise achievement given the unequal distribution of wealth, family 'capital' and privileged access to knowledge and accreditation. Around that time, Basil Bernstein (1970) was to write that 'education cannot compensate for society', primarily a reference to schools rather than to education more widely conceived. It was a theme that was to resonate in many countries of the world. In South America Paolo Freire wrote about a 'pedagogy of the oppressed' (1970). In Italy a group of school children wrote a Letter to a Teacher (1969), describing school as a hospital that 'tends to the healthy and neglects the sick'. In Scotland Gow and Macpherson reported the words of young people as 'flung aside' and 'forgotten'. In Sweden Torsten Husen, in Germany Hartman Van Hentig, in England Ian Lister called for radical alternatives to the traditional one-size-doesn't-fit-all school.

It is not coincidental that this climate should provoke an alternative stream of research which would challenge the prevailing pessimism and bleak narratives of 'compulsory miseducation' (Goodman, 1961). The thesis required an antithesis, and it set in train a search for the counter perspective, to offer empirical evidence which might confirm what was known intuitively and anecdotally, that schools could be better places for children and that in the right conditions a school could make a difference to their lives and learning.

There is now a body of evidence from effectiveness that the school a child or young person attends makes (some) difference to the subsequent progress they make through the educational system (Gray and Wilcox, 1995, Teddlie and Reynolds, 2000, MacBeath and Mortimore, 2001). Given the volume of this research, it is easy to fall into the trap, however, of supposing that there is a consensus about what makes a difference to schools' performance. There has been a tension within the research community, the origins of which go back to the original studies. To many people's surprise the most powerful finding to emerge from James Coleman's pioneering work for the Equality of Educational Opportunity survey was a school's 'social mix'; indeed, this turned out to be considerably more important than the levels of teacher experience or resourcing. It was a finding which Rutter's research was later to echo. 'The academic balance in the intakes to schools was particularly important', he reported. 'Exam success tended to be better in schools with a substantial nucleus of children of at least average intellectual ability' (Rutter *et al.*, 1979: 178). In other words what really mattered was who you went to school with, a case that Thrupp (1999) has made still more forcibly. In this account the main priority for policy-makers should be to seek to influence schools' intakes, an altogether different agenda.

There is a further difficulty for those seeking to use the research to provide pointers to action. Most research on school effectiveness tells us about the pattern of relationships prevailing in a school at the time it was studied. It doesn't necessarily tell us how the school got to be as it is (Gray *et al.*, 1996). Consider, for a moment, the claimed relationship between a school's 'leadership' and its performance. The usual assumption is that a strong head has caused a school to do well and that, conversely, a weak head has caused it to do badly. In truth, however, most research fails to disentangle the causal influences. Strong heads can lead 'good' schools but they can also find themselves in 'bad' ones where, for a variety of reasons, their efforts are frustrated. It is easy to understand why a common diagnosis for a school in trouble is that it needs a change of leadership. However, it demands an act of faith to assume that this is *the* key factor. Changing the leadership may boost the probability of improvement but it is rarely sufficient to guarantee it unless accompanied by much else that needs to change as well.

While school improvement, born in the house of school effectiveness, sought to identify the interweave of processes through which school be*came* effective, in reality, school improvement as a field of research has turned out to be a much more messy area than suggested by the initial, and perhaps overly optimistic, forays into school effectiveness. To use knowledge to change things also provides a much stiffer test of what is really known. The context within which innovation and knowledge are implemented proved to be of crucial importance and the ability of schools to sustain improvement has been shown to be problematic.

How long can schools maintain an upward trajectory? The evidence suggests that school improvement seems to come in bursts. Changes to aspects of practice and provision may be a continuing process that continues over a number of years. But, in most schools, three years seems to represent an upper limit as far as improving measured results is concerned (Mangan *et al.*, 2005). Improvement then seems to tail off. Over a ten year period Thomas *et al.* (in press) found that only a minority of schools (up to 40%) might be able to deliver a second burst. For the majority of schools, then, building capacity and *sustaining* improvement over time seems to pose a formidable challenge.

The evidence on school improvement provides some useful starting points but there is a further problem for practitioners and policy-makers concerned to tackle performance levels in particularly disadvantaged areas. Much of the existing evidence is drawn from contexts where the preconditions for change were probably more favourable.

The SFECC Project

The School Facing Exceptionally Challenging Circumstances Project (SFECC) was conceived in a sense as a demonstration initiative, a model for what could be achieved in highly disadvantaged schools by applying some of the key lessons learned from school effectiveness and improvement research. The project, originally designed to run for a period of five years, would, it was believed, provide evidence that the persistent gap between high and low achieving school could be substantially closed and that effective leadership, professional development, innovative pedagogy, technological resourcing, sound data systems and inter-school networking would be instrumental in achieving that goal.

After several 'false starts' and some attenuation of its original radical vision, the project began in 2002 with the following elements:

- Direct funding to each school of £150,000–£200,000 a year
- A bespoke reading programme to improve literacy in KS3
- Training in the strategic use of data, especially to track pupil progress, but also in the use of CATs data to broaden teaching strategies
- Funding to develop innovative uses of ICT such as video conferencing and interactive whiteboards and a common website
- Training and development of a school improvement group (SIG) in each school
- Training for the middle managers
- Support for the headteachers through strategic sessions run by the DfES

Eight schools were chosen by the DfES to take part in a project which would demonstrate that with the right kind of support and challenge even schools on the edge could turn failure to success. These eight schools were not the 'worst' in the country, although the press liked to portray them in that light, but chosen as a 'sample', representative of many other schools facing exceptionally challenging circumstances. One of the distinguishing features of this 'Octet' (as they came to be known) was that they had not resigned themselves to a hopeless future. These were judged to be schools that with visionary leadership could be turned round, offering wider lessons that could be learned about improvement even in the most apparently hopeless of places.

In selecting these eight to take part in the project the DfES applied four key criteria. These were: 15% or fewer of the students achieving 5 A* to C in 1999 and 2000; 40% or more of the students eligible for free school meals; 39% or more on the special education needs register; plus good or better leadership as reported in their most recent Section 10 inspection. All of these eight schools had a legacy of underachievement which stretched back to 1994. During the seven years from then until the initiation of the project in 2001 the percentage of students gaining 5A*-Cs at GCSE/GNVQ, had not risen above 15%.

A consistent theme which united these eight schools was their undesirability in the eyes of local residents, opting wherever possible either for selective schools, faith schools or schools in 'better' communities. In a competitive environment all of these schools had lost prospective students to other more 'attractive' schools. It is clear from these descriptions of intake that these schools were obliged to devote considerable energy to attracting students while at the same time trying to recruit and retain teachers in what are seen as undesirable areas. These eight schools suffered acutely because of the breach of principles of collaboration and fairness in the schools with whom they were obliged to compete. One headteacher described this as 'the name of the game', as if he were resigned to the inevitability of rules being rigged in favour of his competitors. The impact on the internal life of these schools was profound, not only on the social mix but on the parent constituency, the most informed and ambitious of parents having been 'drained off' to other more desirable locales.

While sharing common indices of disadvantage these eight schools were, in many respects, quite different. They ranged in size from just over 400 students to almost 1200. They included two faith schools and one single sex school. In 2001, three of the schools had some form of post 16 provision while five did not. Four were located in local authorities with grammar schools cheek by jowl with 'comprehensives', while others compete with comprehensive schools employing less overt selection policies. Five of the schools were located in mono-ethnic white wards and served their local communities from which almost all of their students were drawn, and in some cases students were able to walk to school. By contrast, three others drew from scattered and highly transient multi-ethnic communities involving young people in long and time consuming journeys to and from school.

The differences among the Octet are as striking and significant as the common features which brought them together. There is a danger that their surface similarities would conceal deeper lying dynamics with policy makers simply treating them as suffering from the same malaise and prescribing a common remedy. The communities they served, and continue to serve, are widely separated geographically and with varied and sometimes turbulent histories. The terminology of exceptionally challenging circumstances really only becomes meaningful when we look more deeply into the nature of the very different communities in which these schools are located.

What do we mean by exceptionally challenging circumstances?

While the local character of these communities defies attempts to define common features, their common challenges are captured by some or all of the indicators of economic and social disenfranchisement and lack of social capital. Communities in parts of all these cities are characterised by insularity and disillusionment as their work-based identity has been progressively eroded, areas in all of these towns and cities (Birmingham, Folkestone, Grimsby, Halifax, Liverpool, London, Sunderland) show complex historical patterns of decline, typically home to highly transient populations, including people drawn to the casual work and the twilight economics of major urban centres. Among their numbers are asylum seekers and refugees in temporary accommodation and others leaving troubled domestic and social situations behind.

The attempt to build social capital and a sense of community is frustrated by constant flux as the 'community' may only serve as a temporary stop on the way to a more permanent future elsewhere. For a significant number of young people the pattern of their lives is of a series of short term stays in different locations. At the same time there are those who remain long term, either tethered to their area by history or trapped by lack of mobility or economic opportunity. The left behind are in estates with boarded up and firebombed houses or flats owned by private landlords offering little in the way of aspirational housing to young people. In some areas, the character of the local population can shift rapidly and continuously in terms of its mix of background, ethnicities and cultures. For schools this means a constant process of catch-up in order to offer the appropriate services to parents and students.

Educational policy in England in the new millennium continues to stress parental choice, school performance tables, and local competition, on the assumption that market mechanisms are critical in improving schools, despite strong evidence that such forces are socially divisive. The idea that raising attainment in one school can occur with no negative effects in neighbouring schools is an optimistic one; its dark counterpart is that negative effects are to be expected as the market works by rewarding success and punishing failure.

While some recent analyses of aggregate levels of social stratification have suggested that nationally, schools are becoming less stratified (for example Fitz and Gorard, 2000), more recent work has suggested that in order to understand the levels of polarisation, schools need to be placed in the context of the local markets within which they operate. Local schools operate within a hierarchy that is being inensified by market policies, tending to exaggerate the differences between schools.

'Social mix', as a key factor in determining a school's effectiveness and capacity for improvement, plays out in dramatic fashion in these schools. It was a salient factor in all eight schools in which the student body contained a disproportionately high number of students with special learning needs (ranging from 42.2 per cent to 64.7 per cent at the outset of the project). This social and academic mix not only impacts powerfully on the internal dynamic of the school but also affects perceptions and expectations in the local community. In the Channel School in Folkestone, for example, staff described the negative effects of being well known as a school for dealing with students with autism and Asperger's syndrome.

The challenge of adverse social circumstances is to try and compete not only on uneven playing field but with players unable to come to terms with the rules of the game. The goals to be reached are the same as elsewhere but in a situation where little can be taken for granted and the future is always uncertain.

Negative perceptions of schools, in part, derived from Performance Tables (especially at a time when performance statistics did not include any notion of 'value-added') and in part from local 'intelligence', combined to make SFECC schools less attractive than their more favoured competitors. The stigma attached to a 'failing' school or school requiring 'special measures' compounded the demoralising effect on staff and students, particularly in some of the schools which had been constantly in the media spotlight. Nor was the public image of these schools helped by a proportion of the schools' intake being 'over-age' students, refugees, new arrivals or casual admissions.

Family and school

Children and young people live nested lives, writes David Berliner (2005) referring to the contextual layers of experience through which they attempt to make sense of their world. Failure to grasp the complexity of that policy looks for simple remedies, he suggests. So that when classrooms do not function as we want them to, we go to work on improving them. Those classrooms are in schools, so when we decide that those schools are not performing appropriately, we go to work on improving them, as well. But those young people are also situated in families, in neighbourhoods, in peer groups who shape attitudes and aspirations often more powerfully than their parents or teachers.

'Family life' rarely fits the image that such a phrase might conjure up. Carole and her family (Figure 3.1) may be an extreme case but it graphically makes the point about the minefield that some parents have to negotiate to access the service that meets their complex needs.

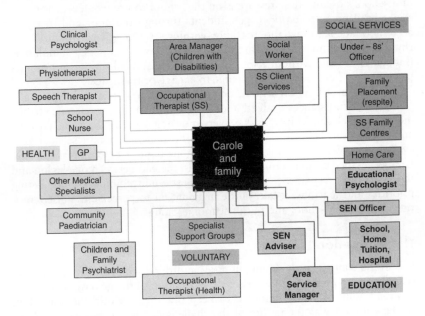

Figure 3.1 Carole, her family and social/educational agencies

Children like Carole, caught in web of circumstance not of their own making, rely on parents or carers who have the skills to successfully negotiate their way through the thickets of welfare and educational agencies. For parents in communities on the edge it means juggling child minding, employment, and domestic upkeep including guarding vulnerable property against ever present threat from a new generation of lawlessness. For children and young people their success is equally a matter of navigation. Success in school is less a matter of academic ability than ability to understand and 'play the system' reliant on motivation, commitment and perseverance in the face of failure – a legacy for young people that may not be within the family inheritance. As we know from numerous studies (Jencks, 1972, Epstein, 2004, Weiss and Fine, 2000), parental length of time in formal education is mirrored by the next generation.

The inflexible structure of the school day does not easily mesh with patterns of home life. Many young people, very often girls, shoulder responsibilities for their younger siblings and sometimes for parents, ill, disabled or simply inadequate to the task of child care and education. From the school's perspective it is difficult to allow exceptions or to know what might be justifiable reasons for lateness or absence, having no immediate links into the home environment except at second hand through social or community workers. The nature of the timetabled day allows for selective attendance at certain periods but also penalises students who miss out; with little chance to catch up they fall progressively further behind due to the relentless pace over the curricular ground to be covered. The periodic structure of the school day, consecutive slices of subjects, requiring successive shifts of focus and expectation is widely accepted as an unsatisfactory way to organise learning but has proved intractable due to 'lock in' the mosaic of factors which conspire to defeat more radical alternatives. As attendance is used as a public indicator of a school's quality the pressure is on the school to use whatever measures might be deemed to work to get students through the door and to try to accommodate learning and teaching within a set of given strictures. Its rhythm, locked into the structure of the school day is 'ruthlessly cumulative' (Pinker, 1998) and without remedial loops and sustained support it becomes progressively harder for young people to engage or re-engage.

Teachers in a London school, one of eight schools 'facing exceptionally changing circumstances', talked about a groundhog day, a reference to the movie in which Bill Murray wakes every morning to relive the same day over and over again. For some young people and their teachers it seemed as if every lesson was a revisiting of what had gone the day before, as if the slate had been wiped clean overnight. Taking into the gap between one lesson and the next, often separated by myriad domestic and community competing priorities and tensions, it takes little imagination to perceive the disconnections between in school and out of school learning.

The evaluation

It is in the context of these communities and the disconnect between home, school and 'community' that we set the evaluation of the government's intervention. While we were enjoined to keep our focus within the black box of the school it was the nature of the challenging circumstances outside of these schools, and imported into them, that we needed to understand. The evaluation of the SFECC initiative was conducted between April 2002 and March 2005 by a team from the University of Cambridge. It was carried out using both quantitative and qualitative methods as mixed methods research. The quantitative research has two main strands: analysis of changes in examination performance in the eight schools over the years 2001–2004, and comparisons over the same time period with a group of similar schools. The qualitative research analysed, through interview, focus group discussion, shadowing, observation and questionnaire, the effects of the project in each of the schools, changes in the eight schools over the three years of the project, with a specific focus on ways in which each of these schools interacted with the community which it served.

The integration of quantitative and qualitative data gave insights into the change occurring in an individual school in order to identify themes significant to the eight schools. Changes in external attainment levels were explored in terms of the changes identified by the schools themselves and the attribution that could be made for these changes.

One main strand of the evaluation was to examine the various government funded initiatives. So, for example we questioned teachers and students on the use and impact of whiteboard technology and observed in classrooms where it was seen to be used well, not so well or not at all. We interviewed teachers who were in charge of the literacy programme and observed lessons. We interviewed young people once or twice each year about their perceptions of change and also periodically interviewed groups of teachers on specific initiatives such as:

- Professional development
- School improvement groups (SIGs)
- Middle management training
- Headteacher networking and mutual school visits
- The uses of data
- Video conferencing

We did not, however, stick to these DfES inspired initiatives but tried to obtain a more holistic picture of these schools and their communities and were directed by the eight schools to practices and innovations that had a life before SFECC, leading us into interviews in the community with social or community workers and in some cases with primary school personnel. In addition to interviews with the head teacher and senior managers we held extended interviews with the eight heads towards the end of the project to get their story which, like all data gathered, was fed back for accuracy and further elaboration.

Professional development

One of the main thrusts and energy of the project was directed towards the development of staff in the SFECC project schools, with most of the centralised funding being used in staff training. Over the life of the project there were many examples of individual personal and career development. Given the turbulence of staffing in many of the SFECC schools, professional development could be seen as an in incentive for staff to stay, and a reward for having done so, often through very difficult times.

A problem was, however, that professional development tended to suggest individual consumption so that enhanced skill and confidence made staff highly attractive to other schools. This worked at cross purposes to staff retention, already a major issue in several of these schools at the beginning of the project (and fluctuated between a major and minor issue in almost all of them over the three years). Without professional development tied more strongly into the organisation rather than as individual enhancement, there is a clear and present danger of new-found expertise being lost.

Pedagogy

Adapting teaching to students' needs and making them more active participants in a class was one of the main foci of professional development and was widely seen as beneficial. Teachers reported an increased interest and positive response from their students as they adopted more finely differentiated teaching strategies. Enthusiasm for VAK (visual, auditory, kinaesthetic learning) and Multiple Intelligences (MI) had been gaining strong currency over the last decade or so in schools throughout the country, and was similarly embraced by many staff in these schools, although viewed with considerable scepticism by researchers and learning theorists who have failed to find any empirical basis for claims made for a VAK approach (Coffield *et al.*, 2004, Bramall and White, 2004). Howard Gardner has also distanced himself from the evangelical embrace of MI, arguing that it was never intended to be used prescriptively and naively in individual profiling and differentiating instruction. None the less, discussion of learning styles did prove to be a catalyst to help teachers recognise the individuality of learners and the blocks to learning which traditional views of intelligence and ability are insensitive to.

The use of interactive whiteboard technology and VAK inspired teaching was also inseparable from the three/four part lesson also widely adopted within Octet schools. Lessons we observed started ritually with objectives on the board, warm-up activities followed by groups work and plenary. So ritual had this become that in one class where a teacher had forgotten to start with objectives she was immediately reprimanded by a student: 'Miss, you forgot the objectives.'

However, though the classroom focus was a given, it was teaching that was given centre stage, with much less emphasis on learning and learning theory, for which VAK and MI are weak substitutes. The assumption that improving teaching through more structured, varied, paced and targeted lessons would improve learning is a contested proposition, at least without some detailed articulation as to how that conjunction might be achieved. As improvement was viewed by the DfES in terms of increased attainment at GCSE (a Key Stage assessment at age 16), deeper learning and the impact of professional development remained unaddressed.

We also found evidence of interactive potential of whiteboards being missed, with teachers using them for traditional didactic teaching or simply deploying them as a projector screen, often leaving students passive and frustrated. The hardware and software were only of pedagogic value when teachers had the knowledge, confidence and expertise to use it and to invest time in the considerable planning needed to exploit the full potential of the resource. Where whiteboards were not embedded in a wider pedagogic repertoire – as simply another tool in the repertoire of skilled teachers – concerns were expressed by teachers and heads about whiteboards being used for their novelty value and a danger of 'death by whiteboard'.

A focus on literacy

It is widely accepted that children have difficulty in learning if they are not proficient readers, a need poignantly illustrated by one Year 7 student:

> When I get told to read in class I don't feel confident ... I get all shaky and scared in case people laugh at me

The DfES's answer was to introduce a secondary school version of a programme written for primary age children, which they were simultaneously piloting elsewhere. The 'Ruth Miskin Literacy' (RML) (now a commercial programme called Read Write Inc.) is a reading, spelling, vocabulary and writing programme for slow or hesitant KS3 readers, which promises to take children to a decoding age (as opposed to a reading comprehension age) of 12 years. It does this by means of a highly prescriptive sequence of activities, programmed into a one-hour lesson four days a week for a year. Teachers and students work through a succession of weekly modules of controlled phoneme and grapheme content, with the level of difficulty increasing each week. RML also stipulates structural arrangements and teaching protocols. Students are taught in groups of between eight and 16 in size, in a quiet controlled classroom environment. Students with behaviour problems and specific learning difficulties are placed in smaller groups and no student is supposed to join the programme part of the way through the year.

By the standards of much classroom practice the RML programme is highly prescriptive and needs to be strictly and faithfully implemented. However, this prescription was judged by many teachers of English, who view themselves as equally knowledgeable and experienced, to be unduly narrow and even naïve. At the time the Project adopted RML there was little independent evidence of its success. In the event, between 20 and 30 teachers were trained in the early stages of the SFECC project and this was supplemented by later training. Many of the trained teachers commented, often with surprise, on the success of the RML programme, both in terms of their own role and in terms of the way that students engaged with the activities. Others remained sceptical. Four of the eight schools judged RML to be highly successful with claims for clear evidence of increased reading ages and marked improvement in attitude. One Head of English, for example, saw RML as addressing shortcomings in the National Curriculum to assist those who, for whatever reason, were behind in reading.

Key to the success of the programme, in the view of those who favoured it, was that it lent itself to an affirming and supportive relationship between a teacher and a small group. Formative feedback and evidence of progress as children make step-by-step achievements are well established as powerful levers, especially in a climate where a nurturing teacher has removed threats and any sense of failure.

However, not all SFECC schools were so positive about the programme's benefits. Indeed some were vitriolic in their dislike of RML and its highly prescriptive approach. Critics (including HMI) observed that students resented being taken out of their normal classes and missing lessons in other subjects, and that a school's 'normal' literacy and SEN programmes were likely to be of demonstrably greater benefit in increasing reading ages. The content of the RML programme was seen as being decontextualised, with little relationship to the curriculum. The rigidity of the programme was criticised both as a uniform one-size-fits-all approach to learning, and for the lack of latitude for invention or adaptation by teachers. Where there was success it was generally ascribed to the skills of the individual teacher, who had managed to build over time a warm and supportive relationship with a small group who, in their 'special' relationship, increased in self esteem. In one school one teacher was highly successful with RML while her colleagues in the school were not. Across the school, the successful teachers were probably those who were flexible in approach and did not slavishly follow programme prescription.

The ambivalent responses to RML and claims for its success are hard to unravel, and raise questions as to the key elements which contribute to success. Possible explanations might include: teacher's own belief in the programme; the intensity of focus; high expectations; praise and reinforcement for success; small class size; the quality of relationships; The Hawthorne Effect; nationally, the pendulum has swung: phonics programmes are back in political favour (Rose, 2006). Furthermore, the reported success of synthetic phonics in Clackmannanshire (Johnston and Watson, 2003) has re-ignited the debate over preferred approaches.[1] Other commentators, meanwhile, suggest that this is a 'war' between analytic and synthetic phonics which misses the essential point that there are a host of differing ways of helping children learn to read (Wyse, 2003).

Using data effectively

Aligned with the focus on teaching and learning were developments in the use of data. A key aim of the project was to encourage the proactive use of data for planning rather than for retrospective rationalisation, data used as formative rather than simply summative. There was, however, a potential conflict, or tension, in the use of data as it was seen as serving two distinct purposes. One was the use of disaggregated data to enhance teaching and learning, while the use of aggregated data was essentially to serve whole school management and accountability purposes. The fact that the DfES was asking the schools to supply extra data for accountability purposes, with the call for attainment data to be sent to the DfES each half term, did not help the cause in the early stages. However, the possibility of using that data in a spreadsheet or database form which would give information at group or class level, allowing schools to plot student trajectories of progress using computer technology, did begin to offer a useful and time saving tool for senior management. In the event, for technical reasons, the spreadsheet developed by the DfES did not actually work, but this did not impede schools from developing their own data systems, many of which were already being implemented. An HMI Report on the Ridings commented:

> All eight schools within the project have focused on the use of data as a tool for raising standards, using a specific software programme. The software has been problematic, but the school continues to make good use of assessment information, using other software. Teachers are

provided with a range of useful information on the pupils in their classes, and there is a clear expectation from senior staff that this information will be used to inform teachers' planning and teaching.

The SFECC spreadsheet led eventually to the development of a fully fledged database system called START but this was only after the project was finished, and had it been fully developed earlier it might have increased the impact of data management and use within the project itself.

Developing and extending leadership

Two strands of the project were concerned with developing leadership in the eight SFECC schools: one, a training programme for subject leaders (though this was extended to more generally cover middle managers) and the other, training to develop a school improvement group (SIG).

The idea of 'upskilling' middle managers and giving them a more significant role in the running of the school is a fairly conventional one, and for example the training of middle managers in the SFECC project was occurring at the same that the National College of School leadership (NCSL) was introducing its 'leading from the middle' programme. Part of the rationale was that if middle managers could take on more of the day to day running of the school, the Senior Leadership Team (SLT) would have time and space for the longer term strategic development needed in today's market-driven climate. In addition, there was increasing recognition that in the subject specialist world of the secondary school, it is subject leaders who need the expertise to 'drive up' standards in the classroom.

The professional development model adopted offers some useful lessons. The middle management training failed not because of the quality of the training but because the training was seen by the schools as an opportunity for particular individuals rather than a means to develop strategically the role of a key group of staff. While the training was carried out at more than one residential session, and participants had a project to complete back in the school, the project was not the schools', but their own. There was little follow through in the schools and for mentoring between middle managers to have succeeded, it would have needed the visible commitment of the SLT in each school to provide the space and time for middle managers to work together across subject boundaries. It also required a validation from the head teacher. Middle managers were locked into the hierarchy of competence, performance management, promotion and so on, and for peer coaching to work it would have required strong affirmation from the top that this was non-threatening and something to be viewed positively.

The School Improvement Group

The creation of a School Improvement Group (SIG) was widely seen as the most successful aspect of the SFECC project. It was not in every case a new initiative but the project gave it further impetus. The notion of a SIG as an engine for change and a major lever for professional learning can be traced back to the James Report (DES, 1972). At its core is the idea that effective professional learning is school-based rather than merely school-focused, and should be linked explicitly to particular development goals.

While the SIG model of improvement bears some similarity to its IQEA predecessor (Hopkins *et al.*, 1996) it has, nonetheless, developed it own identity. Common to both models is the use of a cadre group of staff who act as evaluators of practice and promoters of change. It is a model of improvement that is neither 'bottom up' nor 'top down', but may rather be described as 'middle out' since its influence is designed to flow upwards to senior leadership as well as 'down' to individual classroom level. A key characteristic of the 'cadre group' is that its members co-ordinate development activities, involving many more colleagues in the process.

SIG groups ranged in size from five to nine members, typically representing a wide range of departments and varying experience, from newly qualified teachers to established senior staff with many years service. Almost all the SIGs included a member of the senior leadership team, or an SLT member had direct responsibility for coordinating the work of the SIG with the strategic direction of the school. However, a significant number of SIG members were young and relatively inexperienced teachers who had been given an opportunity to have a say and to start to exercise leadership. While there were attempts in some schools to use SIG membership to support 'weaker' teachers, on the whole the SIGs seemed to derive their credibility and strength from the membership of effective, well-regarded members of staff. SIG training took place on six two-day sessions over a two-year period, and involved a core group of trainers offering a series of workshops at each residential and included topics such as effective teaching, formative assessment, and data to inform teaching and learning.

The challenge comes in terms of the sustainability of a group such as SIG, to continue the level of engagement and enthusiasm achieved without the benefit of external support and training, especially as the composition of the group changes and other priorities emerge. New head teachers often wish to put their own stamp on the school and may undermine the authority and capacity of SIGs for either good or less well intentioned reasons. There is also a delicate balance to be struck between creating an elite group and engendering a wider sense of ownership. A further challenge is to retain staff who have been trained and through that opportunity have enhanced their expertise and 'marketability'. If the SIG model is to be successful in the long term, capacity needs to move beyond the enthusiasms of specific individuals, and the SIG's values and practices – how it works and what it stands for – need to be embedded in the culture of the school. The question arises as to how to develop the SIG group further after a period of funding ceases and whether or not its continuing success is dependent on training, an issue sharpened as 'trained' members leave and new members arrive. In these eventualities the need increases for an embedding within the group of an organisational memory which has a momentum and vitality beyond its individual members.

Even after two years, while the SIG groups had had success with developing in their schools the adoption of surface practices such as icebreakers, plenaries, the three/four part lesson, objectives on the board, use of CATs data and a learning styles matrix, they had yet to provide evidence of a deep impact on learning. Such impact occurs in the long term and a longer term vision for the SIG would be to support teachers in moving beyond these formulaic approaches to a more challenging evidence-led pedagogy (perhaps for instance to begin to problematise the fast developing orthodoxy around 'learning styles).

Networking with ICT

The most signal failure of the project, for which there had been high hopes, was the exchange of information and expertise among the eight schools. At the outset of the project there were high hopes that the eight schools would benefit from harnessing the power of technology to the sharing of good practice. In the event things turned out quite differently. The hope that ICT would deliver a collaborative network of eight schools engaged in frequent and profound discussion through video conferencing and a shared website never materialised. Besides the prospect of the more usual 'talking heads' conversations amongst the different SLTs, video conferencing was promoted by the DfES as having huge potential for dialogue on pedagogy across the schools. The plan was for classroom teachers to use video conferencing to exchange practice focused on interactive whiteboards.

The schools signed up for the vision and timetabled an early afternoon finish for this weekly sharing of curriculum and practice. Each school went through the costly business of buying and setting up the equipment. When the project started and the video-conferencing infrastructure was being put into place, national communication development was well underway and it was envisaged that the equipment in the schools would work through an interconnected, internet protocol. However, what was being proposed demanded not just a national system, but one which supported optimum quality video, so that teachers could actually see each other's work via the link. Unfortunately, this was not in place even by the end of the project. Regional firewalls were preventing signals moving across networks and there were difficulties with particular regional broadband consortia providing an easy feed for video-conferencing. Furthermore, the high costs of using ISDN as an alternative were seen as prohibitive. It could be argued that this was a problem beyond the control of the DfES and that any technical innovation carries the risks of failure, but video conferencing had been talked up as high tech and exciting, and the schools had taken a lot of effort to install the equipment. The consensus among the schools was that all the technical aspects ought have been sorted out before the project was started.

A question of attainment

How well did SFECC perform after three years of costly and intensive intervention? We experimented with a number of different ways of grouping the measures of performance but eventually concluded that the measures of trends over time and value-added should probably be given prominence. On the basis of analysis of varying combinations of data we concluded that the schools could be divided into three broad groups:

a)   where there was evidence of a positive change in performance on (most of) the indicators which suggested that the changes had been substantial and also provided some signs of upwards trends over time and of improvements in value-added;

b)   where there was evidence of a positive change in performance on (some of) the indicators but where the scale of improvement was less substantial and there was less evidence of upward trends or improvements in value-added; and

c)   where the evidence, whilst generally indicative of some improvement, did not amount to convincing evidence of changes in performance over time or of increases in value-added.

Grouping the schools in this way did not prove straightforward. Eventually we concluded that two schools fell into Group A where there was evidence of substantial improvement in GCSE attainment over the period 2001–05 including signs of upward trends on the key indictors. Two schools fell into Group B where the scale of the improvement was generally in an upward direction, while the remaining four fell into Group C where the evidence for change was generally rather modest.

These results were then compared against a comparison group which had not been the subject of government intervention. Originally it contained 24 schools but by 2004 one school had been renamed/closed so no data were available. Consequently the comparison group finally contained 23 schools. Table 3.1 shows the results for the SFECC school as against the Comparison Group in relation to the 5+ A*-C headline measure. Over this period the national percentages reaching this hurdle rose from 50% to just under 54%, a rise of some four percentage points.

The average for the SFECC schools rose by some three or four percentage points a year. Over the period 2001 to 2004, covering the baseline year and the three years when project activity was most intense, the increase amounted to some ten percentage points. The average for the Comparison schools also rose by a similar amount. For both groups of schools the rates of increase were very similar. Both groups secured further improvements during 2005 and ahead of national trends, probably as a result in large measure of the wider range of qualifications brought into the calculation of key targets. However, there was no difference between the two groups overall.

Table 3.1 Proportions achieving 5+ A*-C grades (or equivalent) in the SFECC and Comparison schools 2001–2005

Year	National	SFECC	Comparison Group
2001	50.0%	13.2%	15.5%
2002	52.0%	17.2%	18.8%
2003	52.9%	20.7%	24.3%
2004*	53.7%	23.5%	26.8%
2005**	57.1%	33.7%	33.5%

Notes:* From 2004 a wider range of qualifications have been included by the DfES in the 5+ A*-C grades (or equivalent) indicator. **The 2005 percentages are for pupils at the end of Key Stage 4, *not* aged 15 as previously. The figures in this table have been weighted to take account of differences in cohort size across the schools.

Applying lessons from school improvement research

Can governments change schools? The SFECC intervention was premised on the notion that if everything we have learned about school improvement could be applied to schools on the edge, with funding, support and training, these schools would show dramatic gains and wider policy lessons would be adduced. These assumptions are captured in the publication *School Improvement – Lessons from Research* reflecting the premises on which the project was based. That document summarises four key points, all of which were embodied in the approach to the Octet schools, all of which are none the less open to debate.

Firstly, it is 'at the level of the individual classroom teacher that most of the difference between schools seem to occur' (2005, p4). The implication is that the emphasis of school improvement should be on teachers and their work in the classroom. This premise is derived from effectiveness and improvement studies which show, perhaps not surprisingly, that the teacher effect is more significant than the school effect and that much effort can be wasted on things which have little to do with teaching and learning. Whether this holds as true for schools on the edge as it might elsewhere is a question. Even if teachers are accepted as being the prime focus for school improvement efforts, the question remains how best to achieve this. How can government-led intervention strategies reach every teacher in a school? And to what degree can all teachers be transformed not only in skill and disposition but with the risk taking to confront inappropriate curriculum and testing? Would this imply direct and intensive 'training' of every teacher, bearing in mind the continual turnover of staff? Through cascade training with key staff as mentors and trainers? Creating enough space, resource and support for collaborative lesson planning, peer observation, rigorous and sustained self-evaluation?

The SFECC intervention did focus much of its energy on classroom practice, but primarily through the training of senior and middle leaders and school improvement group members. None of these in themselves, or in concert, could effect the depth of penetration on students' learning needed to revitalise and energise disaffected and alienated young people.

The second premise is that, 'what pupils learn in school is partly dependent on what they bring to school in terms of their family and individual social and economic circumstances. Deprivation is still by far the biggest determent of educational success' (p6). Juxtaposing 'partly dependent' and 'biggest determent' is to sit uncomfortably on the fence. At one end of the spectrum there are children with such strong family support from the earliest age that they arrive at the school gates able to read fluently, already with a wealth of knowledge of the world, eager to learn and impervious to frustrations that classroom learning often entails. At the other end of the spectrum are children so starved of affection and emotional support, in some cases so psychologically damaged as to make 'access' to the curriculum an irrelevance. As we know, where young people lie on that spectrum is closely correlated to socio-economic circumstances, and although every exception tests the rule, there are conditions such as Fetal Alcohol Syndrome which no amount of excellent teaching can repair. Given this, there are strong arguments for investing effort on the wider community, on the kind of inter-agency support now advocated by *Every Child Matters* and *Youth Matters* policy initiatives.

Yet the SFECC project was entirely focused upon the schools, largely ignoring their local communities.

The third premise is that 'sustained improvement over a period of years is unusual, and of course, year to year some schools will fall back' (p6). This implies that school improvement efforts should concentrate upon sustainability (the issue picked up in the fourth point), and that year-on-year improvement is neither to be expected nor necessary for a trajectory of sustained improvement over time. Yet great store has been placed on a school's annual test results, which are themselves only a very limited measure of a school's achievements. Struggling schools in general and schools involved in SFECC in particular were subject to frequent monitoring for example by HMI inspection, and the pressure for short term tangible evidence of 'improvement', notably in the form of GCSE results, was immense. Such intensity of pressure may work at cross purposes to the fourth point – that of achieving sustainability.

Fourthly, 'schools that generate sustained improvement tend to act strategically, first self-reviewing and reflecting, gathering and using appropriate evidence, and then act collaboratively, to build capacity for further improvement' (p7). This is in contrast to what Gray *et al.* (1999) refer to as tactical approaches – ways to increase outcome measures with the focus on the short term, precluding real longer term gains – 'responding simply at a tactical level presents problems for sustained improvement' (Gray *et al.*, 1999, p145). The dilemma of the Octet schools, and all schools in similar circumstances, is that tactical measures are an imperative for survival. It is schools on the very edge of acceptable performance that have to prove themselves in the currency of GCSE and point scores. As headteachers frequently testified, they have very short term and political targets as well as to try to build capacity in the longer term, couched by some senior leaders as a moral conflict which they wrestled with on a daily basis. To deploy the best teachers and invest the greatest efforts in those young people most likely to pay extrinsic dividends at the expense of those unlikely to meet the critical benchmark? To pit the continued survival of the school against the welfare of some individual children? For the most committed and idealistic of senior leaders these were dilemmas that ran like a thread through their everyday thinking and practice.

If governments can change schools these are the dilemmas they have to understand and confront, not with an accretion of new initiatives but with an acknowledgement that some of their funding, curriculum and testing policies constitute a problem rather than a solution for schools in exceptionally challenging circumstances.

Nine lessons for policy and practice

Much of what happened during the life of the project was, in reality, not that distinctive nor was it unique to the eight schools. Many exciting things were already happening in these schools, so that their response to relevance and expectations of the the project were therefore different. Had the project started from where the schools were, rather than from its own menu of interventions, SFECC would have been constructed differently and might have had a different kind of impact. What the project did achieve was to provide a catalyst for schools to review their existing practice, and to test new ways of working. In our conclusion in the final chapter of the book *Schools on the Edge* we attempt to tease out some of the broader lessons.

1   Intervening in schools on the edge is a long-term proposition. Judged in terms of conventional criteria, the investment is risky, and the failure rates historically have been high – higher perhaps than policy-makers are aware of, or care to admit. Furthermore, dividends are slow to emerge. Almost all schools on the edge require considerable and sustained investment.

2   There are systemic reasons why some schools are on the edge. These are not easily addressed by purely *educational* interventions. They require more joined up social and economic policy. Every Child Matters goes some way to recognising the need for more coherent delivery of services but is obliged to work within local infrastructures which do not address wider systematic issues.

3   The longer a school has been floundering, the longer it will usually take to get back on its feet. As a rule of thumb, if the period of difficulties stretches back ten years, it is likely to take five to get back on track and perhaps seven to be confident of longer term success. Five years is seen by policy makers as a long term horizon; on the other hand, children have to take five years to get through with the primary or secondary stages of schooling. We should be cautious about collapsing time.

4   There are few easy generalisations to be made about the contexts and challenges facing schools on the edge – each school is likely to experience different and occasionally unique problems. Lumping them together and attempting to prescribe common remedies is unlikely to be helpful.

5   The fight for some semblance of stability has to be accepted as a never-ending struggle. The mind-set of many of the key participants in schools on the edge (whether they be school leaders, teachers or pupils) is that of 'temporary residents' – in due course they will move on, perhaps sooner rather than later. 'Fail-safes' need to be built into planning, and resourcing will always be more demanding and expensive than in schools were stability can simply be taken for granted.

6   Few schools are adept at introducing and managing innovations success-fully. This capacity is massively under-developed in schools on the edge. However unpalatable, the key lesson for policymakers is that change takes time to plan and implement, and the stage at which most projects end or wind down is often precisely the point at which the feasibility of potential investments can begin to be assessed – possibly for the first time. Demanding that these same schools simultaneously respond to the short-term pressures imposed by performance tables and Ofsted moni-toring can produce the institutional equivalent of schizophrenia. The main legacy in schools on the edge of the 'show-quick-results-at-any-cost' mentality has been a series of failed investments, each in turn adding to the view that 'it might work elsewhere but it won't work here'.

7   Seeking to prescribe the 'what and how' of school improvement in widely differing institutions and social contexts can be counter-productive. Change starts to take root in schools when the staff collectively begin to get hold of a 'powerful idea'. That idea could take a variety of different forms. Policy-makers need to become more adept at drawing up menus of the most promising ideas which schools may approach as 'a la carte',

while ordering 'off-menu' should be also examined and appraised on its merits.

8   Taking a broader view of leadership is essential. A 'charismatic' or 'heroic' headteacher may, in certain circumstances, be needed but the risk is that the template for leadership can be drawn too narrowly, and may in the longer term prove counter-productive. In this respect the setting up of a School Improvement Group (SIG) is significant in distributing leadership. It can create space for teacher leadership and team leadership to emerge and contribute to teacher-led improvement.

9   School improvement groups take a variety of forms but tend to be composed entirely of teaching staff focused on professional development, learning and teaching and school-based issues. If they are to have a wider impact their membership would be enhanced by including other people with a broader community perspective. Whatever their constitution, however, the biggest challenge is to take young people's views about teaching, learning and their connectedness to their lives, in and out of school, more seriously.

A society that is committed to offering all its citizens equal opportunities has no choice about whether to have policies for schools in 'exceptionally challenging circumstances'. Stated baldly, the gap between schools serving mainstream communities and those on the edge is not just large but, in most people's view, unacceptably so. The moral case for intervention should be taken as read but approached with sensitivity, support, receptiveness to research and a firm grasp on the lessons of history.

Note

1 A Teachers TV video with a four way debate among reading experts can be downloaded at http://www.teachers.tv/strandProgrammeVideo.do?strandId=59957&transmissionProgrammeId=275316

References

Berliner, D. (2005) Our Impoverished View of Educational Reform, *Teachers College Record*, 2nd August

Bernstein, B. (1970) Education cannot compensate for society, *New Society*, 387:344–47

Castells, M. (2000) *End of Millennium*, Oxford, Blackwell

Coffield, F, Moseley, D., Hall, E. and Ecclestone, K. (2004) *'Should we be using learning styles? What research has to say to practice.'* London, Learning Skills Research Centre

Coleman, J.S., Campbell, E., Hobson, C., McPartland, J., Mood, A., Weinfeld, R. and York, R. (1966) *Equality of Educational Opportunity*, Washington DC: Government Printing Office.

Epstein J.L. (1992) *School and Family Partnerships* Encyclopedia of Educational Research, Sixth Edition. Alkin, M (Ed.) New York: Macmillan

Freire, P. (1970) *Pedagogy of the Oppressed*, New York, Seabur

Fullan, M. (2000) The Return of Large-Scale Reforms, *Journal of Educational Change*, 2, 1, 5–28

Goodman, P. (1964) *Compulsory Miseducation*, Harmondsworth, Middlesex, Penguin

Gow, L. and McPherson, A. (Eds) (1980) *Tell Them For Me*, Aberdeen University Press

Gray, J. and Wilcox, B. (1995) *'Good School, Bad School': Evaluating Performance and Encouraging Improvement*, Buckingham: Open University Press

Gray, J., Reynolds, D., Fitz-Gibbon, C. and Jesson, D. (eds.) (1996) *Merging Traditions: the future of research on school effectiveness and school improvement*, London: Cassell

Gray, J., Hopkins, D., Reynolds, D., Wilcox, B., Farrell, S. and Jesson, D. (1999) *Improving Schools: Performance and Potential*, Buckingham: Open University Press

Hopkins, D. (2001) *School Improvement for Real*, London: RoutledgeFalmer

Hopkins, D., Reynolds, D. and Gray, J. (2005) *School Improvement – Lessons from Research*. London: DfES

Jencks, C.S., Smith, M., Ackland, H., Bane, M. J., Cohen, D., Gintis, H., Heyns, B. and Micholson, S. (1972) *Inequality: A Reassessment of the Effect of Family and Schooling in America*, New York: Basic Books

Johnston, R. and Watson, W (2003) Accelerating reading and spelling with synthetic phonics: a five year follow up, Scottish Executive Education Department, Insight 4

Knapp, M., Copeland, M., Portin, B., and Wicki (2006) Paper presented at the American Educational Research Association, San Francisco, April 7–12

MacBeath, J. and Mortimore, P. (eds.) (2001) *Improving School Effectiveness*, Buckingham: Open University Press

Mangan, J., Gray, J. and Pugh, G. (2005) Changes in examination performance in English secondary schools over the course of a decade: searching for patterns and trends over time, *School Effectiveness and School Improvement*, 16, 1, 29–50

National Commission on Education (1995) *Success Against the Odds*, London: Routledge and Kegan Paul

Pinker, S. (1998) *Words and rules*, Brattleborough, Vermont: Lingua

Rose, J. (2006) *Independent Review of the Teaching of Early Reading* Nottingham, DfES

Rutter, M., Maughan, B., Mortimore, P. and Ouston, J. (1979) *Fifteen Thousand Hours: secondary schools and their effects on children*, London: Open Books

School of Barbiana, (1969) Letter to a Teacher. Harmondsworth, Middlesex: Penguin

Teddlie, C. and Reynolds, D. (eds.) (2000) *The International Handbook of School Effectiveness Research*, London: Falmer Press

Thomas, S., Gray, J. and Peng, W.J. (in press) Value-added trends in English secondary school performance over ten years, *Oxford Review of Education*

Thrupp, M. (1999) *Schools Making a Difference: Let's be Realistic! School mix, school effectiveness and the social limits of reform*, Buckingham: Open University Press

Weiss, L. and Fine, M. (2001) *Construction Sites: Excavating Race, Class and Gender among Urban Youth*, New York, Teachers' College Press

Wyse, D. (2003) The National Literacy Strategy: a critical review of empirical evidence, *British Educational Research Journal*, 29 (6) 903–16

CHAPTER 4

NEW RELATIONSHIPS FOR OLD

Inspection and self-evaluation in England and Hong Kong

Originally published in *ISEA*, Vol. 34, No. 2, 2006

Introduction

The new 2005–6 school year in England saw the introduction of what is promised to be a 'New Relationship with Schools' (Miliband, 2005). It is a policy initiative so well publicised as to be now referred to simply as NRwS. It is a 'new' relationship because it is designed to address the dissatisfaction with an inspection regime that had often been counter productive in its impact on school and classroom life (see for example, Rosenthal, 2001) as well as acknowledging the growing importance of school self-evaluation. The New Relationship shares much in common with the new rapport between government and schools in Hong Kong. There it is a relationship that has been developing less hurriedly than in England, implemented and monitored over the last three years (Education and Manpower Bureau, 2003). It too was impelled by a recognition that self-evaluation is a significant and growing trend and that inspection of itself does not empower schools to effect improvement. So, in 2003 the six year old Quality Assurance framework was replaced by school self-evaluation and external review, now familiar enough to be known by its acronym SSE and ESR.

In both Hong Kong and England policy makers presented the change as a mature stage of development beyond external inspection and as having both an improvement and accountability purpose. In Hong Kong it is explicitly signalled as SDA – School Development and Accountability (Education and Manpower Bureau, 2003) while in both countries the challenge this presents for schools is to resolve the inherent tension between these two driving motives. Reform in these two countries is evidence of a wider international movement to push down decision-making power to school level while simultaneously pushing up the pressure on schools to render a value-for-money account in both financial and achievement terms (Moos, 2003).

Placing self-evaluation at the heart of school improvement brings with it a new role for the inspectorate. In this brave new relationship no longer will inspectors be the sole arbiters and narrators of the school's story but rather act as mediators, encouraging and supporting schools to speak for themselves. Inside the velvet glove of support and critical friendship, however, is the fist of accountability, intolerant not only of low standards but also of self-delusion. Self-evaluation may be owned by a school staff but is manifestly not a soft option. Schools have to prove their ability to know themselves with appeal to authoritative and verifiable evidence, while the inspectorate has to satisfy itself that a school is truly master of its own destiny.

While bearing strong similarities and deriving from a common rationale there are important differences between the two countries' approaches. These differences are explained largely by the context and culture in which these shifts in policy have evolved. This article examines the convergences and divergence between these two models and the response of practitioners to them. It draws on a substantial empirical base, on studies carried out in both countries in 2004–6.

Sources of data

The data from the English context draws on two studies conducted in 2004–5, one commissioned by the National Union of Teachers (NUT), the other commissioned by the National College of School Leadership (NCSL). Both were conducted by researchers at the University of Cambridge (MacBeath and Oduro, 2004, MacBeath, 2005). The aim of the NUT study was to provide the Union with an independent perspective on the proposed New Relationship through a field study of teachers' and headteachers' views. Interviews were conducted with 192 teachers and headteachers who had completed a short questionnaire on the proposed new inspection model and on purposes and practice of self-evaluation. These school staff were drawn from 45 schools (a 48 per cent response rate from 92 schools invited to participate), located in seven English local authorities, rural and urban and including one inner London authority. Each school included a member of the senior leadership team and three to four randomly selected teachers.

The questionnaires consisted of both closed and open items seeking views on the proposed changes to the inspection system, exploring how teachers viewed the purpose, audiences, and components of self-evaluation. Although providing the team with quantitative and qualitative data, the questionnaires' main purpose was more as a starting point for widening the discussion and probing understanding of the proposed changes and their implications for practice.

The questionnaire items and follow-up discussion were guided by the following five questions:

- What do teachers and headteachers think about current changes in school inspection?
- What should be the purpose of self-evaluation?
- Who should be the audience (s) of self-evaluation?
- What should be the component (s) of self-evaluation?
- Who should determine the criteria for school self-evaluation?

An unplanned part of the study was an opportunity sampling of Hong Kong headteachers and teachers who took part in in-service courses for Hong Kong teachers and school principals in December 2004. 180 school staff completed the questionnaire, a quarter or so adding written comments. Clearly the responses to this questionnaire have to be treated with caution as the sampling was not representative or comparable with the English sample but the very sharp differences in responses do raise some provocative questions about the purposes of self-evaluation worth pursuing in greater depth.

The NCSL study

The aim of the NCSL study was to conduct a systematic meta analysis of self-evaluation, drawing out the key features of its purposes, audiences, frameworks, tools, processes and products; to examine policy developments in the U.K. over the last decade or so identifying trends and shifts in thinking as to the role of self-evaluation and its relation to external inspection; to identify the range of resources and instruments available for evaluating school and classroom practice by teachers themselves and by others who work with schools in an evaluation role, for example, critical friends. The study was set in the evolving context of the New Relationship.

The study had a number of separate components:

- A documentary analysis of Ofsted, DfES policy guidelines, Ministerial and HMCI speeches
- A review of local authority documentation on the New Relationship involving written communication with ten authorities and examination of a survey of web based policy documents
- A web search of all public and private agencies offering support and tools for self-evaluation and inspection
- A short questionnaire to 200 headteachers asking about current approaches to self-evaluation, and tools used (a 32% return).
- A literature review of self-evaluation and inspection including use of terminology such as 'self review', 'self assessment', 'audit' and 'quality assurance'
- Two one hour interviews with Her Majesty's Chief Inspector.

The Hong Kong study

The Hong Kong study was commissioned by the Education and Manpower Bureau to evaluate the impact of SSE/ESR using as a sample the first 99 schools involved in the piloting of the SSE and ESR. The study, undertaken by the University of Cambridge and Cambridge Education[1] had some similar elements to the English studies – questionnaires and group interviews – but these were more extensive, covering a wider group of stakeholders, generating a substantive body of qualitative and quantitative data. The components of the Hong Kong study were:

- Analysis of questionnaires (Q1) on ESR completed by teachers in the 92 schools – 62 primary schools, 23 secondary schools and 7 special schools. 4425 were sent out and 3581 collected, a response rate of 81%
- Analysis of write-in open-ended comments on Q1
- 34 surveys of ESR completed by external reviewers
- 142 surveys of ESR completed by review team members
- Post-ESR questionnaires (Q4) completed by 3,125 school staff in primary, special and secondary schools including senior and middle leaders
- Analysis of write-in open-ended comments on Q4
- Observations and interviews in 10 schools during the ESR process with confidential questionnaires issued to various stakeholders, external reviewers, team leaders and school principals

- Case studies in 8 schools involving one hour interviews with a range of stakeholders including 40 school management committee members, 8 principals, 48 School Improvement Team members, 75 teachers, 78 students and 56 parents.

As a background to the study there were ongoing discussions with members of the Education and Manpower Bureau (EMB) on the history, rationale and conduct of SSE/ESR. During a week long visit to the Chinese University of Hong Kong (CUHK) to discuss issues of self evaluation with University staff there were ad hoc opportunities to visit and sit in on school workshops on self evaluation conducted by staff from CUHK. While this was not a data gathering exercise it did provide something of a cultural backdrop to the reform and gave an insight into an alternative model to the more accountability orientated approach of EMB.

The new relationship in England

England has the longest history of school inspection in the world, since it has the earliest record of inspection, dating back to 1839 (Edmonds, 1999). The concept of a New Relationship was first spelled out by the Government Minister, David Miliband in a high profile policy speech on January 8th, 2004 (DfES, 2004). As spelt out in this speech, and elaborated in subsequent documents, NrWS promised to allow schools greater freedom to define clearer priorities for themselves, to get rid of bureaucratic clutter and render an account of quality and performance to parents and other stakeholders. A School Improvement Partner, described as a 'critical friend', would liaise with schools and support them in achieving greater autonomy, 'releasing local initiative and energy'. The seven elements of the new relationship are portrayed as an interlocking set framed by trust, support, networking and challenge (Figure 4.1).

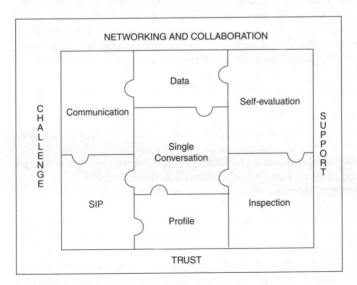

Figure 4.1 Networking and collaboration

The significance of a 'new relationship' has to be understood within the context of the 'old' relationship. Over a decade numerous studies had cast doubt on the efficacy and impact of Ofsted inspection. For example, Cullingford and Daniels' 1998 study reported an adverse effect on exam performance for a sample of schools, although dismissed by the then Chief Inspector of Schools as 'deeply flawed, ineptly executed and poorly argued' (Woodhead, 1999, p.5). None the less, Rosenthal's study in the following year also found 'a significant negative effect of Ofsted visits on school exam performance in the year of the inspection' (2001, p.16), a performance drop explained in part by the diversion of a school's energy into preparing for inspection. A report by Brunel University in 1999 referred to 'anticipatory dread' which impaired normal school development work and the effectiveness of teaching. Ouston and Davies' study in 1998 found that schools that were most positive about the inspection experience were those that did not allow the process to intimidate them. They had a high level of professional self-confidence, enough to challenge the Ofsted team's findings combined with an ability to make their own professional judgements as to what was right for their school. In other words there was already in these schools an incipient, or well developed, self-evaluation culture.

A Parliamentary sub-committee which reported in 1999 acknowledged the stress on teachers and advocated a briefer notice of inspection, recommending that the Chief Inspector 'should be concerned to improve morale and promote confidence in the teaching profession' and that inspectors should 'take account of self-evaluation procedures used by the school'.

The change of heart which led to the formulation of a new relationship may be attributed to the interplay among a number of factors, the mounting evidence of Ofsted dysfunction, evidence of low morale among the profession (for example, Galton and MacBeath, 2003, MacBeath and Galton, 2004), a recruitment crisis and premature exit of teaching staff (Howson, 2002) in conjunction with perhaps the most compelling motive – the high financial cost of Ofsted inspection. In 2004 the Government-commissioned Gershon Report on public spending removed around £400 million from the Ofsted budget, moving those monies to front line services. The coming of a new Chief Inspector, David Bell, was a symbolic opportunity for a fresh start with self evaluation given a new status at the very heart of the New Relationship.

The main features of inspection under NrWS are described in the following terms:

- shorter, sharper inspections that take no more than two days in a school, taking self-evaluation evidence as the starting point
- shorter notice of inspections to avoid pre-inspection preparation and to reduce the levels of stress often associated with an inspection
- smaller inspection teams with a greater number of inspections led by one of Her Majesty's Inspectors
- more frequent inspections, with the maximum period between inspections reduced from the current six years to three years, though more frequently for schools causing concern
- self-evaluation evidence as the starting point for inspection and for the school's internal planning with regular input and feedback from users – pupils, their parents and the community – in the school's development

• a simplification of the categorisation of schools causing concern, retaining the current approach to schools that need special measures but introducing a new single category of 'Improvement Notice' for schools where there are weaknesses in pupil progress or in key aspects of the school's work.

While NRwS inspection has been characterised by some as validation of the school's own self-evaluation, Ofsted is quick to disabuse people of that notion. While self-evaluation is an integral element of the process, inspectors will continue to arrive at their own overall assessment of the effectiveness and efficiency of the school. They reserve their judgment on the capacity of the school to make improvements, 'taking into account' its ability to assess accurately the quality of its own provision – an important caveat as it signals clearly the nature of the relationship between the external and the internal team. There is no pretence that this is an equal partnership.

Prior to inspection schools are expected to complete the self-evaluation form (the SEF) which asks schools to evaluate their progress against an inspection schedule, to set out the main evidence on which this evaluation is based, to identify their own strengths and weaknesses and explain the action the school is taking to remedy the weaknesses and develop its strengths. The school is asked to use the four Ofsted criteria (1 – Outstanding, 2 – Good, 3 – Satisfactory and 4 – Inadequate). While the SEF is described as a critical document in the new inspection process it is, HMCI insists (Oftsed, 2005), not in itself self-evaluation but a *record* of the school's own self-evaluation. As such Ofsted does not prescribe or suggest how schools should go about their own self-evaluation, leaving this to schools to draw on many models and exemplars available.

> *The existence of a SEF itself will not demonstrate that a school has secure methods of review and evaluation, but the quality of completion will be a clear pointer to the effectiveness of the practices (particularly of leadership and management) within the school. … (Ofsted Framework)*

One local authority, Leicestershire County Council, offers the following maxim – 'a school always prepared for inspection, but not always preparing for inspection, is a self-evaluating school'. It alerts schools to the function of the SEF as a summary review of self-evaluation not self-evaluation itself. With a rich body of evidence to draw on, the SEF should, it is suggested, be short, concise, evaluative and evidence-based. And, add the Ofsted guidelines, 'honest'.

> *If you cannot say what you need to in about 20 pages, you are probably describing what you do rather than analysing the impact of what you do. Remember you are trying to convey what parents, pupils and other stakeholders think of the school and give a succinct evaluation. (Ofsted advice)*

The key difference in this reborn self-evaluation is its liberation from an Ofsted predetermined template, schools now being encouraged to use their own approaches to self-evaluation with the self-evaluation form (the SEF) serving simply as an internal summary and basis for external inspection. The small print, which has apparently bypassed most headteachers, adds the barely perceptible caveat that completion of the SEF is not compulsory. That, at least, is the theory.

The challenge facing the New Relationship is the legacy of a decade and a half in which a previous Secretary of State's vision of 'big cats prowling the educational landscape' had become all too real (Learmonth, 2000). Teachers and headteachers interviewed in the NUT study generated a substantial list of concerns including inspectors' excessive focus on accountability, a blame culture, pressure from national exams and SATS, perceived threat from outside audiences against a background of school league tables, negative media publicity, inaccurate inspection reports and lack of genuine consultation with teachers, increasing and oppressive paperwork, ambiguity about the purposes of self-evaluation and imposition of a set of self-evaluation criteria on schools.

Questions of purpose

Almost half of all teachers who completed the NUT questionnaire identified the raising of standards as a fundamental purpose of self-evaluation. Next in priority to raising standards was *providing teachers with tools which help evaluate pupils' learning* (29.7%). 10.4% thought its primary purpose should be the extension of the school's capacity to respond to, and implement change. Few of them (6.3%) identified the primary purpose as *helping staff to share ideas and practice more widely*, while even fewer (3.1%) thought self-evaluation should *provide opportunities for the school to hear the views of pupils*. The smallest response, however, was the 2.1% of teachers who thought the purpose of self-evaluation should be geared towards providing Ofsted with evidence on their schools' quality and effectiveness.

By way of parenthesis, the contrast with the opportunistic Hong Kong sample was striking. 40.8% chose *the extension of the school's capacity to respond to and implement change* followed by 25.0% who chose *providing teachers with tools which help evaluate pupils' learning*. *Raising standards* was selected by only 15.1% as compared to the near 50% in England. While not making too much of these data they raise important issues about perceptions of purpose which we were later able to follow up more rigorously and systematically.

In England (as in Hong Kong) in depth discussion allowed the priority given to different purposes to be further clarified. Raising standards as a top priority was put into a broader perspective. As one primary teacher argued, 'The purpose of looking at the school from the lens of self-evaluation is to make the school a better place for learning. That leads us into raising attainments. ... We're in the business of raising our standards through learning.' A secondary teacher in another school made a similar point – 'Student learning is vital; if we can understand self-evaluation this way, we can make something about our teaching. It will enable schools to respond to and implement change.' A consistent theme was that self-evaluation was for a school's and teacher's own improvement in learning and teaching, not for the benefit of Ofsted or to serve other extrinsic purposes.

Who is self-evaluation for?

We asked teachers to consider a range of potential audiences for self-evaluation and to rank them from 1 to 5. In order to analyse findings we calculated a mean score as a measure of the primacy given to different audiences. The school itself emerged as the first preferred audience for self-evaluation with a mean of approximately 5.0. This was followed by parents with an approximate mean of 3.5. The Local Education Authority (LEA) was ranked third with a mean of around 3.2. Although Ofsted might have been seen as the obvious focus for a school's self-evaluation, teachers did not rank it highly as an audience (a mean of 2.3) while the media was least preferred with the lowest mean (1.0) The case for the school itself as the audience was argued in terms of its own responsibility for addressing what was uncovered.

> *Self-evaluation is to promote open discussion of the results among teachers themselves about strategies for improvement. It is important that the school has the right non-judgemental atmosphere for discussing self-evaluation outcomes. (Secondary school teacher)*

The fear of having self-evaluation results publicised was also a concern for the respondents and appeared to be the major reason for some teachers rejecting the media and Ofsted as primary audiences of self-evaluation:

> *The report should not be in the public domain – teachers are easily identifiable. Why should anyone want to be a teacher when you have to go through this process? ... the school itself should use self-evaluation outcomes. (Primary school teacher)*

On the question of where criteria should come from, 62.2% said these should be of the school's own devising, perhaps with the support of a critical friend, as against 15.5% who said that Ofsted should provide the criteria. As for the components of self-evaluation, pupil motivation (37.8%) and whole school factors such as ethos and culture (25.6%) were rated more highly than value-added measures (20.7%) and Key Stage tests (2.4%). Teacher-pupil relationship was chosen by 8.5% of respondents.

From espoused theory to theory-in-practice

These views espoused by teachers and headteachers have to compared with what they do and how they prioritise issues in practice. In the NCSL study we posed the question 'What approach to self evaluation are you currently using?' Of the 68 questionnaires returned (a poor rate from 200 sent out but not uncommon in a pressured climate), 38 replied simply 'Ofsted' or 'the SEF'. 22 also mentioned a local authority framework, but in almost all cases this was either a customisation of the Ofsted model to the local authority context or an adaptation of the authority model to meet the requirements of the SEF.

What emerges clearly from these two studies is the gap between what teachers and headteachers say self-evaluation ought to be for and how it works in practice. It appears that the Ofsted protocol is now so well embedded both in practice and in people's thinking that the advice that the SEF is not self-evaluation has fallen on deaf ears. Meetings arranged by the National College with about 400 headteachers in four regions of England revealed that either headteachers did not know it was not compulsory or simply decided to play safe by dutifully completing the form.

In light of the background history it is not surprising to find schools avoiding departing too far from mandated protocols, leaving behind some of the more creative and idiosyncratic approaches to self-evaluation that were to be found half a decade ago (Davies and Rudd, 2001). It is symptomatic of what happens in a prescriptive policy environment when government co-opts good ideas and legislates a uniform approach attended by high stakes consequences for lack of compliance.

The school improvement partner

The appointment of a school improvement partner (a SIP) for each school provides further evidence of how top down co-option works. The school improvement partner is described in policy documents (DfES, 2005) as a 'critical friend' who adheres strictly to confidentiality, respects the school's autonomy to plan its development, and starts from the school's self-evaluation and the needs of the community, especially those of the children. So far so good. Further reading, however, reveals that the SIP is chosen by the local authority (a school can reject its new 'friend' only once), that he/she reports to the local authority, to government and to Ofsted on the school's adherence to policy directives. The SIP can initiate action to put a school into special measures, now to be known by its friendlier but equally high stakes appellation – 'improvement notice'.

Herein lies the paradox of a New Relationship, the architecture of which has still to resolve the confusion between support and challenge, accountability and improvement, school autonomy and centralised control.

The new relationship in Hong Kong

The year 1997 marks the watershed in which Hong Kong began to turn its attention increasingly from the West to the North (Wong, 2005). This did not, however, preclude a continued watching brief on the development of school inspection in the U.K. The development of quality assurance through the late nineties and up until 2003 was closer to the Scottish than English model, but benefited from a critical approach to the strengths and weaknesses of both systems. Using overseas as well as local consultancy the Education Manpower Bureau (EMB) identified flaws in its own system as too cumbersome, time consuming and costly, so that to inspect all government schools in Hong Kong would take more than a decade. In response to this, in 2003 EMB set in train a new review process that would include more self-evaluation and a scaled-down inspection/verification process (Education and Manpower Bureau, 2003). As in England, cost and logistics were prime movers but that was not the sole motive. Self-evaluation had been embraced half a decade previously but was seen to still need a much stronger push and support from the centre.

The aim of the new relationship Hong-Kong style is to review all schools over a four-year cycle with self evaluation as the focus of inspectorate visits, the underpinning rationale being that those who are closest to everyday practice are best placed to evaluate, develop and improve it.

And the starting point for this story is that the successful school is a self- evaluating school in which there is a shared belief that school improvement is the right and responsibility of every single member of the school community. The self-evaluating school is singled out by its willingness to improve through learning. (EMB, 2003, p. 7)

During 2003, documentation to support the new approach was developed and a training programme for QAD inspectors was conducted in September 2003 followed by a further training programme for frontline school-based External Reviewers in December 2003.

School self evaluation (SSE) as a prelude to external school review is a process stretching over a period of months in which a school staff are introduced to the purposes and tools of SSE, a number for these provided by the EMB. Principals and school improvement teams (SITS) play a key role in taking staff systematically through the instruments and protocols and trying to alleviate some of the anxieties that accompany any new initiatives. The composition of the school improvement team is at the school's own discretion but in most cases comprises five to eight senior staff, although some schools make a point of including recently appointed teachers. With this background preparation, staff take part in gathering documentation in order to make an evidence-based judgment on the school performance under the 14 headings in the School Self Assessment form (SSA), a close cousin of the English SEF. The external review team (ESR), usually five inspectors plus a co-opted headteacher as external reviewer, visits the school for five days. It starts with the principal presenting the school's work and context, followed by scrutiny of documentation, shadowing of individual students and visits to classrooms by the review team – a form of validity check on the accuracy of the school's self-knowledge.

A question of purpose

A key aspect of the Impact Study was in-depth analysis of the eight case study schools in 2005 followed by a further eight in 2006. These covered nearly a hundred members of staff in each of the two years. In discussions with all stakeholders research started, as in England, with a question of purpose, allowing a deeper exploration of the more impressionistic data from the earlier opportunity sample. Posed with the question 'what is self evaluation for?, school staff (principals, middle managers, SITS and basic rank teachers) offered a variety of answers, the most commonly recurring of which were:

- A mechanism to meet social and global change
- A process of self-reflection and review
- A form of professional development
- An impetus to ownership and teamwork
- A lever for greater effectiveness and efficiency
- An instrument for accountability

These definitions of purpose lean towards a capacity building approach together with an acknowledgement of the need to render an account to external agencies. In Hong Kong, as in England, self-evaluation had been in place in many schools before the advent of SSE/ESR but this new EMB initiative brought with it a sense of urgency. Half of the case study schools had experience of working with higher education teams or developing some form of self-evaluation, yet, paralleling experience in the UK, SSE tended to be seen by many schools as something new rather than as an extension or refinement of what had gone before. Despite espousing broad ranging views as to the purposes and audiences for self-evaluation, in practice Hong Kong teachers, like their English counterparts, tended to see the primary audience for SSE as the external review team rather than the school itself.

The quantitative data from the surveys revealed a widely held view that SSE added to workload, an indicator of the extent to which SSE was perceived as an extra, imposed rather than owned. Only 30.5% of teachers agreed with the statement 'The ESR did not affect much of my daily duties' and only 22.9% agreed that 'ESR did not exert much pressure on me'. The workload issue, as revealed through write-in comments and interviews, was in a climate where successive waves of innovation inclined teachers to see SSE as yet another imposition, requiring a substantial investment of time, primarily in hunting down and assembling documentation. Even schools that had an embryonic self-evaluation culture and welcomed external review as a catalyst for developing it further, there was still apprehension. As one principal put it, it was a fear of 'not being good enough'. As was frequently pointed out, this was less a fear of external review per se than, in a climate of falling rolls, the looming spectre of school closure.

Preparing for review, alleviating anxiety

The pre-ESR briefing was generally seen as helpful in alleviating anxiety. Establishing relationships, building trust, listening to staff's concerns and demythologising the process proved to be of greater value than a simple transfer of information through documentary channels or by other more distant forms of exhortation. However, the most powerful impact on attitudes was through school principals, senior and middle leaders and SITs who were able, over a period of time, to play a key role in clarifying the essential purpose of review, defusing anxiety and maintaining the flow of information so as to manage priorities effectively. If there is a single message to emerge form this study it is the importance of leadership in creating an upbeat climate, inoculating against the anxiety virus and the infectious rumour mill.

The SIT, or school improvement team, is intended to give leverage to SSE. The evidence from case study schools reveals a generally positive influence of school improvement teams. In these schools they have played a wide ranging role in monitoring practice, stimulating collaborative lesson planning and peer observation, and mediating between senior management and the basic rank teachers. As SITs develop their remit and expand their constitution to include more basic rank teachers (and possibly parents and students), they may, in the future, hold the key to the effective embedding of self-evaluation in day-to-day classroom practice.

In the main schools described themselves as well prepared for review. Staff had taken it seriously and professed to benefiting from the experience. In the staff survey following ESR a majority of teachers (59.1%) reported that they were on the whole satisfied with the ESR process, the major dissatisfaction being lack of time, taking teachers away from their teaching priorities.

The Impact Study also identified factors that stand in the way, and those that promote, an effective relationship between SSE and ESR. Those that were most consistently cited as promoting a positive relationship were:

Building confidence, through affirming practice and the validity of the school's own self-evaluation

Giving impetus to cultures of self-evaluation by provision of useful tools and helping schools to build SSE into their planning and practice

Enhancing school improvement, by illustrating how SSE can promote better teaching, better management and leadership

Promoting a positive view of ESR by offering an external perspective and demythologising threat

The most consistent positive comments were in relation to the press for evidence that had helped schools move from a more subjective and impressionistic evaluation of their own performance to a more systematic and rigorous approach to assessing the quality of practice. The aftermath of ESR had, in the case study schools, brought a comprehensive, whole school, view of practice, with planning no longer fragmented in individual subjects but a now more joined-up and systematic process. The inclusion of a range of stakeholders in the process has encouraged schools to view their practice through different lenses, challenging complacency and self-satisfaction where that existed.

Factors cited as inhibiting were:

Questions of purpose. Confusion as to the essential purpose of self-evaluation and review

Apprehension and vulnerability. Build up of stress over a long period having a deleterious effect on morale

Time. The amount of time given to preparation, searching out (and sometimes recreating) documentation, detracting time from teaching and individual student support

Expertise of the review team. Some individual team members lacking in expertise, insight or sensitivity

The two issues most consistently cited as inhibiting were the uploading of the school report on to the web, and the reporting of the 14 areas using grades 1 to 4 (mirroring the practice in England). These strong critiques were taken on board by EMB and both requirements have now been discontinued.

Issues of feedback and reporting

The oral feedback session given by the review team at the end of the visit was generally described as excellent, fair and balanced and clear in its summation of the issues. It was described as encouraging, with 'supportive appreciation', highlighting areas for further action and school improvement. It was emphasised, though, that these sessions needed greater brevity, a closer focus on key issues and greater opportunity for dialogue. Feedback that was too long and too one way could ultimately be counter-productive. There were also pleas from teachers not to be excluded from these sessions.

Review teams were congratulated on their friendliness and professionalism. There were, however, a few exceptions to the rule. In a few cases team members were perceived as compounding misunderstanding or exacerbating anxiety by acting, it was claimed, more like inquisitors than critical friends and intruding in classroom work without prior negotiation or clarification of purpose. It is an issue that points to a need for further professional development and/or more careful selection or de-selection of team members. Evidence from a wide range of stakeholders pointed to a need for better and more sustained professional development, a need for upskilling in analysing documents, shadowing, questioning and probing, accurate listening, affirming and supporting practice, challenging constructively, managing meetings, and writing reports.

The role and contribution of the external reviewer (a principal from another school), while welcomed, pinpointed key concerns as to their experience, training and ability to take a distanced view of their peers. The danger of over identification and collusion was highlighted. The addition of external reviewers serves both as an important signal to schools as to the balance and expertise of the team as well as providing valuable professional development for serving principals. Feedback from the review team, from school staff and from external reviewers themselves highlighted the need for further professional development as paramount.

From the perspective of the review teams themselves the ESR process was very positive. There was a high level of agreement that ESR had been implemented according to the guidelines with a good team co-operation, clear and reasonable allocation of work with attention to procedures and guidance from team leaders. The most critical comments were in relation to time and timing, in particular the tightness of the schedule which encompassed a wide variety of tasks, including a weight of documentation which it is already agreed will need to be less all-encompassing and ritualistic.

The survey conducted six months or more after review found almost complete consensus (more than 8 in 10) that ESR had identified the school's strengths and areas for improvement. When it came to issues which impinged directly on teachers' work responses were less positive, particularly in relation to the use of indicators and their relevance to the work of teachers. Lack of confidence in the use of self-evaluation tools and commitment to learning more in this domain also highlighted priorities for further development.

Taking account of context

The starting point for external review is presentation by the principal of the school's background and social context. For some principals and staff there was a concern that the significance of this tended to be underplayed in the final report and in the common template used by all schools. It was said by a number of schools, particularly those serving disadvantaged communities, that ESR was not sensitive enough to a school's unique mission and strengths and did not give sufficient credit to the context in which teachers worked. Falling rolls, parental choice and external accountability have contributed to a feeling of dissatisfaction among some staff, together with anxiety that uploading of ESR reports on to a publicly accessible website would simply add fuel to the fire. While the falling rolls issue is one that will not go away, and will continue to be a source of concern, the agreement by EMB not to publicise school reports is already easing anxiety.

One of the justifications for review is its brevity and light touch. From a school's point of view, however, this was seen as a potential weakness, not allowing for nuance and complexities to be expressed and unravelled. Because schools worry that something may be missed, preparation for review tends to be exhaustive rather then focused. Evidence tends to be seen as documentary, minutes of meetings and planning documents, often tokenistic rather than 'living' qualitative insights into students' and organisational learning. The transition from inspection to review means that old ideas linger on and it will take time for schools to grasp the essential purpose of review. Its goal is less one of providing a 'true picture' of a school in all its aspects than to validate its self-knowledge and strategic direction.

The question of who self-evaluation and review are really for remains for many staff unresolved. The data reveal clearly that basic rank teachers are less well informed, less confident and less positive than middle or senior managers. This is because they play a minor role in the review process itself and only get access to the teams' findings at second hand after the event, and although their teaching is observed they do not get feedback. Students tended to be informed briefly and even cursorily at morning assemblies and there were only a few examples of students being involved in dialogue over the outcome of the report. Primary school children in particular were often left guessing as to the purpose or outcome of review while policies around parental communication and involvement varied widely form school to school.

These are issues addressed within the Impact Study which, even in its interim stages, is feeding back into reframing of policy and advice to schools. It is a testament to the responsiveness of an inspectorate that it is willing to listen to evidence rather than pursuing a doctrinaire adherence to a preconceived mindset. There is already evidence that the introduction of SSE/ESR has brought a number of benefits, particularly to leading edge schools:

- A deepening understanding of the purposes of ESR and SSE
- Promoting the use of data and evidence as a basis for SSE
- Helping schools to conduct informed discussions as to the value of the SSE and its relationship to school improvement
- Supporting schools in getting better at identifying their strengths and areas for improvement
- Developing a more systematic and informed approach to SSE in schools
- Creating a greater sense of openness and transparency
- Incorporating different stakeholders' perspectives on the relationship between ESR and SSE

Follow-up interviews a year to eighteen months after ESR provide evidence both of a tendency for some staff to relax following review while for others it had led to both restructuring and reculturing with a much more consistent and systematic focus on teaching and learning. It is too early perhaps to judge sustainability and deeper embedding of self evaluation but what is clear is that leadership, of the principal and the SIT, holds the key to effective and meaningful change.

These schools that have made SSE their own are exemplars for other schools to draw on. They provide an invaluable reservoir of expertise for system wide change as these principals and school improvement teams carry more credibility with their colleagues than any government office or university source. Already some of these principals are in demand by their colleagues and one school sponsoring body has set up its own leadership Task Force, a forum in which school principals exchange ideas and self-evaluation practice. A concerted and systematic deployment of school expertise system wide offers the future growth points and the enlistment of 'champions' from among school staff is likely to vouchsafe school self-evaluation and external review at a time of uncertainty and continuing change.

Common challenges

In both Hong Kong and England one could, before the new relationships, find a scattering of schools engaged in self evaluation, drawing on a range of models and sources of support. In England, as in Hong Kong, university staff had for some time been working with schools developing their own approaches and supporting an internal accountability, rather than an external accountability, model. However with the adoption, or co-option, by government of self evaluation, much of that grass roots development appears to have been inhibited (MacBeath, 2005, MacBeath and Clark, 2004). The provision of protocols and templates linked to inspection or review has steered school principals and teachers towards safer waters. In England the SEF was widely seen as the self-evaluation mechanism while in Hong Kong the SSA tended to be seen in the same way. The adherence to this one-off review moved Chief Inspectors in both countries to insist that this form filling exercise with an eye on external review was not self-evaluation but rather a shorthand or summary of ongoing practice.

While both systems adopted the four point scale for their SEF/SSA self reporting, there were some salient differences in the approach to its completion. In Hong Kong the form was the subject of discussion and negotiation with a whole school staff. For example, in one primary school staff came together for the whole of a Saturday to go through each of the 14 indicator areas one by one discussing their ratings in small groups, supporting their case with appeal to evidence and finally agreeing a grade. In schools where there was an inability to agree on a grade this often resulted in a majority vote. By contrast, in England the SEF tends to have been completed by the headteacher[2], sometimes in his or her summer holidays, with or without wider consultation among the senior leadership team.

The difference in approach is explained largely by the timing and pacing of reform in both countries. In England the New Relationship was announced and implemented within a very short space of time so that headteachers found themselves having to adopt a rapid response mode just in case the inspection visit would be announced on the Monday followed by a visit on the Wednesday. The much longer time frame in Hong Kong afforded schools a lengthy lead in and allowed prescient principals to engage a whole staff in thinking through a studied response. However, the length of lead-in was also an inhibitor for some schools who would spend nine months or more in preparation including in one, perhaps apochryphal case, the Saturday before Christmas day.

The public reporting of these summative grades, schools' own rating being raised or lowered by the inspection/review team, proved to be a source of contention in both countries. The decision by the Chief Inspector in Hong Kong to dispense with the 1–4 labels was a brave move signalling a desire for a more nuanced profile of a school's quality. While in England the school report is made public in Hong Kong the mandatory uploading of the report to the web has now been discontinued.

The composition of the inspection/review teams bears some similarities in respect of widening the scope to include co-opted headteachers and, in

England, lay members. Neither country yet has included teachers or students in the review team but their inclusion is likely to be seen as much a less heretical idea in the future as parent and teacher voices are increasingly taken into account in self-evaluation.

While in England proportional review has been discussed for a number of years, in Hong Kong it has not yet been embraced. The piloting phase of SSE/ ERC is still to be completed and evaluated but the logic of proportionality is clearly accepted as something for the future. It is a mark of a maturing self-evaluation system that good schools need less and less policing by an external agency. What is referred to in England as 'light touch' inspection may in future take the form of a one day visit or less, by way of reassurance or even celebration of a school's ability of telling its own story with evidence-based conviction. Hong Kong is moving more slowly to the logic of proportional review as the wide differential between the most and least confident self-evaluating schools is exposed.

Conclusions

At the very heart of the issues in both countries are issues of trust, networking, support and challenge. These are the four framing words in the seven piece NrWS jigsaw in England (Figure 1). The implication is that a New Relationship has to be founded on these and cannot work unless these are in place. These four key precepts apply with equal force in Hong Kong. Yet what is implied by the word 'trust', for example? Should it be taken to mean that teachers trust the goodwill of the government's intentions? That teachers can trust that inspectors will be fair? Does it mean that the government trusts the professionalism and integrity of teachers? Or that inspectors trust the integrity and honesty of the school's own self-evaluation? Few, if any, of these are realistic aspirations given the asymmetry of the power relations between inspectors and schools.

However friendly the rhetoric, in England the bottom line was clearly articulated by David Miliband the English Junior Minister. 'Accountability drives everything. Without accountability there is no legitimacy; without legitimacy there is no support; without support there are no resources; and without resources there are no services' (North of England Speech, 2004). It is within this political imperative that a school and its inspection team have to negotiate where trust resides and is tested. In Hong Kong, as in England, trust is a matter of history and an asymmetry of power. In that country there is not the same long shadow cast by the oppressive Ofsted regime of the 1990s, but trust cannot simply be assumed or piously extolled within a relationship that is bound to carry consequences for the future of a school at a time of shrinking population and falling rolls.

Trust is elusive of measurement and resides deep within cultural history. In England there is a long standing tradition of dissent within the profession and Teachers' Unions, and although senior leaders conform to the demands of Ofsted, within the rank and file there is much less dutiful compliance than is to be found in Hong Kong. There teachers are typically still to be found in their schools at seven or eight in the evening, three or four hours after the last child has left. It is this profound sense of duty which SSE/ESR is able to exploit as, within a school, no stone will be left unturned, no document unexamined in the prelude to external review. Getting it right is a deeply embedded cultural imperative. For the Hong Kong inspectorate it is also the greatest challenge as schools are not easily convinced to ease off, do less and work smarter rather than harder.

A sense of duty and compliance to demands of external authority, while stronger in Hong Kong, is not absent in England. There is within the profession an innate sense of accountability, if not in the form that governments now mandate. The contention that has become a running sore is not about what teachers owe to their pupils and parents but the guise in which such responsibility is presented. Richard Elmore (2005) makes an important distinction between internal and external accountability. Internal accountability describes the conditions in a school that precede and shape the response of schools to pressure that originates in policies outside the organisation. The level or degree of internal accountability is measured by the degree of convergence among what individuals say they are responsible for (responsibility), what people say the organization is responsible for (expectations), and the internal norms and processes by which people literally account for their work (accountability structures). Elmore concludes that with strong internal accountability schools are likely to be more responsive to external pressure for performance.

This is the meeting ground of pressure and support. When there is a measure of professional trust it is possible for there to be support, as this implies a relationship in which people experience a genuine intention on the part of the other to help without a hidden agenda, without a sense that support come with caveats and some form of payback. This is why critical friendship is best exercised when there are no hidden agendas, no differential power bases, not premised on accountability but on improvement first. As research has consistently shown (Doherty *et al.*, 2001, Swaffield and MacBeath, 2005) colleagues from other schools or universities can play this role.

However well intentioned and however supportive, the School Improvement Partner in England or the Review Team in Hong Kong, whose role is necessarily political, cannot be a critical friend in the essential meaning of that term. External review can, however, offer an honest form of external validation which does not pretend to be other than what it is, its purpose and functions clearly understood. In England the Ofsted strapline Improvement through Inspection will continue to mislead if the purpose of validation is not also understood there as well.

In England the government have co-opted the term 'intelligent accountability', a phrase ironically coined by Baroness O Neill's critique of 'perverse indicators' (2002). It was intended as a shot across the government bows, not as a validation of what she described as unintelligent accountability. Intelligent accountability grows from collegial networking within and between schools. It proceeds from strong professional and inter-professional alliances. It is nourished by the support of trusted advisers and critical schools friends. When there is strong and resilient internal accountability it can turn outward to system-wide demands. Schools and teachers are likely to respond more positively and thoughtfully to external pressure and critical review when they are confident in the knowledge that they have a rich and unique story to tell, one which rises above and goes beyond the mean statistics and pushes against prevailing orthodoxies of competitive attainment.

Notes

1 Cambridge Education is an independent company, its head office located in Cambridge
2 Evidence from NCSL development sessions with headteachers in four English regions

References

Cullingford, C. and Daniels, S. (1998) *The Effects of Ofsted Inspection on School Performance*, Huddersfield: University of Huddersfield.

Davies, D. and Rudd, P. E. (2001) *Evaluating School Self-evaluation*, Slough: National Foundation for Educational Research.

Department for Education and Skills (2004) *Strategies for Improving Schools: A Handbook for School Improvement Partners*, London: DfES.

Department for Education and Skills (2004) *A New Relationship with Schools: School Improvement Partners' Brief*, London: DfES.

Doherty, J., MacBeath, J., Jardine, S., Smith. I. and McCall, J. (2001) Do schools need critical friends? in: J. MacBeath and P. Mortimore (Eds) *Improving School Effectiveness*: Buckingham: Open University Press.

Education and Manpower Bureau (2003). Enhancing School Development and Accountability through Self-evaluation and Accountability, Circular 23/2003, June 12.

Elmore, R. (2005) *Agency, Reciprocity, and Accountability in Democratic Education*, Boston, Mass: Consortium for Policy Research in Education.

Galton, M. and MacBeath, J. (2002) *A Life in Teaching?*, London: National Union of Teachers.

Gershon, P. (2004) *Releasing Resources to the Front Line; A review of Public Sector Efficiency*, Norwich: HMSO.

Howson, J. (2002) 'The relationship between head teachers' length of service in primary and secondary schools and selected PANDA grades'. The National College for School Leadership.

Learmonth, J. (2000) Inspection: what's in it for schools?, London: RoutledgeFalmer.

MacBeath, J. and Galton, M. (2004) *A Life in Secondary Teaching?*, London: National Union of Teachers.

MacBeath, J. and Clark, W.R. (2004) *The Impact of External Review in Hong Kong*, Cambridge: Cambridge Education.

MacBeath, J. and Oduro (2004) *Inspection and Self evaluation: a new relationship?* London: National Union of Teachers.

Miliband, D. (2004) North of England Speech, Education Conference, Belfast: 8 January.

Moos, L. (2003) *Educational Leadership: understanding and developing practice*, Copenhagen: Danmarks Paedagogiske Verlag.

National College of School Leadership (2005) *Self Evaluation: a guide for school leaders*, Nottingham: NCSL.

Office For Standards In Education (2004) *A New Relationship with Schools*. London: DfES, Ofsted.

O'Neill, N. (2002) *A Question of Trust*, Cambridge: Cambridge University Press.

Ouston, J. and Davies, J. (1998) 'OfSTED and afterwards: schools responses to inspection' in Earley, P (ed) (1998) *School Improvement after OfSTED Inspection: school and LEA responses*. London: Sage Publications.

Rosenthal, L. (2001) 'The cost of regulation in education: do school inspections improve school quality?' Department of Economics, University of Keele.

Swaffield, S. and MacBeath, J. (2005) School self-evaluation and the role of a critical friend, *Cambridge Journal of Education*.

Woodhead, C. (1999) 'An Inspector responds.' *Guardian Education*, 5th October edition p.5.

Wong, K.C. (2005) Interview at the National College of School Leadership, Nottingham, June

CHAPTER 5

REVIVED BY POST MORTEMS; BRIEFING; RESEARCH FOCUS

Originally published in *TES Magazine*, 16 April, 1999

An 18-country study has shown that school self-evaluation is not a cosy option – but it can provide remarkable insights, according to John MacBeath.

Eurocrats call it 'the beautiful project'. Some of them have pronounced it the jewel in the crown of European Community education initiatives. Evaluating Quality in School Education involved 101 schools in 18 countries, all committed to using a common approach to school self-evaluation. Although it received funding for only one school year, 98 of the schools wanted to continue the work beyond the funded period. As one English school put it: 'We have learned more in this short year than we ever thought possible. The project has brought new vitality and new energy to the staff.'

The genius of the project was in its common approach in all 101 schools while respecting their very different contexts and cultures, from Iceland to the Greek Islands and Malmo to Madrid. There were four elements common for all schools – a set of self-evaluation guidelines containing 30 methodologies, the appointment of a critical friend to support the school, networking workshops and conferences both nationally and internationally, and a self-evaluation profile.

This was used at the beginning of the project to give schools a baseline perspective of their organisational health and well-being. The evaluation consisted of 12 indicators, each rated on a four-point scale from positive to negative, with three further assessment categories – improving, stable and declining.

This assessment was not, however, simply the task of the senior management team or teachers but also involved students, parents and governors (or school boards). Each of these groups was asked to reach a consensus, then to send two representatives to the school evaluation group. This consisted of 10 people, representing five sets of 'stakeholders' with different perspectives on school quality and improvement.

The group was then charged with drawing up a self-evaluation profile for their school, and choosing up to five of the 12 areas to explore in greater depth over the following year. This process was the centrepiece of the project.

Consensus rarely came easily. Dealing with disagreement, however, proved to be a salient indicator of the school's inner strength and capacity for improvement.

Of the 101 schools, 44 chose quality of learning and teaching as a priority for further evaluation. Methodologies included questionnaires, focus groups, photo-evaluation, shadowing and spot-checks. And many schools incorporated their researches into the curriculum. In one Spanish school, students administered a questionnaire to younger children, analysing the data as part of their socio-cultural studies programme.

Classroom observation was a popular methodology. This sometimes took the form of peer observation, teachers evaluating one another in a climate of trust. More challenging still was observation by students, for many of whom it was an eye-opener. One Greek student wrote: 'For the first time as a student I did something I will remember my whole life. I attended a lesson in our school as a simple observer. During the lesson I filled in a questionnaire based on my observations. I realised that some students are interested in the lesson, while others neither paid attention nor took part. I wondered who is to blame ... To what extent are we students responsible, or our teacher?' From this toe in the water, students became more rigorous and critical. In one Finnish school, teachers agreed that students could conduct unannounced classroom observations. The teachers said it had provided a salutary inside view, more penetrating than the cursory observation of a visiting inspector.

Perhaps the greatest gain was the challenge and the sharing of experiences across 18 nations. Irish teachers visited Finnish schools, English schools played host to the Dutch and Danes. A new teacher from St Kentigern's in West Lothian who thought he was going to conduct a friendly workshop with a dozen Hungarian teachers found himself addressing 250 heads in Szeged.

In Luxembourg, a student from Sarah Bonnell school in Newham found herself on a question-and-answer panel facing questions (not all friendly) from the European Association of Teachers. She described how her students rallied round before the Office for Standards in Education inspection to help 'bury the bodies'.

Echoing the words of a teacher she described the contribution of self-evaluation as 'leading you to where the bodies are buried'.

At the start and end of the project schools were asked to rate its value and impact. On three items there was a significant positive gain. Some 82 per cent of schools replied that self-evaluation helped to improve teaching (as against 55 per cent at the beginning). Even more (84 per cent) said it improved management (53 per cent before) while 95 per cent pronounced self-evaluation as 'valid' (compared with 56 per cent). Improvement through self-evaluation? The evidence is convincing. But there is an important rider. 'Self' in this context is not a cosy, introspective process. As we have learned, welcoming, confronting and dealing with this kaleidoscope of data is the first hallmark of the learning school.

CHAPTER 6

INSPECTORS WORTHY OF KAFKA

Geraldine Hackett

Originally published in the *TES*, 4 December, 1998

Leading professors of education this week went before MPs to savage the Office for Standards in Education for inspection methods that could have come from the pages of a Kafka novel.

Peter Mortimore, director of the Institute of Education at London University, told MPs on the House of Commons education select committee that the team that had arrived at his institution included untrained inspectors who carried out the work in an atmosphere of mistrust.

'There was a sense that we were at war with an OFSTED team that was determined to pull down our grades,' said Professor Mortimore.

He added that the chief inspector of schools had decided to re-inspect the Institute, despite the fact that its provision for teacher training in English and maths had been highly rated only 12 months earlier. He told MPs: 'Some of the inspectors had not had any inspection experience, but that was only part of the problem. OFSTED gave no impression that it had prepared the methodology or criteria.'

Committee member, Gordon Marsden, MP for Blackpool South, said the written evidence on the Institute's inspection had read like Kafka, and the inspection had been carried out by Kafkaesque characters.

Part of the written evidence before the committee's current inquiry into OFSTED also suggested that the fear of inspection could lead to universities withdrawing from teacher training, which could have serious implications for teacher recruitment.

In the most serious attack on OFSTED's credibility since the select committee began its inquiry, Professor Mortimore and John MacBeath, professor of education at Strathclyde, said the organisation had lost the trust of many who work in schools, local education authorities and universities.

Professor MacBeath suggested that in 'rubbishing' education research, the chief inspector had undermined the efforts of those concerned with improving schools.

MPs were told that many of the HMIs who transferred to OFSTED when it was created in 1993 have left and there is now a serious shortage of capable and qualified inspectors.

Professor Mortimore said that many of those who had left made little secret of the fact that they found the culture and methods of OFSTED unacceptable.

Harvey Goldstein, professor of statisticial methods at the Institute of Education, said OFSTED had only attempted a partial assessment and that had cast doubt on inspectors' ability to judge between the crucial grades that decide whether lessons are satisfactory. However, an independent study was needed on the reliability of different teams of inspectors.

CHAPTER 7

SHOULD WE SUGAR COAT THE PILL, MISS?

John MacBeath and Archie McGlynn

Originally published in John MacBeath and Archie McGlynn,
Self Evaluation, What's in it for Schools? (London: Routledge,
2002), pp. 110–111

This short extract captures the awareness of young people as to the high stakes nature of inspection and their willingness to play the game and help out their school.

Sugar-coating

These seven sins are reflected in a recent study by a Cambridgeshire teacher (Dannaway, 2001). Summarising her students' views of the inspectors' visit, she reported five key changes in the school.

- The relative *change in attitude* of staff and students: 'Everyone is telling us what to say and how to act. What's this – a dictatorship? Are we expecting Stalin or Hitler next week?'
- *Special lessons* being put on for show for the inspectors. Students discussed at great length how their motivation changed when the normal style of teaching was taken over by more challenging lessons and a general disruption to their routine.
- The *look of the school*, which they felt became more polished and suitable for visitors at any time of the day; staff bemoaning the fact they had put on the show constantly, ever ready for an inspector's visit.
- *Trouble was well hidden* during OFSTED week. 'Trouble students' were sent away to an outdoor pursuits centre to partake in a week-long alternative education programme.
- The *changing atmosphere* in the school was described as a rising continuum of stress. Students noted how stress and anxiety permeated the atmosphere of their school leading up to the inspection, as did a feeling of fear and expectation during 'the visit' itself. This was dispelled in the week after OFSTED when, 'everything returned to normal'.

When it was suggested that the students write their experiences for the local newspaper their response was 'Should we sugar coat it, miss?' With some further counsel from the headteacher the pupils' comments, largely favourable but mildly critical, appeared under the headline 'OFSTED and us – no problem'. Dannaway concludes:

At times, as I strain to remember some of the heated atmosphere that surrounded our discussions during my research sessions, I do think about the fickle nature of youth. When I look at the newspaper and read the students' words I admire their courage and their naivety. In the end what was important to them was their school, their name, their words and their faces in a well read local paper printed clearly for all to read. If I learnt something from this experience it's that kids don't *sugar-coat the truth* because somewhere along the way they decide what is public and what is private.

Reference

Dannaway, Y. (2001) 'Should we sugar-coat the truth then, Miss?', Unpublished M.ED paper, Faculty of Education, University of Cambridge.

CHAPTER 8

THE TALENT ENIGMA

Originally published in the *International Journal of Leadership in Education*, July–September 2006, Vol. 9, No. 3, 183–204

The talent enigma juxtaposes the discourses of 'talent' as an inherent individual quality to be sought out and recruited as against talent as inherent in organizations which grow their own. This article explores this issue in the context of an international 'crisis' of school leadership, examining how that crisis is constructed and how it impacts in differing contexts. Included here is discussion of the implicit assumptions of leadership qualities that schools require and, in other cases, explicit discussion of competencies deemed to be in short supply. In countries where no such shortages existed, the focus was less on the problems of recruitment and greater emphasis on growing and nurturing talent of prospective leaders and of school leaders already in situ. Recruitment issues and the debate over talent also served to bring into sharper focus the importance of succession and sustainability and leadership as distributed across the school community. This article examines these issues in light of the notion of the 'war for talent', reviewing the nature of the obstacles to recruitment, some of the proposed solutions, and taking issue with some of the assumptions on which the 'crisis' rests.

The war for talent

There is a war for talent. This is the McKinsey thesis in their book of that title (Michaels *et al.*, 2001). It depicts a corporate world in which exceptional leaders are hard to find and in which holding on to gifted managers and executives is the major challenge facing business sustainability. The McKinsey thesis finds a close parallel in the recruitment and retention 'crisis' in school leadership, now the subject of a substantive literature, much speculation, considerable media interest, and a growing corpus of empirical data. A critical survey of that literature raises a number of questions:

- Is the recruitment and retention crisis real or a manufactured myth?
- What is the substantive nature of the issues?
- What are the implications for a reframing of school leadership?

Underlying all three of these questions is the talent enigma. Like the long-standing nature/nurture contest, 'talent' is viewed from different perspectives as either innate or acquired. The question in search of an empirical answer is,

'Do talented people create great organizations?' or 'Do great organizations create talented people?' In the educational context this conundrum might be framed as, 'Do exceptional leaders grow successful schools?' or 'Do successful schools grow exceptional leaders?' In both of these juxtaposed perspectives, however, talent is treated as an individual quality rather than potentially as something that may be distributed, that may lie between people and be defined in the synergy that manifests itself in 'great groups' (Bennis 1997, Surowieki 2004).

The assumptions that policy makers bring to these questions and how they answer them are likely to have far-reaching implications for approaches which address the recruitment 'crisis'.

The crisis: real or manufactured?

Between 2000 and 2002, a group of Australian researchers (Thomson *et al.*, 2003) subjected news articles on the putative recruitment crisis in the school principalship to a 'deconstructive narrative analysis'. While including articles from English and Australian newspapers, their particular reference point was the USA, where the volume of newsprint on the subject exceeds the combined output of many other nations. The authors point to a contradiction in the two narratives, one of 'sleepless nights, heart attacks and sudden death accountabilities', the other of the 'saviour principal . . . who is able to create happy teams of teachers, students, and parents for whom all reform is possible' (2003:128). This duality needs to be understood, Thomson and colleagues argue, within a policy rhetoric of failing schools and 'best' practice. While not denying the validity of long hours and high stress, the authors conclude that this is a partial representation. The issue is partial because, although patently a matter of concern, recruitment, and retention are highly context sensitive and play out very differently at country level, state, regional, or province level, as well as at district and individual school level.

The war for talent: a matter of culture?

The 'crisis' is located primarily in studies conducted in the USA, Canada, Australia, New Zealand, and the four countries of the UK. Common to all of these is a similar language and common attribution of causal factors. By contrast, in most Asia-Pacific countries there is no perceived crisis and no shortage of applicants for principalship. In Singapore, for example, this is due to a keen sense of succession allied to strong central forecasting and direction from the Ministry, which ensures a continuous supply of principals, identified early and trained to fill vacant posts (Walker *et al.*, 2003). In Hong Kong, where by contrast recruitment is highly decentralized, there is no recruitment issue, rather a thrust at government level for forward planning and nurturing the qualities of leadership which extend beyond the school principal (Cheng, 2005). In Korea, the over-supply of teachers creates a selection rather than a recruitment problem; while in Japan, promotion procedures effectively stifle turnover and the retention issue is not one of attrition but one of potential stagnation. In Japan, the average age for promotion in primary and lower secondary schools is the early fifties for teachers, and the late fifties for upper secondary school principals (Hallinger 2003).

European countries reveal changing patterns in recent years. For example, in the Netherlands, the last few years have witnessed a transition from surplus to 'alarming' shortage (Lovely 2004). In Sweden and France, recruitment is now beginning to reach a critical stage; while in Germany, it differs widely from one state to the next. In Spain, there is still a surplus of applicants for every teaching job, ensuring a potential line of succession for the foreseeable future.

In all of these countries, the leadership issue is directly related to the continuing supply of teachers. As Darling-Hammond and Sykes (2003) show in the US context, disparities at the principal level reflect teacher recruitment policies at the state level. Some states, for example, enforce redundancy (i.e. retirement) requirements for fully qualified and credentialed candidates from other states, making it difficult for people to enter the local teaching force. Additional barriers include late budget decisions by state and local government, teacher transfer provisions that push new hiring decisions into August or September, lack of pension portability across states, and loss of salary credit for teachers who move. Most districts have salary caps for experienced candidates, while few districts reimburse travel and moving. Darling-Hammond and Sykes conclude that the differential nature of supply and demand has to be understood in relation to the state-level obstacles which feed into, or generate, a 'crisis'.

The war for talent: a matter of social economy?

'A job is always somewhere and where matters', write Thomson *et al.* (p.128). In the countries where recruitment and retention are problematic there tend to be significant differences by state, province, or region. This is, in part, a geographic issue, but in larger part, a socio-economic one, although these two are interrelated. In New Zealand, a 1999 study by Wylie *et al.*, reported that, in rural areas the recruitment issue was at crisis point, while in other more favoured parts of the country, no such issues existed. In England, applicants for primary headship ranged from none at all in the least favoured areas to 156 in the most sought after. For secondary headship, the range was from six to 200 (Earley *et al.*, 2002). There is a parallel in Roza *et al.*'s, 2003 study of 83 metropolitan districts around the USA. They found that the average district reported 17 applicants for principal positions, but that the range was from four to 40 or more. In Australia, Brooking *et al.* (2003) suggests that beneath the surface 'crisis', deeper structural issues are in play, so that the recruitment picture is not, in fact, one of undifferentiated hardship but one acutely responsive to market-driven economies in which experience and expertise flow into the most advantaged areas and follow the laws of supply and demand.

The US Bureau of Labor Statistics calculated in 1998 that an imminent shortage would be from areas, typically in the inner city, characterized by high-poverty students, low test scores, high staff turnover, and unusually large numbers of inexperienced teachers, provisionally certified, or people teaching out of their specialist field (Hertling 1999). A study of recruitment and retention in New York City (Papa *et al.*, 2002, quoted in Lashway 2003) reported a flow of urban principals to schools with higher test scores, better qualified teachers, and lower proportions of students on free meals, thus leaving inner cities with a less qualified cadre of school principals—in essence a self perpetuating downward spiral.

A similar picture emerges in areas where schools struggle to recruit new leaders. In UK schools located in troubled communities re-advertisement for applicants was nearly three times as common than in the more well-off English 'home counties' (Howson 2002). Following a first advertisement, 98% of London primary schools interviewed no candidates.

Retention rates also reveal wide differentials. Howson's (2002) study found that schools with A and A* grading (the premium level of exam performance) had the highest percentage of headteachers staying in post for six years, while schools with E or E* grading had the lowest percentage staying that long. These low-performing schools also had the highest percentage of heads staying for between zero and three years, demoralized by the unequal struggle for resources, support, and job satisfaction.

In countries struggling economically, the issues assume a sharper edge. A 2004 World Bank report (Moreno 2004) on schools in the Ukraine and Bulgaria found that school leaders spent 70% of their time on raising finance, and the remaining 30% on conflict resolution. Such a picture would not be unfamiliar to headteachers in the most disadvantaged areas in the UK or the USA. In England, a recent study of 'schools in exceptionally challenging circumstances' (MacBeath *et al.*, forthcoming) described the headteacher's day as fragmented by a constant search for sources of finance and staff, casting the recruiting net globally to capture teachers from South Africa, Canada, and Australia or anywhere reasonably-qualified English speaking staff could be found. In embattled communities, where only the most committed or most desperate of staff wished to work, the daily pressures of community life spilled over into schools and classrooms (Cullen 2004). The complex array of day-to-day issues that senior leaders face in these trying circumstances militate against long-term survival and increase the likelihood of burn-out. To remain in post in such unpredictable and energy sapping circumstances, it was found, requires exceptional dedication, resilience, and unwavering hope and optimism.

The war for talent: gender matters?

In this complex mix, gender also plays its part. A metropolitan district in the north-west of England attracted 40 applications from men and only two from women. A further discriminatory layer is by school type, where a sharp gender bias remains between primary and secondary schools. Fidler and Atton (2004) reported a ratio of 30:70 women to men appointments in primary schools and an almost mirror image (69:31) in secondary schools in 2001. In Earley and colleagues' 2002 study gender and ethnicity emerged as a compound factor: The nationally-based research revealed a significant imbalance in English schools of White ethnic women in primary and White ethnic men in secondary schools. Brooking and colleagues (2003) also report principal retention in New Zealand as particularly acute in small primary schools. In these schools, mainly led by women, time for professional leadership has been seriously eroded by the exigencies of self-management.

The attrition of talent

The differential nature of the issues from place to place, by school phase and type needs to be borne in mind when examining the causal factors which appear to be common across national boundaries. Williams' (2001) list of 22 'dissatisfiers', derived from research with Canadian principals (time, change, support, resourcing, accountability, and parent demands heading the list), resonate with lists from other countries and revolve around policy changes which stem from very similar ideological premises across national boundaries. However, while there is a striking similarity in explanations adduced as to the unattractive nature of principalship/headship, an understanding of how these issues play out in different contexts is a precursor of any proposed solutions.

The story to be told is not one of 'linear causality'—a convenient fiction, an oversimplified narrative (Thomson *et al.*, 2003). These authors argue for a more nuanced understanding of causal factors. The following summary of such factors, primarily from North America, Australasia, and the UK, has therefore to be seen as a mosaic in which complex patterns shape and reshape the dynamics of the war for talent and the premises on which that notion rests.

The changing nature of school leadership

Notions of highly talented individuals being sought out and who transform practice are no longer tenable propositions, wrote Southworth (2002). Such a view receives widespread endorsement from those who argue that the nature of school leadership has changed irrevocably and that thinking needs to change commensurately (for example Fullan 1991, Hargreaves 2004, Cheng 2005). Devolution of decision-making to school level, a world-wide phenomenon, has created a whole new raft of demands, as well as new freedoms. As power is pushed down, accountability is pushed up (Moos 2003), and paradoxically, while enjoying more power, school leaders are reporting less room for manoeuvre (Fink and Bryman, 2006).

The discomfort of change is explained in varying ways. One narrative locates it in the loneliness and impossible exigencies of the principalship, while a contrary view depicts 'visionary champions', keen to put their own personal stamp on the school, being hemmed in by the imperative for more widely-distributed leadership (Gronn 2000). Wallace and Hall (1994) describe this as 'a high pain/high pain strategy', which through the empowerment of other actors diminishes the singular power of the individual leader.

Although clearly more acute an issue in challenging circumstances, the task of leading a school in the twenty-first century can no longer be carried out by the heroic individual leader, single-handedly turning schools around (Gronn 2003). Drawing on Coser's (1974) notion of 'greedy institutions', Gronn applies this to individual leadership as 'greedy work'—all consuming, demanding unrelenting peak performance from superleaders, no longer a sustainable notion.

'Unrelenting change' is a story told in many different places, as policy initiatives flow across the principal's desk in a seemingly endless stream (Mulford 2003). Mulford finds that it is the multiplicity and simultaneity of initiatives that school leaders find most difficult to accommodate. The problem is less one of change, per se, but of change driven by external sources which undermine the power and discretion of school principals to exercise the leadership talents for which they were recruited. Instead, they find themselves in compliant managerial roles, delivering agendas decided elsewhere, but for which they are nonetheless held to account.

Whatever happened to talent?

Talent, whether spotted and enlisted, or developed and nurtured, may undergo a slow erosion, as a range of contextual factors work together to diminish energy and creativity. The following eight factors that recur most frequently in the literature focus on what happens to individual leaders to wear them down and sap their abilities to manage creatively, diminishing what is generally seen as a limited pool of talent. It raises the question of a possible corollary—if systems and organizations are able to destroy talent, might they, with different prevailing conditions, also be able to create it?

Stress

Stress is one of the strongest recurring themes in the literature, its source lying in constant change and the changing nature of the job. In Canada, Leithwood (2002) reported a rise in stress levels 'considerably exaggerated over the past two years in Ontario as a consequence of the speed with which policy changes have been introduced'. Decentralization and the competitive nature of a market economy bring with them a need to work harder, more demanding hours, and progressively higher stakes. Much of the stress is explained in terms of principals/headteachers having more responsibilities than power (Thomson *et al.*, 2003), carrying on their shoulders the responsibility for the success or failure of their schools. Delivering success, in the currency of test scores, in a turbulent socio-economic context, where few things stand still enough to be measured, or measured with meaning, adds a layer of stress for principals who no longer feel in control of their schools. The strongest correlate of stress is the feeling of being out of control (Martin 1997). Lack of control, and even more significantly the perception of being out of control, is correlated with chronic illness (physical and psychological) and premature death.

In Boyland's study of 266 schools in the UK (quoted in Mulford 2003), 71% of long term absences for men over 45 were attributed to stress, while the figure was 58% for women in the same age group. A survey of 800 teachers by the International Stress Management Association (ISMA) found substantially different responses between English and French teachers. While 22% of sick leave in England was attributed to stress it was 1% in France. More than half of the English teachers as opposed to a fifth of the French sample reported recently having considered leaving teaching (cited in the Newsletter of the ISMA (Stress News 2002)).

Workload

The issue of workload is closely related to reports of stress and appears to be common to many countries. In the USA, workload has been a continuing source of concern for half a decade (Hertling 2002, Lovely 2004). Jones' (1999) study of headteachers in the UK finds close parallels with Livingstone's study in the same year of primary school heads in New Zealand, and Louden and Wildy's (1999) study in Australia. One effect they report is for school leaders to devote less time to the core business of teaching and learning and more time to administrative tasks. Time, it is argued, has become fragmented, the demands of the urgent leaving inadequate space for reflection and for discussion with colleagues. In Hong Kong, where no shortage as yet exists, school principals aired their concerns about workload as a critical issue and disincentive to effective leadership (MacBeath and Clark 2006).

The UK Parliamentary report on Education and Employment (1998) concluded that 'the extra responsibilities that go with being a head in a primary school contributed to primary headship not being an attractive option'. In that same report, the then Deputy General Secretary of the National Union of Teachers (NUT) claimed that:

> The reason why people are not applying for headteacher posts is that it is an enormously high stakes, high-risk job without an understanding of their professional responsibilities or the fact that they may face a snow-ball of additional professional responsibilities in the future. Basically, no one knows what the ground rules are when they apply for a headteacher post. That is the big issue.
>
> (9th Parliamentary report on education & employment, 1998, item 166).

Accountability and bureaucracy

Feelings of stress and workload are closely related to issues of accountability and bureaucracy. Shen *et al.* (2004), quoting Portin *et al.* (2003), describe the principalship in the USA as 'a powerless position mired in bureaucracy'. In the UK half a decade before, accountability, and attendant bureaucracy were identified by Draper and McMichael (2000) as significant disincentives to applying for headship. While headteachers widely recognized the importance of accountability it was the bureaucratic aspects that appeared to demotivate, aspects such as excessive form filling and paperwork, combined with a constant pressure to justify actions taken and the feeling of not being in control of one's own destiny. Giving testimony to the Parliamentary Select Committee, Peter Mortimore said that 'the responsibilities are pretty daunting and chances are you are going to be blamed and shamed for things which perhaps are out of your control' (Parliamentary Report, Item 167).

'Blame and shame' are also cited as causes of principal demotivation in New Zealand (Livingstone 1999), while in the USA, the added threat of litigation is seen as compounding the problem. Accountability has acquired negative connotations, because it is not only highly demanding, but often directed at the wrong things.

Personal and domestic concerns

Many of those who go into teaching do not see themselves as managers or leaders. Commentators (for example in Tucker and Codding 2003) describe the challenges of 'crossing the professional border' into school leadership and cite anxiety and information perplexity as explaining reluctance to put themselves forward. For many teachers it would seem that the balance between classroom teaching and family life is threatened by the 'burden of headship'. Researchers in both the UK (James and Whiting 1998) and Australia (d'Arbon *et al.*, 2001) suggest that many staff are content to remain as classroom teachers because the principalship implies not only longer hours, but may possibly also involve greater travel away from the home base, and they do not want to be separated from children. 'Trailing the spouse', sometimes involving dislocation of family and home or temporary separation, are cited as further disincentives. The decision to apply for headship positions is for many prospective school leaders, determined ultimately by their reflection 'on the balance of lifestyle' and weighing the incentives and disincentives of the job (James and Whiting 1998).

Salary

Salary is frequently cited as an issue, with comparisons frequently made between levels of responsibility of school leadership with leadership in other occupations. In Australia, 'disaffection with salary of the principal rated strongly as a deterrent to persons applying for the principalship' (d'Arbon et al., 2001). The researchers report that people's perceptions about salary ranged from the lack of sufficient differential between positions of responsibility and the salary being based on the size of the school, rather than simply level of responsibility. Comparisons were made with similar positions of responsibility in industry or commerce 'where the management of human and material resources was seen as equivalent but not as highly recompensed' (d' Arbon et al.: 12). Principals, it is claimed, also earn less per hour than their staff, as they work 30% longer hours in a week.

Social factors

At a time when many people view schools as one of the few intact social organizations, students arrive with very different attitudes, motivations, and needs than students of generations past (Normore 2004). We are living in a society where social relationships, parenting, and the attitudes of young people are experiencing dramatic and often unforeseen changes. The increasing diversity of the student population, multiplicity of language, and ethnic backgrounds, short-term refugeeism, the casualties of war, transience of the student body, concentrations of poverty in inner cities, and depopulated rural areas, all bring their own, often formidable, challenges. Problems such as drug abuse, intimidation, and violence create dilemmas which are often beyond the power of leadership to resolve, but which have repercussions within the school walls. For schools, particularly in challenging circumstances, there is an increase in the incidence of confrontation and conflict, heightening the need for mediation and intervention, and negotiation with parents and other social agencies (MacBeath and Galton 2005). Headteachers in urban schools spend proportionately more time outside their school than their counterparts in other locations.

The teacher supply line

As headteachers are sourced from the ranks of teachers, a decline in teacher recruitment poses a challenge to principal recruitment and selection. As Dorman and colleagues suggest, 'if there is a shortage of teachers, then it is logical that there will be a shortage of principals' (2001: 4). An OECD Education Policy Analysis in 2001 warned of a 'meltdown scenario' caused by a growing teacher exodus from the profession, positing widespread public dissatisfaction with the state of education in the face of a deep teacher-recruitment crisis and a growing sense of declining standards, especially in the worst-affected areas. A year later, a report by the General Teaching Council in Wales (GTCW, 2002) described the fulfilment of that forecast, with one in 10 teaching posts remaining unfilled. Its Chief Executive claimed, 'Clearly, heads don't believe they have enough choice of applicants to make the appointments they want. . . . In some cases, they had no choices at all'.

The 'crisis' in teacher recruitment impacts directly on recruitment for the principalship which must accommodate a changing profile of the profession and the nature of teachers' career paths. As Moore Johnson (2004) found in the US context, teaching is no longer a career for life, no longer are first-career entrants prepared for the job in traditional ways, operating privately and autonomously in their own classrooms. Between 24% and 40% of teachers in her study, depending on the area, were mid-career entrants. Those who came from industry looked for opportunities to work in teams and to have expanded influence. The 'hole in the bucket' inflow and outflow of staff is, she argues, an expression of a shifting socio-economic situation but one that can be attenuated by school leaders attending to the expectations that teachers bring with them.

A US study by Ingersoll (2003) reported 30% of teachers leaving within three years, while 50% are no longer in post after five years. Ingersoll offers a reminder of how vulnerable organizations are to mobility of personnel, suggesting that a key issue governing organizational resilience in a time of change is 'substitutability'. He points out that schools, and in particular secondary schools, are in many ways unique institutions in the specificity of roles they require. Teaching is a profession that loses new recruits very early and schools are victims of the 'revolving door' syndrome, suffering from lack of flexibility in their ability to address the issues creatively.

There are things that enlightened leaders do, however, suggests Johnson (2004). Hiring of staff needs to be 'information rich'. Heads need to offer new entrants appropriate and fair teaching assignments. This needs to be accompanied by collegial support, professional development, and an infrastructure which allows them opportunities to share the problems they face, especially when it comes to discipline.

At the same time simply keeping teachers in place for pragmatic reasons can lead to stagnancy. A degree of turnover is necessary to counter what Johnson (2004) describes as 'schools organized for a retiring generation', talent matched to the needs of schools as we knew them in the past.

Intensification

The changing social context, the revolving door of staffing, workload, stress, personal issues, and perceptions of unfair remuneration cannot be treated singly as causes. They are a compound of factors and may be summarized as an intensification of the principal's role. The result is more than the sum of the parts. The implications for school leaders are 'to give more of themselves to their work; to give more time, to give more energy, to identify strongly with the goals and needs of the organization, and to learn how to collaborate effectively with co-workers' (Barker, quoted in Hertling, 1999). In the world of twenty-first century schooling, leaders must be able to 'leverage accountability and revolutionary technology, devise performance-based evaluation systems, re-engineer outdated management structures, recruit and cultivate non-traditional staff, drive decisions with data, build professional cultures, and ensure that every child is served' (Hess 2003:1). He adds that teaching experience or traditional preparation programmes do not equip candidates for these challenges, which demand a paradigm shift in how leadership is conceived, supported, and rewarded.

These are systemic, rather than simply individual issues, because intensified job roles are highly vulnerable. Over-reliance on 'superheads' not only incapacitates resilience at the level of the organization but damages the system as a whole. In summary, 'it changes what it means to be a professional' (Gronn 2003). These acute charges imply a reconstruction of professional identity and career trajectory:

> Rather than systems trying to recruit people into what is seemingly both an unattractive job and a heroic mission, perhaps some work needs to be done on rethinking the work of principals. To do this though would require that systems develop different priorities . . . now is the time to engage in fundamental rethinking of the principalship.
>
> (Thomson *et al.*, 2003: 129)

Solutions in a time of crisis

What solutions are then proposed in a time of crisis? On what assumptions do those putative solutions rest? Foremost among solutions, is more informed, aggressive, and targeted recruitment. This is McKinsey's 'war for talent'. It rests on a belief in a limited pool of exceptional people for whom there is such intense competition that recruitment becomes something of a strategic battle.

Aggression does not sit easily in an educational context with a long liberal tradition which frowns on competition and sees it as a zero sum game (Hargreaves and Fink 2005). Competition between schools, argue Hargreaves and Fink, is ultimately destructive and diminishing of educational purpose. In a market-driven climate, schools which poach teachers and students from their neighbours see their schools rise as others fall, diminishing the social capital of their neighbours and the systemic social capital more broadly conceived. The analogy of school as an individual unit warring with competitors may indeed reflect the prevailing climate in many countries, but diminishes sustainability and is ecologically destructive.

Sustainability and attention to ecology do not appear to be foremost considerations in the search for talent which, the literature suggests, is conservative, often backward-looking, timid, and impatient. In Scotland, Draper and McMichael (2000) report an indecent haste in fulfilling vacant posts by impatient authorities who simply desire to keep the school running and, in doing so, opt for the lowest common denominator, 'a safe pair of hands'. This is allied to a timidity in recruitment, playing safe rather than risk taking (Middlewood and Lumby 1998), school governors in England being tempted by the familiar known quantity rather than the hazards of an unknown quantity.

A Canadian study (Williams 2001) found evidence of 'cronyism' and warns of screening out candidates for the wrong reasons, particularly apposite to individuals who are seen to be critics of the status quo. This allows 'the nature of the future to be determined by a combination of strategic default and expedient hiring' (p. 167).

Expediency, safe hands, favoured candidates, and default positions are issues which combine to inhibit more adventurous recruitment and selection. Expedient decision-making and playing safe can play into gender and ethnic stereotypes. The gender ethnic imbalance reported by Earley *et al.* (2002) underlines a widely expressed need for targeting of under-represented groups to consider the principalship as a realistic option, and selection policies which support rather than counter such strategies. Initiatives to target minorities include advertising, using recruitment agencies, intelligence networks, and access courses such as Women into Management and courses for 'emergent leaders' from Black and ethnic minority backgrounds. Targeting applies as much to the untapped internal resource as to the external world.

In a time of crisis, the war for talent not only becomes more hard fought but its very urgency may act as a deterrent to thinking differently about leadership, succession, and organizational development. But, crisis may also create opportunities to think differently, to challenge traditional assumptions of talent and what schools or school coalitions need to grow and transform.

Numerous commentators, for example Hess (2003), suggest strategies for identifying non-traditional candidates. Should it be assumed, he asks, that only former teachers can do the job? What about individuals with leadership skills acquired in other fields? The current inhibitor in many countries of traditional certification requirements may be a significant blockage to applications for school leadership positions. Hess argues that giving thought to alternative pathways, or doing away with certification rules altogether could dramatically expand the talent pool.

The assumption that teaching experience is a precondition for assuming the principalship is challenged by a number of sources. Roza and colleagues (2003), for example, found that in the US context, superintendents valued other qualities ahead of teaching experience. Responding to a forced-choice question, 83% chose 'experience leading professional colleagues' as the most important requirement, whereas just 14% chose classroom-teaching experience. The researchers did not, however, ask superintendents whether they would consider hiring a principal with no teaching experience.

Portin and colleagues (2003) interviewed principals from a wide spectrum of schools and concluded that the single most important leadership skill was diagnosing and acting on the needs of the school. While some leadership functions require special knowledge, it is always possible to turn to colleagues for this kind of advice. The principal's job is to see that the job gets done, not to personally accomplish it. Other alternative approaches that have been suggested, and in some cases successfully implemented (Court 2002), are co-principalships where two or more people share the position of head/principal on a part-time or full-time basis. Those in co-principal positions experience less isolation and stress.

If not more aggressive, a more informed and creative marketing of schools is now required if schools are to capture the right kind of leadership and, as a result, continue to survive, and perhaps even prosper.

Incentives as solution

Incentives are the very essence of recruitment in the business world. Incentives common in that milieu are relocation assistance, reduced rent or utilities, reduced-price homes, and tax credits. These are rare in education, but may increasingly be seen as necessary to attract potential leaders, particularly to inner city and hard-to-staff schools.

The educational research literature tells us more about disincentives to apply for leadership positions than about incentives likely to attract people to the job. Heading lists of incentives tend to be those that focus on conditions of work, time and space, support, and continuing professional development. Principals need 'time and space to become leaders rather than being plagued by bureaucracy' (Mulford 2003). Mulford advocates a 'loosening of ties' that bind principals to structures and systems which leave them little room for manoeuvre and professional sustenance.

Efforts to improve job conditions should not overlook the idealistic orientation of many educators, who entered the field because they wanted to make a difference. Pounder and Merrill (2001) found that when assistant principals were asked to consider the desirability of a high school principalship, they gave the most weight to psychological benefits, particularly the opportunity to influence education. From that perspective, the opportunity to lead a troubled school may actually be an incentive, but only if the position provides the authority and support to focus on improvements that matter to people, and on pedagogy, as opposed to performativity.

A summary of sources suggest the following incentives:

- Opportunities to lead and not simply manage;
- A measure of independence from external control;
- Flexibility and latitude for decision-making;
- Recognition of the professionalism of school leadership;
- Time and space to focus on values and what matters in education;
- Alliances and support from peers;
- Opportunity to build and work with teams;
- Opportunities for ongoing professional development;
- Life work balance; and
- Salary and reward.

While salary is not generally seen as the most decisive factor, it compares unfavourably with remuneration and commensurate responsibilities in the business world, while school leadership is often more demanding, stress inducing, and intensive (Gates *et al.*, 2003). Headteacher and principals' compensation is also relative to teacher compensation and the nature of the gap is a sensitive issue, as a large gap may simply accentuate the difference between 'management' and 'staff'. On the other hand, a small differential may offer little incentive to move from teaching to headship. As Gates and colleagues suggest, teachers considering a move into senior leadership may be put off when they realize that the cost is longer hours and greater responsibility not commensurate with reward. The principalship is a lonely job, and the first few months can be a particularly challenging time. The new incumbent may have to work with unsuccessful candidates and, in some cases, deal with subversion or outright opposition.

All searches need to be guided by a recognition of the specific context and culture of the school and a consideration of best fit (Fidler and Atton 2004). Rather than the search for the best headteacher, the question should be: 'Who is the most appropriate headteacher in the particular circumstances of the school?' This can, of course, be a conservative and 'cosy' position, unless the 'fit' is framed in terms of questions such as 'Who is best placed to take us on from where we are? Who can challenge and lead practice in a way that can be heard and owned by staff?'

Solution as fast tracking

Fast tracking is a recruitment strategy designed to spot emerging talent and to cultivate it at an early stage. In England in 2002, the Government introduced a fast track initiative to ensure that the most able new teachers could progress quickly to leadership posts. Teachers are selected for this special programme during their pre-service year at university and given extra support and tuition through twilight leadership seminars and by experience in a diversity of school contexts, including schools in challenging circumstances, so that they acquire and develop skills in school leadership at different levels of the organization.

Solution as professional development programmes

Professional development is a key strategy in preparing for the principalship, but one that is often either missing, or simply ineffective, preparing principals for obsolete work environments. Many countries have been moving in recent years to national programmes or 'academies' for preparing future school leaders, sometimes administered by the government, sometimes by 'arms length' agencies or entrusted to universities.

Huber and West (2002) examined the aims, content, methods, and voluntary/compulsory status of programmes, differentiating these into centralized and decentralized approaches. The international literature reveals a greater complexity than this simple model allows. For example, leadership programmes in England and France are centrally prescribed and devolved or 'franchised' to regional centres. In Germany, as in Canada, USA, and Australia, education policy is a state or province matter and practice varies widely on a national basis, running alongside a range of entrepreneurial approaches by private providers and universities. In Scotland, there has been a national programme for a number of years but, like Sweden, delivered through university sites. Ongoing discussions there propose a National Leadership Academy, conceiving it more as a network than a central geographical location. In England, the establishment of the National College for School Leadership (NCSL) was in recognition of the disparate nature of provision and the nature of the gap that existed between theory and practice.

There is a potential Catch-22 in leadership programmes. Their very effectiveness may both solve and create problems. In the Scottish context, Cowie *et al.* found that the extra workload involved in the programme could compound problems for already overworked headteachers, especially in challenging circumstances, adding to the detriment of work/life balance. Cowie and colleagues conclude that success and failure is linked to the context and culture of schools. The professional development opportunity is, he suggests, 'a double edged sword', because while of demonstrable benefit to schools, without adequate support and sensitivity to context, it may be counter productive: 'Even exceptionally able participants may find it difficult to survive in stagnant schools with poorly developed systems' (p.4).

Professional development is also a double-edged strategy with regard to retention. On the one hand, it can provide the support and stimulation for heads to remain in their schools with renewed vigour and commitment, but on the other hand it may provide the incentive to move on, either to other schools, to positions in local authorities, or into private consultancy: 'Some heads today do not choose to spend an extended time in headship. They wish to explore other avenues in their education career, including advisory, consultancy and school improvement roles' (Flintham 2003). Retention at a systemic level means finding ways of capitalizing on the investment within the wider system.

Earley *et al.* (2002) reported a small minority of headteachers (17%) saying they had been prepared for the role, while only one in eight said they felt well equipped to deal with the nature of issues they were presented with in school leadership and management. Acting headship is one form of induction that gives first-hand experience of the job, although as Draper and McMichael (2000, 2003) found, it is just as likely to deter people from applying for the job as providing a path into the headship.

After interviewing hundreds of principals in the USA, Boris-Schacter and Langer (2002) concluded that the job should be modified to alleviate some of the stress and time pressures. They suggest that districts could spread the burden by reconfiguring the job description, either through a co-principalship, a rotating principalship, or some other form of distributed leadership. Different forms of co-principalship are suggested by Court (2002) such as job sharing which relieves the full-time pressure on one person, dual leadership which is convivial and collaborative, or other forms of a more extended collective leadership.

Like teacher training, leadership preparation has traditionally been front-loaded (Lashway 2003), with an intensive period of formal preparation and certification, followed by informal, self-guided, and sporadic professional development. There is a widespread recognition of the need to provide a seamless continuum of professional training which lasts throughout the leader's career, paying particular attention to the critical induction period in which the principal's career choice is either validated or undermined. The old sink-or-swim initiation has been replaced by structured experiences in which mentoring plays a major role (Malone 2001).

Solution as mentoring, coaching, and critical friendship

Schools are more likely to improve when they enjoy external support. That is the conclusion of Baker and associates (1991), who compared schools which drew on external support and those that didn't. External support assumed myriad forms. The three most cited in the literature are mentoring, coaching, and critical friendship. Although very closely similar in practice there are some fine but important conceptual distinctions which separate these practices.

On a spectrum of intervention to facilitation, coaching is at one end and critical friendship at the other, with mentoring being somewhere in between. Critical friendship is a form of support in which friendship comes first and critique follows, as the relationship grows and judgments are made as to what may or may not be appropriate in the context. The key difference from mentoring or coaching is in the nature of the partnership, which is construed as a mutual learning opportunity and is intended to be reciprocal (Swaffield 2004). While coaching is a form of partnership, it is one in which the power or authority in the situation shifts toward the coach, who is more directive and interventionist than either a critical friend or mentor. Mentors, like critical friends, can be a sounding board or a listening ear and, by virtue of their greater experience, can offer advice and guidance to those less experienced than themselves. Like coaches, mentors work on a one-to-one basis, while critical friends may work with a range of people in an organization. While all three approaches share much of a common purpose, the distinguishing feature of critical friendship is to emphasize the capacity building and distributed character of leadership, rather than the more individualistic orientations of coaching and mentoring.

Solution as networking

Networking with peers in other schools is a form of collegial support that is now recognized as a powerful form of professional renewal and widely used in the business world. One example is Xerox's creation of communities of practice in which people collaborate across agency boundaries to address common issues and work toward common solutions (OECD 2003). In OECD's report on *Schooling for tomorrow* (2004) it is claimed that 70% to 90% of practitioner knowledge is 'tacit', created not through hierarchies or transmission of research but through 'knowing who knows' (Van Aalst 2003).

In England, the Networked Learning Communities (NLC) programme brings together clusters of schools, local education authorities, higher education institutions and the wider community to work collaboratively to improve opportunities for students and staff. Learning with and on behalf of others is described as a moral purpose, exposing oneself, one's school and one's pupils to the diversity and challenge that come from other contexts, becomes 'a positive force for knowledge-sharing and innovation'. In a similar vein, the US principals interviewed by Boris-Schacter and Langer (2002) spoke of the need for sharing, reflection, and the in-depth professional development that were most effective when built into the working week and incorporated school visitations, meetings with community-based groups, and attendance at support groups.

Networks may be horizontal (for example school-to-school, on a collegial basis) or vertical (linking a school with centres of particular expertise). Networks may link principal to principal or have a more diffused focus on organizational development. Networks may be face-to-face or virtual. They may operate locally, nationally, or across national borders, offering new perspectives and challenging inert ideas.

MacBeath *et al.* (2005) provide examples of school heads, deputy heads and teachers fundamentally rethinking their own assumptions when confronted with differing practices and differing conceptions of the purposes and nature of leadership. The flatarchies of Danish schools and 'leaderless' Swiss primary schools (where there are no principals, only teachers) are so challenging for senior leaders inured to hierarchy that they find major difficulty in coming to terms with the absence of a command structure. Yet the cognitive dissonance such innovative structures provoke has released new energy and new approaches to the talent question, focusing attention on the treasure within.

Solution as the treasure within

In some areas of England there are moves to appoint school improvement co-ordinators whose task it is to look within classrooms for the hidden talent. What these efforts reveal is a reluctance of teachers to apply for senior leadership positions because they are daunted by the visible stress and workload of headteachers (MacBeath and Galton 2005). These may be implicit or, in some cases, made explicit by what school leaders communicate to their staff about the pressures of their job. This is a disincentive to internal recruitment. Shen and colleagues (2004) identified eight salient factors in the US context which dissuaded teachers from applying, including workload, constraints, and stress of the position, the consequent impact of the position on individual and family life, status of the position, and autonomy in exercising it, the work environment, location, and size of the school, nature of the community served by the school, and safety and support. These perceptions may, however, be jaundiced by lack of broader knowledge, lack of alternative perspectives, and by a school climate which has not attended to the needs of the next generation of leaders.

While leadership development programmes recruit candidates on a local or national basis schools may, of their own volition, support and encourage emerging talent. In recent years academics, policy makers, and schools themselves have been giving more thought to succession planning, long a feature of the most successful companies (Collins 2001). In the USA, Anderson (1991) recommended developing a pool of qualified candidates inside the school by creating career ladders. For career ladders to work, there must be adequate opportunities for individuals to enjoy a diversity of experience which qualifies them for the principalship. For example, Anderson suggests that assistant principals should not be treated as 'single-facet administrators', good only as disciplinarians or directors of activities, but be provided with opportunities to develop in a more well-rounded way. Barker (1997) advises school districts to be more far-sighted in identifying the professional and personal benefits of the principalship and then 'selling' those benefits to talented teachers.

Distributing leadership

The emphasis on distributed leadership is a Third Millennium theme, which resonates across national boundaries. It is in one sense a pragmatic response to the impossibility of individualistic, or heroic, leadership, but also a recognition that schools cannot build capacity, sustainability, or plan for succession without seeing opportunities for leadership be dispersed through the school community. In England, The Parliamentary Select Committee on Education and Skills, Fifth Report states that:

> It is crucial that heads do not feel expected to carry sole responsibility for all aspects of their school's activities, because such a load, in a large secondary school, is not sustainable long term. [117]

In a study of eleven schools in three English authorities (MacBeath, Oduro and Waterhouse 2004) headteachers were interviewed on their views of distributed leadership, then shadowed in order to examine how these views worked out in practice. The tasks these heads undertook and the people they spent time with over the course of the day gave substance to, or sometimes belied, their leadership philosophies. What emerged were six ways in which distribution was conceived and effected, from a formal distribution downwards through a hierarchy of positions to more opportunistic notions of distribution, where staff and students without formal status took the initiative to lead. What researchers described as 'cultural' distribution was characterized by a practice of sharing leadership so deeply embedded in people's thinking and practice that leadership was genuinely without deference to hierarchy and flourished from the ground up. It grew both individual and distributed talent.

The talent enigma

Where leadership can be perceived in the flow of activities of a school, shared and developed collegially and democratically, 'talent', its nature and nurture become a more contested issue. Taking issue with the McKinsey study Gladwell (2002) wrote:

> The talent myth assumes that people make organizations smart. More often than not, it's the other way around.
>
> (p.2)

The author challenges the assumption that an organization's intelligence is simply a function of the intelligence of its employees. People believe in stars because they don't believe in systems, and 'the organizations that are most successful at that task are the ones where the system is the star'. (p. 2). This is a view that receives some support from major studies. Collins and colleagues (1994, 2001) argue that the principles of successful enduring companies not only apply internationally in virtually every country of the world but across public sector agencies, including education:

> Gone forever—at least in our eyes—is the debilitating perspective that the trajectory of a company depends on whether it is led by people ordained with rare and mysterious qualities that cannot be learned by others.
>
> (1994: 2)

A study of 1000 leading professionals (Groysberg *et al.*, 2004: 2) found that top performers quickly fade after leaving one company for another:

> Most companies that hire stars overlook the fact that an executive's performance is not entirely transferable because his personal competencies inevitably include company-specific skills. When the star leaves the old company for the new, he also leaves behind many of the resources that contributed to his achievements. As a result, he is unable to repeat his performance in another company—at least not until he learns to work the new system, which could take years. The authors conclude that companies should focus on cultivating talent from within and do everything possible to retain the stars they create.

The tension between the search for talent and the creation of talent from within are themes that run through the educational literature. Qualities of leadership are grown within institutions, and retention issues do not simply apply to keeping good headteachers in post, but building succession by both recognizing and nurturing talent. These themes are to be found in work on communities of practice (Wenger 1998), learning communities (Mitchell and Sackney 2002), the growing body of literature on teacher leadership (Frost, Durrant and Head 2000, Gronn 2000, Liebermann and Miller 2004), the personification of the school as a school that learns (Senge, 2000) and the 'intelligent school' (McGilchrist, Myers and Reed 2004). The common theme in these literatures is that, where there are genuine learning cultures that offer opportunities to lead and allow people the experience of assuming responsibility for others, professional expertise flourishes and hidden talents emerge.

The talent orientation blinds people to an alternative view of leadership, not as role, status, or position, but as activity (Spillane 2006). In the Leadership for Learning Project mentioned above it took a long time for participants to come to terms with a conception of leadership as activity, a concept hard to make sense of in the day-to-day practices of their schools. Yet, with exemplification from other schools of how students, office staff, newly qualified teachers, caretakers, and cooks could and did take initiative, effect change, and inspire those round around them, the concept became less alien. Seeing things through this different lens was helpful in making the talent enigma less enigmatic. With fresh eyes and new ways of seeing, daring to lead and to follow came closer to everyone's grasp.

While ordinary people are capable of doing extraordinary things, this is not to deny that there are also extraordinary people who may, from an early age, evidence a capacity to change their world and the world of others around them (Goleman 1996). It would be a short-sighted school or school district that did not cast its net wide in a search for people who are able to bring new challenges and fresh thinking to schools which have for too long looked solely inwards. But as Michaels and colleagues (2001) conclude, cultivating the treasure within and seeking the challenge from without are complementary rather than antagonistic strategies. Successful companies are those which create room for talent to grow, that build a high-performance culture, combining a strong performance ethic with an open and trusting environment. Informal feedback, coaching, and mentoring are described as enormous developmental levers. At the same time, it is important to be always on the prowl for new ideas, looking in new ways and in new places.

References

Anderson, M. E. (1991) Principals: How to train, recruit, select, induct, and evaluate leaders for America's schools. Eugene, Oregon: ERIC Clearing house on Educational Management, University of Oregon 133 pages. ED 337 843.

Baker, P., Curtis, D. and Bereson, W. (1991) Collaborative Opportunities to Build Better Schools (Bloomington, IL: Association for Supervision and Curriculum Development).

Barker, R.A. (1997) How can we train leaders if we do not know what leadership is? Human-Relations, 50(4), 343–62.

Bennis, W. (1997) Organizing Genius: The Secrets of Creative Collaboration (London: Nichoas Brealey).

Boris-Schacter, S. and Langer, S. (2002) Caught between nostalgia and utopia. Education Week, 34, 36–37.

Brooking, K., Collins, G., Court, M. and O'Neill, J. (2003) Getting below the surface of the principal recruitment 'crisis' in New Zealand primary schools, Australian Journal of Education, 2, 146–158.

Cheng, Y. C. (2005) Multiple Thinking and Multiple Creativity in Organization Learning (Hong Kong: Institute of Education).

Collins, J. (2001) Good to Great: Why Some Companies Make the Leap—and Others Don't (London: Random House).

Collins, J. and Porras, G. (1994) Built to Last (New York: Harper Business Esssentials).

Coser, L.A. (1974) Greedy Institutions: Patterns of Undivided Commitment (New York: The Free Press).

Court, M.R. (2002) Alternatives to the lone(ly) Principal. SET: Research for Teachers, 3, 16–20.

Cowie, M. (2005) A silver lining with a grey cloud? The perspective of unsuccessful participants in the Scottish Qualification for Headship Programme across the north of Scotland, Journal of In-service Education, 31(2), 393–410.

Cullen, J. (2004) Leadership development in struggling schools. Paper presented at the International Congress of School Effectiveness and Improvement, Rotterdam, January 6–9.

d'Arbon, T. and Dorman, J. (2003) Leadership succession in New South Wales Catholic schools: Identifying potential principals. Educational Studies, 29, 2–3.

d'Arbon, T., Duignan, P., Duncan, D. J. and Goodwin, K. (2001) Planning for the future leadership of Catholic schools in New South Wales. British Educational Research Association Annual Conference, University of Leeds, September 13–15.

Darling-Hammond, L. and Sykes, G. (2003) Wanted: A national teacher supply policy for education: The right way to meet the 'highly qualified teacher' challenge. Education Policy Analysis Archives, 11, 33.

Dorman, J. P. and d'Arbon, T. (2001) Assessing impediments to leadership succession in Australian catholic schools. School Leadership and Management, 23(1), 25–40.

Draper, J. and McMichael, P. (2000) Contextualising new headship. School Leadership & Management, 20(4), 459–473.

Draper, J. and McMichael, P. (2003) Keeping the show on the road? The role of the acting headteacher. Educational Management & Administration, 31(1), 61–81.

Elmore, R. and Burney, D. (1999) Investing in teacher learning: Staff development and instructional improvement. In L. Darling-Hammond and G. Sykes (eds), [??] Teaching as the Learning Profession. Handbook of Policy and Practice (San Francisco: Jossey-Bass), pp. 263–291.

Fidler, B. and Atton, T. (2004) The Headship Game: The Challenges of Contemporary School Leadership (London: RoutledgeFalmer).

Fink, D. and Brayman, C. (2006) School leadership succession and the challenges of change, Educational Administration Quarterly, 42(1), 62–69.

Flintham, A. (2003) Reservoirs of Hope (Nottingham: National College of School Leadership).

Frost, D., Durrant, J. and Head, M. (2000) Teacher-Led School Improvement (London: Routledge).

Fullan, M. G. (1991) The New Meaning of Educational Change (New York: Teachers College Press).

Gates, S. M., Ringel, J.S., Santibañez, L., Ross, K.E. and Chung, C.H. (2003) Who is Leading Our Schools? An Overview of School Administrators and their Careers (Santa Monica, California: RAND).

General Teaching Council of Wales (2002) The Teacher Recruitment Survey.

Gladwell, M. (2002) The talent myth: Are smart people overrated? New Yorker, 22 July, 28–33.

Goleman, D. (1996) Emotional Intelligence (London: Bloomsbury).

Gronn, P. (2000) Distributed properties: A new architecture for leadership. Educational Management and Administration, 28(3), 371–338.

Gronn, P. (2003) The New Work of Educational Leaders: Changing Leadership Practice in an Era of School Reform (London: Paul Chapman).

Groysberg, B., Nanda, A. and Nohria, N. (2004) The risky business of hiring stars. Harvard Business Review, 82(5), 212–222.

Hallinger, P. (2003) Leading educational change: Reflection on the practice of instructional and transformational leadership. Cambridge Journal of Education, 33(3), 329–352.

Hargreaves, A. (2004) Sustainable leadership. Keynote address delivered at the International Conference on School Effectiveness and Improvement, Rotterdam, January.

Hargreaves, A. and Fink, D. (2005) Sustainable Leadership (San Francisco: Jossey-Bass).

Hertling, E. (1999) Conducting a principal search. ERIC Digest 133—December 1999.

Hertling, E. (2002) Retaining principals. ERIC Digest.

Hess, F. (2003) A License to Lead? A New Leadership Agenda for America's Schools (Washington, D.C.: Progressive Policy Institute). Available online at http://www.ppionline.org (Accessed May 2004).

Howson, J. (2002) The Relationship Between Head Teachers' Length of Service in Primary and Secondary Schools and Selected PANDA Grades (Nottingham: The National College for School Leadership).

Huber, S. and West, M. (2002) School leader development: Current trends from a global perspective. In P. Hallinger (ed.), Reshaping the landscape of school leadership development: A global perspective (Lisse, Netherlands: Swets & Zeitlinger).

Ingersoll, R.M. (2003) Is there really a teacher shortage? (Center of the Study of Teaching and Policy, University of Washington, Seattle). (www.ied.edu.hk/principal conference).

James, C. and Whiting, D. (1998) The career perspectives of deputy headteachers. Educational Management and Administration, 26(4), 26–34.

Johnson, S. M. (2004) Finders and keepers: Helping new teachers survive and thrive in our schools (San Francisco: Jossey-Bass).

Jones, N. (1999) The real world management preoccupations of primary school heads. School Leadership & Management, 19(4), 483–495.

Lashway, L. (2003) Finding Leaders for Hard-to-staff Schools, ERIC Digest 173, December.

Leithwood, K. (2002) School leadership times of stress. OISE newsletter. Available online at: www.utoronto.ca/orbit/school_leader_sample.html (Accessed June 2006).

Leithwood, K. and Jantzi, D. (2000) Principal and teacher leader effects: A replication. School Effectiveness and School Improvement, 4(10), 451–479.

Lieberman, A. and Miller, L. (2004) Teacher Leadership (San Francisco: Jossey-Bass).

Livingstone, I. (1999) The Workload of Primary Teaching Principals: A New Zealand Survey (Wellington: Chartwell Consultants).

Louden, W. and Wildy, H. (1999) Short shrift to long lists: An alternative approach to the development of performance standards for school principals. Journal of Educational Administration, 37(2), 99–121.

Lovely, S. (2004) Staffing the Principalship: Finding, Coaching, and Mentoring School Leaders. Association for Supervision & Curriculum Development.

MacBeath, J. and Clark, W. (2006) Final Report of the Phase II Impact Study on the Effectiveness of External School Review in Hong Kong in Enhancing School Improvement Through School Self-Evaluation. (Cambridge: Cambridge Education).

MacBeath, J., Frost, D. and Swaffield, S. (2005) Researching leadership for learning in seven countries (The Carpe Vitam project). Education Research and Perspectives, 32(2), 24–43.

MacBeath, J. and Galton, M. (2005) A Life in Secondary Teaching? (London: National Union of Students).

MacBeath, J., Gray, J., Cullen, J. Frost, D., Swaffield, S. and Steward, S. (forthcoming) Schools on the Edge (London: Sage).

MacBeath, J., Oduro, G. and Waterhouse, J. (2004) Distributed Leadership in Schools (Nottingham: National College of School Leadership).

Malone, R. J. (2001) Principal mentoring. ERIC Digest 149 (Eugene, Oregon: ERIC Clearing House on Educational Management).

Martin, P. (1997) The Sickening Mind (London: Flamingo).

McGilchrist, B., Myers, K. and Reed, J. (2004) The Intelligent School (London: Paul Chapman).

Michaels, E., Hartford-Jones, H and Axelrod, B. (2001) The War for Talent: How to Battle for Great People (Harvard Business School Press).

Middlewood, D. and Lumby, J. (1998) Human Resources Management in Schools and Colleges (London: Chapman Business).

Mitchell, C. and Sackney, L. (2002) Profound Improvement (Lisse, Netherlands: Swets & Zeitlinger).

Moos, L. (2003) Educational Leadership: Understanding and Developing Practice (Copenhagen, Danmark: Paedagogiske Verlag).

Moreno, J. (2004) Unpublished speech to the Lynch School of Education Leadership Summit, Boston, November.

Mulford, B. (2003) School Leaders: Changing Roles and Impact on Teacher and School Effectiveness (Paris: OECD).

Normore, A. (2004) Recruitment and selection: Meeting the leadership shortage in one large Canadian school district. Canadian Journal of Educational Administration and Policy, 30.

OECD (2001) Teacher Exodus – the Meltdown Scenario (Paris: Education Policy Analysis).

OECD (2004) Schooling for Tomorrow (Paris: Education Policy Analysis).

Plumbley, P. (1976) Recruitment and Selection (London: Institute of Personnel Management).

Portin, B., Schneider, P., DeArmond, M. and Gundlach, L. (2003) Making Sense of Leading Schools: A Study of the School Principalship (Seattle: Center on Reinventing Public Education).

Pounder, D. G. and Merrill, R. J. (2001) Job desirability of the high school principal-ship: A job choice theory perspective. Educational Administration Quarterly, 37(1), 27–57.

Roza, M., Celio, M. B., Harvey, J. and Wishon, S. (2003) A Matter of Definition: Is There Truly a Shortage of School Principals? (Seattle: The Center on Reinventing Public Education).

Senge, P. (2000) Schools that Learn (New York: Doubleday).

Shen, J., Cooley, V.E. and Wegenke, G. (2004) Perspectives on factors influencing application for the principalship: A comparative study of teachers, principals and superintendents. International Journal of Leadership in Education, 7(1).

Southworth, G. (2002) Leadership in English schools: Portraits, puzzles and identity. In A. Walker and C. Dimmock (eds), School Leadership and Administration: Adopting a Cultural Perspective (London: Routledge).

Spillane, J. (2006) Distributed Leadership (San Francisco: Jossey-Bass).

Stress News (2002) Available online at: www.isma.org.uk/stressnw/teach erst ress1.htm

Surowiecki, J. (2004) The Wisdom of Crowds (New York: Random House).

Swaffield, S. (2004) Critical friends: Supporting leadership, improving learning. Improving Schools, 7(3), 267–278.

Thomson, P., Blackmore, J. Sachs, J. and Tregenza, K. (2003) High stakes principal-ship—sleepless nights, heart attacks and sudden death accountabilities: Reading media representations of the United States principal shortage. Australian Journal of Education, 47(2), 118–132.

Tucker, M. and Codding, J. (eds) (2003) The Principal Challenge: Leading and Managing Schools in an Era of Accountability (San Francisco: The Jossey-Bass Education Series).

Van Aalst, H. (2003) Networking in Society, Organisations and Education in OCED. Schooling for Tomorrow: Networks of Innovation: Towards New Models for Managing Schools and Systems (Paris: OECD).

Walker, A., Stott, K. and Cheng, Y.C. (2003) Principal supply and quality demands: A tale of two Asia-Pacific states. Australian Journal of Education, 2, 197–208.

Wallace, M. and Hall, V. (1994) Inside the SMT: Teamwork in Secondary School Management (London: Paul Chapman).

Wenger, E. (1998) Communities of Practice, Learning, Meaning and Identity (Cambridge: Cambridge University Press).

Williams, T. R. (2001) Unrecognised Exodus, Unaccepted Accountability: The Looming Shortage of Principals and Vice-Principals in Ontario Public School Boards (Ontario: School of Policy Studies).

Wylie, C., Mitchell, L. and Cameron, M. (2002) Sustaining School Improvement— Ten Primary Schools' Journeys (Wellington: New Zealand Council for Educational Research). Available online at: www.oise.utoronto.ca/orbit/school_leader

CHAPTER 9

SCHOOL LEADERSHIP CRISIS

Neil Munro

Originally published in *TESS*, 6 November, 2009

More than half of headteachers would not recommend their 'lonely' job to anyone

Headship is a lonely and emotionally-demanding job, to which only 8 per cent of teachers aspire.

This dramatic finding is revealed in a major and long-awaited report issued this week, which foreshadows a potentially serious crisis in the recruitment and retention of high-quality headteachers in Scotland.

Commissioned by the Scottish Government, the study found that 22 per cent of male heads and 24 per cent of females would not recommend headship to anyone. Overall, more than half – 53 per cent – said they would not urge others to go for the top job, or were not sure.

The chief reasons were their long hours and the demands of accountability to inspectors and local authorities. The majority of heads said they worked for more than 50 hours a week, with 45 per cent spending up to 65 hours on school-related tasks.

Six out of 10 heads said experience of inspection was a significant factor in their dissatisfaction, specifically 'unfair, or unbalanced, representations of the school and too public an exposure of weaknesses'.

The 'emotionally-demanding' nature of the job was a concern for nearly 70 per cent of heads; 72 per cent worried about the impact on their lives outside work; and 46 per cent said it was lonely at the top. A further 72 per cent blamed the 'public grading of school performance' for their disillusion.

The research, carried out by a team from Cambridge, Edinburgh and Glasgow universities, canvassed the views of 1,137 heads and 1,218 teachers. Almost three-quarters of teachers – 73 per cent – said they had no intention of pursuing the official route to leadership, the Scottish Qualification for Headship.

John MacBeath, professor of education at Cambridge University, who led the study, said: 'The vividness of the language used by heads in their interviews to describe the task of leading a school is testimony to the emotional nature of the work: "fire-fighting"; "battles"; "ground down"; "frazzled"; "washed out"; "sucking people dry".'

'At the same time, "passion", "exhilaration", "commitment" and "pride" were recurring themes. One head described having a "love affair" with the school, another as having "an emotional relationship with the school" and another as "being married to the school".'

'This deeply personal investment in their schools ("my school") tells the story of headship and explains why frustration looms so large in their accounts.'

Although Education Secretary Fiona Hyslop has signalled the importance of this study in several speeches – and initially promised to publish it 11 months ago – her department does not appear enamoured of the findings which were given a low-key release yesterday on the Scottish Government's website, with no political fanfare.

CHAPTER 10

'VACANCY. HEADTEACHER REQUIRED, SCOTSMAN 7/24/365 . . .'

John MacBeath and Peter Gronn

Originally published on www.scotsman.com on 8 November, 2009, entitled *Heads Need Hearts to Survive in Scottish Schools*

Guess whose is the first car in the morning in the school car park and the last to depart at night? Who eats their lunch on the run—that's if they eat at all? How many working professionals have a job description ranging from changing light bulbs through to preparing strategic plans? How many people work with a range of children from neighourhoods of grinding poverty and generous wealth? How many have to endure being verbally (and sometimes physically) abused by parents? But who else experiences the joy of watching children flourish and seeing staff growing in confidence and expertise?

Welcome to the world of the Scottish headteacher. An exceedingly complex and demanding world which requires an extraordinary level of mental agility, interpersonal savvy and emotional resilience. It is a job in which a person is expected to be both 'on top' and 'on tap' 7/24/365, only a mobile phone call away from the next demand, the next problem, the next unanticipated dilemma.

Interviews with headteachers and teachers across the country told similar stories, of professional sacrifice and personal reward. The all-consuming nature of the job revealed in comments such as: 'It's like day and night. I couldn't switch off', 'I eat, sleep and breathe it. It's just in my blood'. Yet, 'It's my choice'.

For many it was a studied choice to work in troubled areas. These heads wanted to make a difference to the lives of children growing up in fractured neighbourhoods and multiple disadvantage. But care taking could be demanding and 'draining' work, dealing with the 'heartbreak' of children's lives in neighbourhoods in which instability was the only constant. One is only as good as one's last success. At least that's what Scottish headteachers, their deputies and teachers told us when we spoke to them. In the current global financial meltdown, there is concern about bonus payments for CEOs and their staffs. Scottish heads must be shaking their heads in disbelief. They don't earn bonuses and most do not expect or want them. But if this is the case, employers need to ask themselves: is it reasonable to expect headteachers to work during weekends and their annual holidays? We found that some do because they want to, although most do because they have to or because they feel duty-bound.

Schools are different from the commercial world. It is rare for people to undertake public service roles for personal or financial gain, or ego gratification. Most heads and teachers don't seek the limelight. What motivates them is a passion to serve and to improve the lives of children. It has mostly always been so. But there is a fine line between provision of a service and exploitation. Particularly when resources are scarce and the political pressures on education are intense there is a tendency to try to require staff to do more with less and to squeeze out ever more productivity. In these circumstances, there is a delicate balance to be struck between making demands on headteachers that challenge and stretch them, while not making the job so burdensome that sufficient numbers will still retain their enthusiasm for the task.

As the report that we have co-authored suggests, this is where Scottish headteachers find themselves at the moment. The reality for them is that when, for whatever reason, circumstances in schools go pear-shaped, it is heads who are the fall-guys. The range of stakeholders that is willing to finger heads for mistakes is truly staggering: parents, employers, inspectors, unions, the media, community and government. We can think of no comparable occupation (perhaps apart from politicians) which requires its leaders to satisfy so many conflicting interests.

Are the problems associated with headteacher recruitment and retention peculiar to Scotland? No, but the solutions have to be. Intensified patterns of employment, work–life imbalance and stress are not unique to heads (let alone Scottish heads) for they are being experienced across the professions and globally. Pointing to this commonality, however, is not an excuse for inaction in the case of Scottish heads, many of whom are feeling badly let down and unsupported. We found that they cope with these occupational pressures in different ways and with varying success. Just as there is no one-size-fits-all way to run a school, there are different responses to work demands. For some, no challenge can be too great—it's as if their motto is 'pile on the pressure'. Others are less sanguine and lie awake at night worrying. Still others feel overburdened and ground down.

So what, specifically, are the problems and how are they to be rectified? Broadly our report details the ways in which heads feel that their relationship with their employing authorities has gone badly out of kilter. Unless a head is in a big school (mostly secondaries) she or he is on their own. That is, they lack the luxury of an HRM infrastructure to support them. This means that they have to field many inquiries and requests, particularly from local authority officers, that might otherwise be delegated to business managers and bursars. The effects of this lack of resource are compounded by the requirement to complete numerous audits, such as health and safety, and inspections. Lots of control lines generate huge compliance requirements. There has to be room here for streamlining. The current situation is far from 'intelligent' accountability. One of Scotland's unique advantages is its scale: it is sufficiently compact and integrated to be able to tackle the issues without alienating key stakeholders and sectors.

Apart from rectifying this relationship balance, there are two other ways in which Scotland can build on its strengths. First, there is an urgent need for a re-assessment of risks and sharing the burden of risks. Being a head teacher has become a high-wire act. The major gripe of heads is that when the going gets tough for them they lack local authority support. As our report makes clear, this experience is not uniform nationally and some authorities cannot be faulted in this regard. The balance of relations between local authorities and heads has become skewed against headteachers in ways that restrict their autonomy. Parental complaints and media intrusion are two hot spots. There is a widespread perception that authorities are inclined to support parent complaints in a default way, rather than backing heads. This makes for vulnerability. Likewise with media reporting: there is a need for clear guidelines and support for heads when they go public on behalf of their schools. Heads have to be allowed to take risks and their employers have to back them.

Second, ways have to be found of incentivizing the system. Scottish education already performs remarkably well with succession planning and leadership development, and it has done so without being tempted to invest huge resources into a national leadership college. Prospective heads now have two pathways available to them as options for satisfying the Standard for Headship, the Scottish Qualification for Headship and the Flexible Route to Headship. Few other standards-based preparation systems in the world provide such options. Its other great strength, for which Scotland is the envy of other systems globally, is the Chartered Teacher scheme for teacher leaders. Incentives include salaries, but salaries alone are not the answer. Answers to the question of what keeps headteachers in their job, and equally, what might influence teachers to leave their comfort zones and apply for senior leadership roles, will require close collaboration between professional associations, employers and government.

CHAPTER 11

LEADERSHIP AS A SUBVERSIVE ACTIVITY

Originally published in the *Journal of Educational Administration*,
Vol. 45, No. 3, 2007, 242–264

Abstract

Purpose – Leadership is as widely used as it is misused and misunderstood. This paper seeks to argue that in an educational context it is important not only to revisit and reframe conceptions of leadership but also to see it as having an essentially subversive purpose. The paper aims to discuss subversion in an intellectual, moral and political sense, as a sacred mission to confront the 'noble lies' of politicians, the superficiality of the designer culture and the line of least resistance opted for by overworked and demoralised teachers.

Design/methodology/approach – The empirical base for this paper is a seven-country three-years study entitled Leadership for Learning which brought together staff from 24 schools in seven countries to explore the connections between learning and leadership and to arrive at some common understanding which could be tested in practice across national and linguistic boundaries.

Findings – While recognising the unique contexts and differing cultural traditions as diverse as those of Australia and Austria, the USA and Greece, engaging in an international discourse through face-to-face workshops, virtual conferencing and exchange visits led one to five key principles held in common.

Originality/value – The paper offers intriguing and insightful discussion into the subject of leadership as a subversive activity.

Keywords Leadership, Learning, Culture

Paper type Research paper

Leadership as a subversive activity. The words contained in this title are all, to a greater or lesser extent, in common usage, yet with such a diverse range of meaning that some conceptual ground clearing is required.

Five years ago the *Daily Mail* newspaper in the UK declared that 'the world cries out for strong leadership'. The journalists who penned those lines could not have foreseen where such an aspiration might lead, nor did they appear to have a sufficient sense of history to recall the trail of havoc left by strong leadership and its impact on the lives of weak and willing followers.

Advocacy of 'strong' leadership also runs through much of the corporate and educational literature and is international in its scope:

> Accountability systems, and US views of leadership, tend to treat school leaders or principals as the primary agents of accountability in schools. The mythology of US education is heavily tilted in the direction of 'strong leaders make good schools'.
>
> (Elmore, 2005, p. 11)

Yet 'strong leadership' is an equivocal term, concealing more than it reveals. It conjures up images of charismatic figures striding through the corridors of their schools, making their presence felt and, when moving on leaving a depth of imprint behind them. Often, these larger than life figures left their schools because, by virtue of their apparent success, they were called on to turn other schools around.

Strength in leadership may, however, imply something entirely different from the image portrayed by the juxtaposition of the two words 'strong leadership'. As the Collins (2001) studies of successful corporations in the USA illustrates, strength runs both deeper and wider. The leaders of those successful companies were described as modest and self-effacing, surprised to be singled out as effective leaders.

Those corporate leaders also invested leadership in their colleagues. In Spillane *et al.* (2001) they 'spread it out'. They recognised that holding tight to information, influence and power may enhance the individual but enfeeble the body politic:

> The most notable trait of great leaders, certainly of great change leaders, however, is their quest for learning. They show an exceptional willingness to push themselves out of their own comfort zones, even after they have achieved a great deal. They continue to take risks, even when there is no obvious reason for them to do so. And they are open to people and ideas even at a time in life when they might reasonably think – because of their success – that they know everything.
>
> (Hesselbein *et al.*, 1996, p. 78)

The problem is that conceptions of 'leadership' are too easily confused with expert knowledge, role and status, with what people represent rather than what they are or what they do. A president, judged by 63 per cent of the US public to have 'strong leadership qualities' at the time of his re-election in 2004, was seen by less than half of those polled a year later to possess those qualities.[1] Public perception may be fickle but, ultimately it can be said that 'by their deeds shall you know them'.

Dixon (1994), in his compelling book 'On the psychology of military incompetence' the myths of the heroic leaders are exposed, together with 15 aspects of incompetence derived from famous disasters. These human frailties are, however, not restricted to the military but are often deeply embedded in organisations that lack the necessary subversive qualities. People who do not conform to this rule-bound stereotype have found it hard to survive within conformist and authoritarian regimes. Describing Major-General Damien-Smith, Dixon says the military had 'never forgiven him his brilliance and unorthodoxy' (p. 162). A 'dislike of intelligence (in both senses of the word)' is to be found in the academic world and in the business world. Judi Bevan's study of *The Rise and Fall of Marks and Spencer* explains its decline in the late 1990s in large part due to a leadership incapable of listening to divergent views, together with a sycophantic followership too timid to confront hierarchical authority.

In workshops in which business and educational leaders are asked to choose those of the 15 incompetences, which resonate with their own organisational learning disabilities (Senge, 1990), those most frequently opted for tend to be:

- An inability to profit from past experience.
- A resistance to exploiting available technology and novel tactics.
- An aversion to reconnaissance, coupled with a dislike of intelligence (in both senses of the word).
- An apparent imperviousness to loss of life and human suffering amongst the rank and file.
- A tendency to lay the blame on others.
- A love of bull, smartness, precision and strict preservation of the military pecking order.
- A high regard for tradition and other aspects of conservatism.
- A lack of creativity, improvisation, inventiveness and open-mindedness.

Of all of these, the most striking is the fourth – imperviousness to loss of life and human suffering. It is chosen, often with tongue in cheek but with a serious underlying intent. Although business environments are not immune to stress and consequent ill health, they perhaps suffer less from the intensification of workload that impact on the well-being and job satisfaction that teachers and school principals experience now on a daily basis. Delivering success, in the currency of test scores in a political and social context where few things stand still enough to be authentically measured, is a source of stress for principals who no longer feel in control of their schools and teachers who no longer feel in control of their teaching (Galton and MacBeath, 2002; MacBeath and Galton, 2004). The feeling of being out of control, concludes Martin in his book *The Sickening Mind* (1997), is highly correlated with chronic illness (physical and psychological) and with premature death.

As Dixon's treatise shows, leadership is made visible by its explicit failings as well as by its transparent successes. As examples from the military, from business and from education show, leadership is expressed in activity. It cares little for positional authority. It pays regard to the nature and quality of what individuals, or groups, do to affect and enhance the lives of others. It is measured not only by the activity of the appointed leader but by the activities of those around him or her. The Chinese book of wisdom, the Tao, poses these challenges – Can you lead without ego? Can you lead your people without seeing to control? Can you create without possessiveness? Accomplish without taking credit? (Tao 10).

Focusing on activity brings new insights. We begin to see things, perhaps for the first time – the quiet unassuming figure in the staff room taking initiative to comfort a colleague whose distress is not apparent to others, too engrossed in their own conversations. In so doing this 'servant leader' creates a precedent, sets an example and establishes a norm for others to follow. In probing the 'density' of leadership in a school (see, for example, Sergiovanni,

2001) we are led to ask – Who is it that intervenes to defuse conflict? Who takes control in a crisis? Who helps to shapes people's thinking? It is very often in the informal context, on field trips or residentials, where leadership emerges in new forms. Stripped of institutional constraints and institutional mandate, leadership arises spontaneously. In these less circumscribed environments there can be greater scope for leadership to be subversive. In the words of the radical Scottish dominie Mackenzie (1965) it was the 'escape from the classroom' (as he titled his most famous book) that brought new insights into the human condition, and troubled the complacency of the *status quo*.

Mackenzie was a headteacher and his teachers and students always returned to their classrooms, but their habits of seeing had been disturbed by questions, which were not the pseudo questions that framed so much of routine curriculum and assessment. They were their own, sometimes subversive, questions rather than those to which the answer had already been tirelessly rehearsed. While too often in breach of their essential purpose, schools are by their very nature subversive places. Yet the failure to walk that line is less because of personal inadequacy than by what teachers are required to teach, where, when and how they are required to teach it. Mary Alice White portrayed it in these metaphorical terms:

> Imagine yourself on a ship sailing across an unknown sea, to an unknown destination. An adult would be desperate to know where he is going. But a child only knows he is going to school . . . The chart is neither available nor understandable to him . . . Very quickly, the daily life on board ship becomes all-important . . . The daily chores, the demands, the inspections, become the reality, not the voyage, nor the destination.
>
> (Mary Alice White, 1971)

It is both the nature of the voyage and a visionary destination that are the hallmarks of a learning school, a school that is committed to restless inquiry, to aggressive curiosity and healthy scepticism (Warren-Little, 1993). The subversive nature of learning is captured by Gardner in his view of what learning is about and what schools should be for:

> I want my children to understand the world, but not just because the world is fascinating and the human mind is curious. I want them to understand it so that they will be positioned to make it a better place. Knowledge is not the same as morality, but we need to understand if we are to avoid past mistakes and move in productive directions. An important part of that understanding is knowing who we are and what we can do . . . Ultimately, we must synthesize our understandings for ourselves. The performance of understanding that try matters are the ones we carry out as human beings in an imperfect world, which we can affect for good or for ill.
>
> (Gardner, 1999a, pp. 180–181)

As subversive places schools require a quality of leadership which is a constant irritant, not allowing a slide into intellectual complacency, constantly reminding colleagues of education's sacred mission. If it were ever true that schools reflect society then to maintain such a view in the current climate would be a gross dereliction of that mission, and a disservice to children and young people growing up in the twenty-first century world we have created for them. To fail to offer an alternative to the banality of mass media, the conceits of the designer culture and a sex-obsessed popular culture would be to betray a subversive legacy of thought which stretches back to Socrates, and has reached us by way of Piaget, Dewey, Bruner, Vygotsky and other leading minds who worked tirelessly to keep to the fore the vision of learning as a constant process of subverting common sense, challenging received wisdom and 'inert ideas' (Whitehead, 1929).

The prescribed graduate text when I taught in the USA in the 1970s was 'Selected educational heresies' (1969), a compendium of thinkers who are remembered because they upset conventional wisdom and required us to think again.

Subversive leadership is intellectual, moral and political. It is intellectual because moral and political leadership are grounded in knowledge and wisdom. There are many people who are instinctively, intuitively and consistently ethical in their conduct without any clearly thought through rationale for their behaviour, but the exercise of leadership requires more than that. It demands rational explication and justification to those who might be persuaded to follow. Intellectual subversion is restlessly and creatively discontent. It cannot accept children being short-changed whether by government policies, by teachers unaccountable for their actions, or by young people who settle for the mediocre. Its expectations of high standards are too intellectually acute to be equated with the paucity of 'standards' as conceived by timid legislators or with the perverse indicators by which governments measure success. Subversive leadership is intolerant, not in a bullish or confrontative sense, neither personalised nor necessarily even direct, but implicit in the fostering of a climate in which critical inquiry is simply the way we do things around here.

Intellectual and moral subversion go hand in hand. Responsibility is a moral commitment and one that is consciously and rigorously applied. It believes in accountability but one that derives from a strongly held value position rather than mandated targets. It rests on 'the connective tissue' of trust, a fragile commodity, hard to construct and easy to destroy (Elmore, 2005, p. 20). Trust, Elmore argues, is a compound of respect, listening to and valuing the views of others; personal regard, intimate and sustained personal relationships that are the very stuff of professional relationships; competence, the capacity to produce desired results in relationships with others; and personal integrity, truthfulness and honesty in human concourse.

When these essential values are undermined and threatened, moral leadership acquires a political edge. Moral leadership cannot accept, endorse or perpetuate what is manifestly wrong. Its stance is in Luther's famous dictum 'Hier stehe Ich, Ich kann kein anders' (here I stand, I can no other). This is, of course, much easier for academics to argue than for school leaders to enact. In advocating subversion we have to be alive to leadership dilemmas, a continuing struggle with compromise, which bring sleepless nights in the wake of pragmatic decisions taken for the greater good. The following comment from an English headteacher had an alarmingly familiar resonance with schools in many other countries:

I have three pistols to my head: one is the need to prepare the school for another visit from the inspectors because we are in 'special measures', another is the need to present a case to the local authority which is threatening to close the school and another is the need to improve the attainment figures so we can be lifted out of the status of being 'a school in challenging circumstances'. And then there is the small matter of trying to lead and manage the school on a day-to-day basis and meet the needs of our students and the community.

(quoted in Frost, 2005, p. 76)

In the context of a three-year study into a school in exceptionally challenging circumstances in a UK inner city, a headteacher spoke candidly and in confidence to me about his choice to prioritise the school efforts and resources on the borderline achievers at the expense of the low achievers. It was a strategy simply to vouchsafe the survival of his school. It was a decision set in a context in which inner-city low performing schools are threatened by performance tables and parental choice, exercised in a climate of disinformation and high stakes accountability. It was, he agreed, a decision taken uneasily and with regret. The policy context is one, as Andy Hargreaves has argued, which:

> . . . divides high capacity schools in socio-economically favoured districts which support professional discretion and autonomy, and build professional community among teachers, from low capacity schools in poorer districts which receive prescriptive improvement strategies that perpetuate dependency among poorly certified, low-skilled staffs.

(Hargreaves, 2004, p. 39)[2]

The pragmatic and uneasy compromise of this one English headteacher did not stop him speaking publicly, arguing the case for policy change in newspapers and making his voice heard in Downing Street.

The political context

We are, writes the US academic Alterman (2004), living in a 'post-truth political environment'. He argues that the value of 'truth' has been superseded by a new set of norms in which truth is pragmatically and politically determined and in which veracity has no intrinsic value. These themes find direct parallels in the British context in his book (Oborne, 2005), 'The rise of political lying' which charts the rise in British politics of distortion, going beyond mere spin and half-truths to a process of systematic deception. 'It was almost as if there were a parallel world,' writes Oborne, one inhabited by ministers, their spokesperson and spin doctors, with another world inhabited by everyone else. Rather than connecting these two worlds with the truth, ministers 'make statements on what they would have liked to be the truth' (p. 10). As he points out, 'conventional wisdom', the term coined by the economist Galbraith, meant in its original form, convenient truth.

In the world of schools 'truth' is a core value, however much it is also subject to curricular 'spin'. Being truthful to the disciplines of knowledge lies at the very heart of the school's educational mission, and adherence to truth is the warrant for the school's integrity and the social glue which holds relationships together. Yet schools find themselves caught up in a statistical deceit not of their own making.

In the USA the famous 'Texas miracle' under the governorship of George W. Bush was shown to be a deception of a high order. An analysis by Boston College's Haney (2000) concluded that the dramatic rise in pass rates for high school students on the Texas Assessment of Academic Skills (TAKS) and decrease in dropout rate was illusory, in part due to a doubling of the numbers 'in special education' and therefore excluded from grade ten tests, and a significant rise in grade retention (students held back for another year), including as many as 30 per cent of black and Hispanic students. In fact, rather than the reported 20 per cent increase, Haney's analysis showed a sharp decrease despite heavy coaching for the test. In Chicago, Levitt and Dubner (2005) have shown teachers' cheating on tests has been widespread, not because teachers were intrinsically untrustworthy but because a high stakes environment destroys the fragile trust that Elmore writes about.

In uncompromising language Starratt (1998) talks to teachers and school principals about learning as a moral enterprise and that teaching to the test is a 'ransacking' of the world of ideas and devaluing the integrity of the learner and the teacher, who is complicit. Without deeply grounded morally subversive leadership teachers will collude with, rather than challenge, larger systemic corruption.

In England the government's much vaunted rise in literacy and numeracy attainment under New Labour was similarly shown to be fraudulent. Tymms' (2005) meta-analysis at the Curriculum Evaluation and Management Centre in Durham found government figures to be hugely overstated – their 2004 figures, 84 and 74 per cent respectively for Key Stage 2 (age 11) English and maths; his figures, 60 and 66 per cent respectively. This did not endear him to secretaries of state from whom he might seek funding in the future, but the pursuit of truth is an academic, as well as a school, moral imperative.

Schools leaders have neither the time nor the expertise to delve as deeply into claims of government statistics but they do have a duty to remain attuned to alternative sources of evidence, and to other voices. Subversive leadership needs to maintain and nurture a healthy scepticism as to politically inspired miracles.

While in a competitive globalised world governments hold schools to account for the moral and social welfare of their charges (in rhetoric at least), more important, in their eyes, is the contribution that schools make to the health and wealth of the economy. This is most clearly demonstrated in the growing influence of the Organisation for Economic and Social Development (the OECD) and its PISA reports comparing attainments of young people in participating OECD countries. These are taken extremely seriously by politicians, contributing to what Berliner and Biddle (1995) have described as the 'manufactured crisis'. It is one, although largely unsupported by evidence, which holds that schools and teachers are harming the economy through their attachment to woolly 'progressive' thinking and child-centred methods. The political sleight of hand is to connect measured success in school subjects with the vitality of the economy rather than the more plausible explanations of family influence or private tutoring, for example. In her well-argued critique of the specious links between schools and the economy, Wolf writes:

> Our pre-occupation with education as an engine of growth not only narrows the way we think about social policy. It has also narrowed – abysmally and progressively – the vision we have of education itself.
>
> (Wolf, 2002, p. 254)

As Wolf argues, positive correlations between education and earnings can be accounted for by 'natural ability', by the contribution made by the family, by peers and by other forms of out-of-school learning. It opens to serious examination, therefore, whether the huge and anxious investment in raising test scores and staying in school longer for more and more young people will actually be of benefit to national competitiveness in the global economy.

Confronting the noble lie

For Plato, his Republic would only ever be viable if the leadership class were to convince the populace of a 'noble lie' fabricated to ensure that people were happy with their station in life and did not aspire to grandiose ambitions which could undermine the carefully designed infrastructure of the Republic. Famously, Michael Barber, close attendant on policy making in the Blair government, perpetuated his own version of the magnificent myth. In keynote lectures, delivered nationally and internationally to a variety of audiences, he interpreted four decades of the policy/practice interface in these terms. He characterised the 1970s as the era of 'uninformed professionalism', 1980s the era of 'uninformed prescription', the 1990s as 'informed prescription', with the 2000s as 'informed professionalism'.

How myths become internalised is illustrated in extracts from headteacher interviews conducted in the course of a four-university research project 'Learning how to learn' (MacBeath, 2006). Referring to the 1970s and 1980s, a secondary headteacher claimed 'a short period of time ago nobody was interested in achievement in schools'. A primary head makes a similar claim, referring to a previous time when 'teachers took no responsibility for children's learning at all. They had no expectation of them at all'. It is this easy and unthinking internalisation of the myth that Giroux (1992) warns us about. He signals the danger of the 'omniscient narrator' – the agency or authority that tells the story on our behalf. There is no grand narrative that can speak for us all, says Giroux. Leaders, whether principals or teachers, have an intellectual, moral and political responsibility for the knowledge that is organised, produced, mediated and translated into practice. If teachers are not alert and alive to the what and how of their practice there is a danger that they come to be seen as simply the technical intervening medium through which knowledge is transmitted to students, 'erasing themselves' in an uncritical reproduction of received wisdom (p. 120).

Mainstream political leadership does not address questions of culture, identity, or voice, speaking volumes in what it ignores. In so doing it stifles any real discussion of issues of power, hierarchy, exploitation, and the professional accountability that teachers owe to one another. Rather than internalising the master narratives, argues Giroux, it is incumbent on leadership to examine how ideas and panaceas become constructed, what they mean, how they regulate our social and moral experience and how they convey particular political views of the world, so pre-empting debate as to what knowledge counts and what is worth learning.

Giroux's writings help us to grasp something of the relationship between schooling and political life, asking us to bring new insights to the traditional ways in which we conceive of the roles of students, teachers, principals and of schooling itself. At the kernel of Giroux's work is a plea for new 'spaces' and a new critical discourse about learning, ideology and power.

The power of inertia and inert ideas was vividly illustrated by the reception given in England to Bramall and White's (2000) book 'Why learn maths?' (2000). It was met with disbelief and reflex opposition as if posing the question was equivalent to challenging the existence of a deity. While agnosticism and atheism are now in the mainstream of western thought, the questioning of maths' sacred place in the curriculum appears to be a heresy too far.

In this disingenuous world of myth and contradiction the task of leadership is not to create a parallel world of its own, insulated from the 'real' world and the counterfeit world of political spin, but to confront deception and obfuscation with its own truth.

The new world of growing up

Three decades ago Holt (1969) wrote that 'schools are bad places for children'. This, along with many other radical critiques of schooling, cast doubt on the school not only as unable to create authentic independent learners but as actually stifling the creativity and curiosity which children brought with them. The challenge for schools in the era in which Holt was writing, and the issues that schools face three decades later, are qualitatively different. Schools may have changed little but the world of 2006 is a different place from that the parents of this generation's children grew up in.

In his brilliant trilogy spanning a decade Castells (1996, 1999, 2000) identifies three key inter-related elements of the Network Society – informational capitalism, social exclusion and perverse integration. Access to information and the ability to discriminate and exploit it for personal benefit is what increasingly separates the knowledge haves from the knowledge have-nots. And year on year the gap widens. This is closely tied to social exclusion. As Putnam (1999) and Martin (1997) have shown, social exclusion recreates itself from generation to generation. Young people spend more and more time alone, in homes, families, surrogate families or institutions with few supportive social networks. For the less passive and victimised, the route back into the economy is through a shadow economy of borderline legality, petty criminal and criminal activity – a route back which Castells terms as 'perverse integration'.

Many of the hazards of childhood and adolescence now all too familiar seem to have been newly invented or discovered. Depression, addiction, attention deficiency and bipolar disorders appear as new phenomena among children and young people, to some degree only now recognised but also seen as emergent in response to a changing social fabric. Research by Abela (2003) found that clinical depression in the young was a phenomenon largely characteristic of the last two decades, attributing increasing rates of depression among the young to growing materialism, fixation on financial success, a premium on physical appearance and social recognition, a more fragile sense of self in proportion to self worth being judged by attaining external goods and pursuit of extrinsic goals (within which we might include obsession with school performance). He concludes that as societies become more materialistic, depression rates rise in tandem.

The World Health Organization (2005), found that many mental disorders seen in adulthood have their beginnings in childhood and adolescence, estimating that 8 per cent of all girls and 2 per cent of all boys in the UK showed symptoms of severe depression. In the five to ten age group,

10 per cent of boys and six per cent of girls were affected, and among the 11–15 age group, 13 per cent of boys and 10 per cent of girls.

Many of these young people, they pointed out, received no care or treatment, their conditions often barely understood by teachers, parents or social services. Depression is associated with suicide in the young, the third leading cause of death among young people in Europe. Similar findings are reported in Australia (Sawyer, 2001), where 14 per cent of children and adolescents were identified as having mental health problems. Many of those had problems in other areas of their lives and were at increased risk for suicidal behaviour. Only 25 per cent of those with mental health problems had attended a professional service during the six months prior to the survey.

Common to these data from European, North American and Australasian countries is the disproportionate incidence of mental ill health in disadvantaged neighbourhoods. Poorer people are also six times more likely to be admitted to hospital with schizophrenia, and ten times more likely to be admitted for alcohol-related problems (World Health Organization, 2005).

Schools may not always be the best places for children because they lack the capacity to address a challenge that is too big to contemplate and the competitive pressure on attainment may simply exacerbate the problem rather than counter feeling of inadequacy and low self worth. Teachers are the first to recognise that the limited scope of a classroom lesson with its tight objectives and demand for coverage leaves little or no room to deal with things that really matter.

We can see all too clearly a process of what Foucault (1973) termed 'normalization', a tacit acceptance of the status quo as inevitable. This is held in place, he argues, by political power focused on what people have not done (nonobservence), in other words, a failure to reach required standards. So deviant behaviour is sanctioned and normalised.

The intensification of teachers' work means that there is little energy left for subversion or dissent. The sanctions are too great when domestic and familial concerns take priority. Keeping your head down and getting on with it is the counsel of many teachers, despite their job satisfaction being progressively eroded. It poses the question for school leadership – How do we, as a learning community, accommodate the categorical demands of market realities, while at the same time not abandoning pedagogies of hope, possibility and transformation?

Subversive activity may conjure images of radical action, civil disobedience and a manning of the barricades, but subversion in its three forms, intellectual, moral and political, may imply a softer revolution.

Leadership for learning: the Carpe Vitam Project

Over the course of three and half years we came to understand a lot about the potential and limits of leadership as a subversive activity through an international project encompassing schools in seven countries and eight cities. The Leadership for Learning Project (known as Carpe Vitam after its Swedish commissioning body) was an international research and development project focusing on the process by which schools made, and then grew, the connections between learning and leadership. It was funded for three years (2002–2005) by the Wallenberg Foundation in Sweden, with further financial support from participating countries. The project was directed from the University of Cambridge[3] in collaboration with eight different groups of university researchers and their nominated schools in eight cities – Athens, Brisbane, Copenhagen, Innsbruck, London, Oslo, Seattle and Trenton (New Jersey).

The three journeys, which these schools undertook in collaboration, were a search for common ground and common meaning, which could apply in their widely differing contexts. The monocultural schools in Innsbruck, Oslo and Athens contrasted starkly with schools in Brisbane, London and Trenton, serving local communities with a highly diverse ethnic mix with concomitants of poverty endemic to such socio-economic profiles. Among young people in a Brisbane school 55 different languages other than English were spoken with birthplaces that extended to 60 countries other than Australia, with certain parts of the city continuing to attract students from Pacific Rim countries, European countries such as Yugoslavia, Romania, Hungary and Poland, as well as from troubled African countries such as the Sudan. There was a measure of common ground here with one of the London schools in which 55 per cent of the school population have English as an additional language while 35 per cent are on the school's register of Special Educational Needs. The profiles of attainment, as in many of our schools, were more a reflection of the demographics of their communities than of the quality of classroom learning and teaching:

> . . . cos we're a small school, from year to year you get odd things like . . . one year all your bright kids might be Bangladeshi girls, which is wonderful 'cos you're guaranteed results! Another year, like our current Year 11, all our bright pupils are actually white boys, which has all sorts of problems! So you have to change what you do. We change our pupil grouping. We try not to just be set in our ways. There is constant reflection. And so I think that's part of the learning and constantly looking at what we're doing, and do we need to change it?
>
> (Deputy head teacher, secondary school, Tower Hamlets, London)

The culture is depicted as fragile, on the edge of chaos, imported by students, by media and by disgruntled or demanding parents. Some minority groups are distinguished by high aspirations and high achievement while others traditionally fail to thrive within conventional school arrangements. Yet despite the widely diverse communities they serve, all schools shared some common elements of a global culture in which the prescriptions for school learning seemed increasingly out of touch with the society in which young people are growing up. All experienced the tension between political pressures on attainment. All were touched by PISA comparisons, increasing the pressure on school performance and accountability demands, framed in terms of test and examination performance. All were subject, although to widely differing degrees, to external monitoring and accountability.

The project was implicitly framed within a political context as, during its three year lifespan, there were elections in Austria, Australia, Denmark, Greece and Norway, the UK and the USA, observed by participants with high levels of anxiety, and with an acute awareness of the implications of this for school and classroom practice. While four of these countries saw the re-election of the same political parties, only in Greece was this greeted with a sense of relief, while three of these countries (Austria, Denmark and Norway), witnessed a sharp swing to the right. This was particularly challenging in the two Nordic countries – Denmark and Norway, in which a commitment to democracy, historically and culturally, was traditionally reflected in the flatarchy of their schools in which teachers enjoyed a high level of autonomy and students played an active role in their own learning. In these two countries, in particular, the introduction of targets, performance indicators and New Public Management runs shrilly across the cultural grain.

Moos (in Denmark) and Moller (in Norway) have written extensively on the leadership challenges faced in their countries (for example, Moos, 2002; Moller, 2002; Moos and Moller, 2003) by the hegemony of English language and policy cherry picking by government keen to keep up with their European neighbours. As most educational publications are produced in the UK, the USA and Australasia, and as research findings are accessible only in the English language, Nordic countries find themselves not only adopting others' language but also its underlying constructs. In Moos and Moller (2003, p. 360) these are described as 'cultural isomorphs', deceptively similar but essentially different, creating a barrier to understanding of the essential differences that lie beneath words:

> Language is co-opted as an agent of ideology . . . So participatory discourse becomes overshadowed by an administrative discourse, and is distorted into a technology of control. Traditional norms of democratic accountability are open to question while the tenor of debate about democratic leadership undergoes gradual change.
>
> (Moos and Moller, 2003, p. 361)

English and US principals and teachers, well versed in the new performativity lexicon, and inured to the structures of NPM, found in the Norwegian and Danish schools they visited, a resistance and resilience which encouraged them to return to their own schools with new insight and new determination to teach and lead differently. It gave them renewed energy, optimism and a sense of agency.

It was 'agency' that proved to be the most unsettling and subversive of ideas within the Carpe Vitam project. For some it presented a mental hurdle, struggling to see how it could be accommodated within conventional structures and strictures. In order to find and to map the common ground, to establish shared language and a collective discourse, we began to frame a set of principles of leadership, which could begin to bridge the theory practice. By subjecting them to testing in the daily round of school and classroom life these were progressively reframed. The principles, which follow here, are by nature inherently subversive.

Principles for subversive leadership

A focus on learning was our first guiding principle for leadership. The problem with such a statement is that it can be taken as too self-evident, too easy to sign up to. That is, after all, what schools are for and ultimately what school leadership is about. Yet the vocabulary of learning, whether in English or in other languages, has proved as often to inhibit thinking as to promote it. It has become too familiar and too habitual, leading us to see what we already know rather than knowing what we see. It has been rendered unproblematic, and in part its co-option by politicians and policy makers is treated as synonymous with school attainment, while 'lifelong learning' is seen to apply to something that happens once the 'real' learning of school days are over.

Expanding a focus on learning so as to give it a finer, more cutting edge we arrived at five elaborations on the principle, expressed as follows.

Leadership for learning practice involves a focus on learning in which it is assumed that:

- Everyone (students, teachers, principals, schools, the system itself) is a learner.
- Learning relies on effective interplay of emotional, social and cognitive processes.
- The efficacy of learning is highly sensitive to context and to the differing ways in which people learn.
- The capacity for leadership arises out of powerful learning experiences.
- Opportunities to exercise leadership enhance learning.

These principles evolved, and continue to take shape, through continuing dialogue and as they are tested against practice and the 'real world' of schools' classrooms. In theory few might demur from these principles, but they are radical in implication for both learning and leadership. Taken together as a philosophy and a guide to practice they are subversive of much common sense, current policy and conventional wisdom.

The names Freire and Illich fail to resonate with a current generation of students and entrants to teaching, inducted into Barber's world of 'informed prescription'. Freire and Illich's ideas, too big to be accommodated within the small compass of conventional classrooms and mainstream literature, gave way in the 1970s and 1980s to more sensible policies and the pragmatics of 'reschooling', not simply coincident with the rise of the Reagan–Thatcher world view. However, Illich's conceptions of convivial tools and convivial sites for learning resonate powerfully with the principles of Carpe Vitam.

Illich did not presuppose a teacher, a curriculum and a set of pre-determined objectives. As the above principle states, learning is highly sensitive to contexts and social milieu and learning preferences. One exemplification of Illich's theory, and related to our first principle, comes from a recent series of 'hole in the wall' experiments in India in which computers were placed in a wall 'kiosk' in slum villages (Inamdar, 2004). The researchers found that groups of children who had never before seen a computer were able to learn very quickly how to navigate their way through them to produce surprising results. Numerous experiments were conducted to find out how it was that children could learn without being taught, what was termed 'minimally invasive education' (MIE). In total, 103 children of the Grade 8 level, across three villages, were administered the curricular examination for 'Computer Science' for that grade. Results showed that children who had learned at MIE kiosks were able to complete this curricular examination without being taught the subject. They scored at nearly the same level as children who had been taught the computer curriculum in school throughout the school year.

Interviewed by a journalist, one of the authors of the project, Mitra related the following anecdote:

One day there was a document file on the desktop of the computer. It was called 'untitled.doc' and it said in big colorful letters, 'I Love India'. I couldn't believe it for the simple reason that there was no keyboard on the computer (only a touch screen). I asked my main assistant – a young boy, eight years old, the son of a local betel-nut seller – and I asked him, 'How on earth did you do this?'. He showed me the character map inside (Microsoft) Word. So he had gotten into the character map inside Word, and dragged and dropped the letters onto the screen, then increased the point size and painted the letters. I was stunned because I didn't know that the character map existed – and I have a PhD.

(Businessweek Online Daily Briefing, March 2, 2000)

'The results of this study throw new light on pedagogy,' concluded the research teams (Mitra and Rana, 2001). Some children actually learned better without formal school instruction, others did appear to need some form of 'scaffolding', while there were others for whom a more structured approach was needed, whether from their peers or from informed adults. But as the many snapshots and video illustrations showed, learning was highly social. Children learned from and through one another. They distributed intelligence. They networked their knowledge. Experts and leaders emerged while others played the role of 'connectors' and 'mavens'[4] who put their peers in touch with the intelligence sources and knew how to access the most expert current knowledge (see Gladwell, 2000).

A century ago Dewey wrote:

> . . . without insight into the psychological structure and activities of the individual, the educative process will, therefore, be haphazard and arbitrary. If it chances to coincide with the child's activity it will get a leverage; if it does not, it will result in friction, or disintegration, or arrest of the child nature.
>
> (Dewey, 1897, p. 78)

Dewey's insights and lessons from the Indian research relate directly back to our first Carpe Vitam principle and challenge much of what we take too easily for granted about learning, leadership and their inter-connections. Back in the 'real world', a Norwegian teacher who had been part of the project from the start and was in it because she was already a good teacher, wrote after our final conference in Athens:

> I have become more focused on learning in my own teaching, and I know that influences my work. I have also seen how important it is that we as teachers have time and space for discussing our teaching with colleagues, with a focus on learning. So much time is used on organization, administration and frustration. I think at my own school we focus too much on problems instead of opportunities and solutions.
>
> It has provided an improved and extended perspective on my own work and means that I am asking different questions compared to before taking part in the project.

Focusing on learning had, for this one teacher, changed priorities and mindset. A change in mindset means asking different kinds of questions, ones that are not only more subversive of the teaching and learning interface but that led directly into questions of leadership, her own and that of her colleagues. Opportunities for learning enhance leadership and – setting in train a virtuous circle – opportunities for leadership enhance learning.

A second principle

We articulated the second principle in the following terms to underline again the importance of conditions, context and culture.

Leadership for learning creates and sustains conditions that favour learning, when there are:

- Cultures which nurture the learning of all members of the school community;
- Opportunities for all to reflect on the nature, skills and processes of learning;
- Physical and social spaces that stimulate and celebrate learning;
- Safe and secure environments that enable pupils and teachers to take risks, cope with failure and respond positively to challenges; and
- Tools and strategies which enhance thinking about learning and the practice of teaching.

The mark of a learning organisation, or a learning 'community', as Mitchell and Sackney (2000) prefer in an educational context, is the transparent openness to learning of all its members. How can children learn if there are no models of inquiry, reflection, risk taking, empathy and moral courage to be emulated? Perkins, our critical friend to Carpe Vitam used this metaphor to highlight the importance of learning and conditions, which make that possible:

> Imagine learning to dance when the dancers around you are all invisible. Imagine learning a sport when the players who already know the game can't be seen . . . As educators, we can work to make thinking much more visible than it usually is in classrooms. When we do so, we are giving students more to build on and learn from. By making the dancers visible, we are making it much easier to learn to dance.
>
> (Perkins, 2003, p. 1)

Learning is a social activity, as our first principle claims, but is has to be modelled in a milieu within which we observe and internalise norms, in which learners both 'catch' and 'spread' ideas. Knowing and remembering occur because knowledge and memory are invested in, and accessible from the behaviours and intelligences of people with whom we share and create ideas.

The dance was a metaphor that entered the Carpe Vitam discourse at an early stage. In the initial Cambridge conference which launched the project, Michael Schratz, leader of the Innsbruck team, talked about the dance of change while Archie McGlynn (former HMCI) posed the question 'How do you tell the dancer from the dance?'. It took three years of work with schools before these ideas came to have real meaning, as the dance of change came to be perceived and identified less in persons and roles but in the 'dance' itself, the flow of activities in which a school is engaged (Gronn, 2003).

In activity theory (Engeström, 1999), it is the activity itself which is centre stage. The context of the activity is not simply an outer container or shell inside of which people behave in certain ways, as passive objects, but as actors who recreate the context through the artefacts with which they engage, including other people – a fusion of internal mental processes and the external social world. Learning is then understood, not seen simply as the property of an individual to be interred in memory and disinterred for examination purposes (Freire, 1970) (banking concept), but concerned with how intelligently intellectual, human and material resources are deployed to formulate and resolve problems. We lodge and retrieve our thinking and memory in other people to whom we are close and, through this transactive and transformational process, develop our individual and shared capacity for intelligent behaviour.

How communication flows through a staff is a condition which underpins learning at student, teacher and senior leadership level. In a Brisbane school it was said that prior to the arrival of the new principal, 'nobody knew how anyone did anything. It was all done by word of mouth and ad hoc and by the seat of your pants' (Principal interview, 2004). The recognition of this communication lacuna gave rise to trans-disciplinary learning teams, designed to increase the learning exchange across the school, within an explicit leadership for learning framework. It was underpinned by a conviction that changing the professional mindset is a necessary prelude to changing the student mindset, putting the oxygen mask on your own face before putting it on the child's face.

Intellectual subversion is a slow process but one in which leadership makes available the tools that inspire ideas and give leverage to practice. Developing, sharing and modifying tools to widen teachers' and students' repertoires was one of the project's main activities and one of its key contributions to the fusion of theory and practice. As Csikszentmihalyi argues, the tools of learning extend beyond the classroom and need to cater to the breadth and complexity of young people's experience:

> A good society needs more than schools with a broad curriculum and up-to-date science labs. Education takes place in the whole community . . . If we wish to have a society in which freedom coexists with responsibility, we must ensure that the environment in which young people grow up provides complex experiences.
>
> (Csikszentmihalyi, 1990, p. 273)

The third principle

Following from the second principle, the third emphasises the role played by dialogue – the process by which learning and leadership are made explicit, not only conceptually but in practical application.

Leadership for learning practice involves an explicit dialogue which:

- makes LfL practice explicit, discussable and transferable;
- promotes active collegial inquiry into the link between learning and leadership;
- achieves coherence through the sharing of values, understandings and practices;

- addresses factors which inhibit and promote learning and leadership;
- makes the link between leadership and learning a shared concern for all members of the school community; and
- extends dialogue internationally through networking, both virtually and through face-to-face exchange.

The whole Carpe Vitam Leadership for Learning project could be viewed as an extended dialogue. Much of the thrust of the project was about facilitating the meeting of minds. As well as the more conventional tools of research – interviews and questionnaires – dialogue came through the discussion of data as it was fed back to schools, through the creative development and sharing of school portraits, the critical appraisal and testing of tools, and conference workshops which provided a forum for more extended and in-depth interchange of ideas. These occasions also afforded participants a discursive space for deep reflective discussions with colleagues from the same school – something that proved difficult in the busyness of everyday life.

Dia logos, in the original Greek meaning flowing through it, is something qualitatively different from conversation, discussion, and debate. It is hard for teachers to shed an outer skin which has calcified over many years in classrooms where dialogue is a rare commodity no matter how much teachers strive for it, and in which 'instruction' is the norm. 'Instruction' is the US term, containing within it an implicit message as to the stereotypical nature of classroom transactions. In contrast, the emphasis within our third principle links the importance of dialogic teaching (Alexander, 2003) and the dialogue that takes place in inter-cultural exchanges across linguistic borderlands. Including the international dimension in the second principle is to remind us that new forms of words help to reframe our thinking. Through dialogue the shallowness of 'instruction' is exposed and, within cross-cultural discourse, it was important for teachers to wrestle with the ideas inherent in terms such as 'Bildung' and 'paedogogisk'. Both of these terms, alien to the English ear, signal something deeper and more growth promoting than the notion of 'delivery', the word which policy makers seem to believe, describes what teachers do with curriculum. Within such a paradigm, devoid of dialogue, Elmore (2005) argues:

> The transfer of agency from teacher to student is minimal because the nature of the task locates the knowledge with the teacher and the obligation to learn with the student – knowledge is transferred, agency over learning is not.
>
> (2005, p. 8)

Seeing things through a different cultural and linguistic lens shakes the foundations of our 'thought world', one which contains 'a set of basic assumptions that are taken as axiomatic; that is, it is assumed that they exist, that they are shared by the majority in the field and their presence is evoked whenever a practice is challenged' (Czarniawska, 1997, p. 68). Challenging the assumptions that are brought to what is 'seen' and the way in which it is judged, Czarniawska coins the term 'outsidedness' to denote a form of knowing – by difference rather than by similarity:

> It aims at understanding not by identification ('they are like us') but by the recognition of differences – 'we are different from them and they are

different from us; by exploring these differences we will understand ourselves better'.

(p. 62)

At the culmination of the project a Brisbane principal attested to intellectual subversion in these words – 'a significant change in their mindset about being in the school and what is important' (Principal interview, May 2005). In Seattle the research team reported that, two years into the project, intercultural travel, both geographical and intellectual, had helped to dislodge many of the preconceptions that principals and teachers brought with them. The dialogue had helped them to see past 'cursory practice' to deeper-lying principles:

> By the time of the Copenhagen Conference (2004), enough exchange and interchange had occurred to allow the schools to see both their own and other schools' experience in relation to a more developed set of principles. The examples provided were around how their schools, and others, compared and differed from principles rather than cursory practice-to-practice comparisons (Seattle Research Report, 2005).

Dialogue need not be a verbal process, as the following illustrations from one of the English schools illustrates:

> At Barnwell School the challenge was to make practice visible on a large scale . . . The strategic team constructed a mock-up of a brick wall on a notice board at the entrance to the staffroom . . . Whenever a teacher used a post-it to record an observation it would be posted on to the wall. Soon, posting observations took on a degree of competitiveness and it was clear which departments were contributing most because of the colour of the post-its. As the wall grew, members of staff found that it was worthwhile to stop and read the post-its as they passed on their way into the staff room. These classrooms' observations therefore became the catalyst for cross-cutting conversation about teaching and learning.
>
> (Frost, 2005, pp. 21–22)

The fourth principle

We came to the project with a belief in distributed, or shared, leadership, but it was only through the journeying between theory and practice that we began to get a firm grasp of what this means and what principles might flow from it.

Leadership for learning practice involves the sharing of leadership by:

- creating structures which invite participation in developing the school as a learning community;
- symbolising shared leadership in the day-to-day flow of activities of the school;
- encouraging all members of the school community to take the lead as appropriate to task and context;
- drawing on the experience and expertise of staff, students and parents as resources; and

- promoting collaborative patterns of work and activity across boundaries of subject, role and status.

Shared leadership was something that most of our Carpe Vitam schools aspired to but it was understood quite differently in different settings: in some cases distributed as in delegated, in other cases as initiative spontaneously exercised, and in other interpretations as teamwork. Each of these differing conceptions reflected the cultural and organisational context in which they were embedded. The more hierarchical the structures of the schools the more distribution seemed to rest on a downward flow, a trickling down which might not ever reach the lowest layers of the organisation. In this respect historical inertia played a part. In Greek schools, for example, there was initially a strong resistance to the upsetting of the status quo in which the distinction between leaders and followers had long been institutionalised and accepted as the immutable reality of school life. Nor was it easy for English schools initially to risk loosening the structures which maintained effective control and held schools together.

A Seattle principal, speaking well towards the end of the Carpe Vitam project, acknowledged shared leadership as a slow and pragmatic process, feeling out the strengths and weaknesses of staff, and learning the importance of flexibility and fluidity:

> As a leader, you must be flexible and fluid . . . and (able to) go with the flow. Every day is different. It's important to involve everyone in leadership . . . to know the staff, recognize their strengths, build on their strengths, move them in a direction you want them to go or they want to go, in moving forward teaching and learning. We're on the right road . . . but still need more shared leadership. In some ways, I feel like we're just beginning.

Spillane's work on distributed leadership helped to lay bare some of the assumptions on which these notions rest. He describes principals who have told him they plan to distribute leadership by pointing out to them that, if they have eyes to see it, leadership is already distributed. It is inherent in what he calls 'reciprocal interdependencies' (Spillane *et al.*, 2001, p. 34). Whether taking action, innovating or creating knowledge, individuals play off one another. What A does can only be fully understood by taking into account what B does, and vice versa, each bringing differing resources – skills, knowledge, perspectives to bear:

> We contend, in other words, that the collective cognitive properties of a group of leaders working together to enact a particular task leads to the evolution of a leadership practice that is potentially more than the sum of each individual's practice. Consequently, to understand the knowledge needed for leadership practice in such situations, one has to move beyond an analysis of individual knowledge and consider what these leaders know and do together. Depending on the particular leadership task, the knowledge and expertise of school leaders may be best explored at the group or collective level rather than at the individual leader level.
>
> (Spillane *et al.*, 2001, p. 12)

In Spillane's terms, distributed leadership is made manifest in 'negotiated order' between leaders and followers. While leaders can often draw on their positional authority to support the beliefs and actions they advocate, followers can influence leaders by drawing on personal characteristics, access to information, their special knowledge or expertise, and so may influence leadership strategies through subtle forms of manipulation, subversion and 'creative insubordination'. In other words, followers are an essential element of leadership activity. Not, might we add, that those roles are static. Those who lead may also follow, while those who follow may also lead, depending on context and the task at hand. In Denmark this was exemplified in the fluidity of leaderless, self-governing teams:

> In the self-governing teams there is no formal leader. Instead, they make use of everybody's resources by talking about teaching, students and learning.
>
> (Denmark Country Report)

In the discussion of shared leadership a major theme was the role of students as decision-makers and leaders. Students are the school's largest untapped knowledge source in a school, says SooHoo (1993): 'the treasure in our very own backyard', arguing that a school which overlooks that intelligence source is inevitably poorer as a consequence. Historically they have been the last to be consulted about school quality and effectiveness, yet, as a developing literature attests, they may get closest to the heartbeat of the school (see, for example, Rudduck and Flutter, 2004).

In both Brisbane and Seattle student leadership was also a key theme, as an Australian teacher described it:

> There are a lot of students in this school and a lot of students in a leadership role, which is very impressive, and they take it on quite well too . . . it's not just at the top, it's spread throughout and there are various leaders at various levels.
>
> (teacher, Brisbane school)

In Denmark student leadership was described in terms of their initiative in leading their own learning and that of their classmates. As one student claimed in interview:

> We have great freedom and take responsibility for our own learning . . . The independent responsibility for learning makes me inclined to learn more . . . We choose what we want to work with on our own, but the teachers keep tabs on you if you start reducing the demands you make on yourself . . . If somebody gets a good idea in relation to the task or has some kind of insight beforehand, it seems natural that he or she takes on the leadership for a period.

Reflecting on the leadership for learning journey at the end of the Athens conference a Norwegian teacher wrote:

> I have gained an understanding of the way of conceptualizing leadership with a focus on many people (who) can take part/initiate leadership in

many contexts, and that leadership is focused on the core activities within the school, i.e. learning. Learning happens in the interaction, and that's why it is so important with sharing.

The fifth principle

The fifth principle emerged late in the Carpe Vitam project, less an after-thought than a reminder from the US contingent to make explicit what we understood by the term 'accountability' and how it played out in concert with the other four principles. It was framed thus:

Leadership for learning practice implies accountability by:

* taking account of political realities and exercising informed choices as to how the school tells its own story;
* developing a shared approach to internal accountability as a precondi-tion of accountability to external agencies;
* maintaining a focus on evidence and its congruence with the core values of the school, reframing policy and practice when they conflict with core values;
* embedding a systematic approach to self-evaluation at classroom, school and community levels; and
* maintaining a continuing focus on sustainability, succession and leaving a legacy.

Accountability is a particularly problematic concept, rooted as it is in political structures and with redolent connotations that evoke strong responses in different cultures. The fifth principle aroused vigorous debate. It was introduced at the Athens conference. Words such as 'delicate', 'challenging', 'complex' and 'worrying' were all used to describe the term as it did not translate easily into other languages, literally or conceptually. Despite attempts at definitions and clarification, the demand was made repeatedly for 'greater clarity' and a shared understanding that could be accepted across countries and cultures.

Accountability was widely perceived as a matter of external pressure rather than a professional imperative and, indeed, something that was instinctive in pedagogical and leadership practice if not couched in the forms of language and data on which government bodies rely. It is a fundamental tenet of leadership as a subversive activity to take account of political reali-ties and within that context to find ways of telling the school's own story both to government, and equally importantly to its immediate stakeholders – parents, students, teachers and support staff.

Internal accountability is measured by the degree of convergence among what individuals say they are responsible for (responsibility), what people say the organization is responsible for (expectations), and the internal norms and processes by which people literally account for their work (account-ability structures) (Elmore, 2005). This is a form of self-evaluation in which schools speak for themselves, with a focus on what really matters. It is not about counting the numbers, ticking the boxes or completing the dreary and formulaic audit process, which much inspection and quality assurance frame-works presuppose.

Self-evaluation is the process by which schools make their intellectual and moral journey, measuring the distance they have travelled not in the simplistic trajectory of aggregated attainment scores, summative tools that say little about deep learning. The tools of authentic, professionally driven self-evaluation, by contrast, are set in a social context. They encourage dialogue. They serve a primarily formative purpose. They are congenial, flexible and adaptable to new situations and new challenges. They are not restricted to what happens in classrooms or to students' learning. They apply to teacher and organisational learning. They measure how teachers are progressing in their thinking and practice and how the school is developing as a community of learners. They relish accountability because it is the platform for telling a story rooted in evidence of the most profound kind.

Elmore writes:

> Schools construct powerful accountability environments out of the way they do academic work, whether they are aware of it or not. These environments can operate to pull the organization toward higher levels of collective action and higher levels of student learning, or they can operate to pull schools apart into highly variable and weak learning environments.
>
> (Elmore, 2005, p. 18)

Self evaluation is implicit in strong internal accountability and enshrined in the fifth principle, 'developing coherence among leadership activities and demonstrating how they impact on learning'. The confidence that flowed from grasping the value of this is attested to in reports from many of the Carpe Vitam schools. In Trenton, for example, it was reported by the US (East) research team that a focus on learning as a fundamental aspect of accountability had led to significant change at school level. Involvement in the project had clarified the importance of a focus on learning and the conditions for learning as a counterbalance to a focus on statutory standard assessments alone. In the report from the Trenton schools it was said that 'focusing on deepening learning through engaging students in meaningful activities and exciting conversations' had provided the impetus to develop a shared approach to internal accountability, paving the way for a more intelligent accountability at district and federal policy levels.

As in other aspects of the principles there is evidence of slow movement to some common ground but from very different starting points. What is held in common are forms of imposed accountability that disempower rather than empower teachers. When there is strong internal support and conviction as many of these Carpe Vitam schools report, there is resilience and vitality to tell the school's story in their own register and in terms of their own core values.

Teachers need to be helped to assert rather than retreat from accountability measures. 'Strong leadership' revisited means having the intellectual grounding, moral courage and the micro-political nous to show that there is a better way. In his keynote last year Keith Walker spoke of fostering hope: a leader's first and last task. Without denying the difficulties, leadership requires 'keeping confidence unimpaired'. Hope, writes Bohm (1983), fires a neuron in the brain. Hope makes us more intelligent. Hope breeds confidence and confidence seeds and nurtures learning. Without hope schools become hope-less places. Hope is what keeps us going and make subversion both desirable and possible.

Notes

1 *Newsweek*, September 9, 2005.
2 Interview conducted in the context of the research project Schools in Exceptionally Challenging Circumstances, to be published in late 2006, see references – Schools on the Edge.
3 The Cambridge team: John MacBeath, David Frost, Sue Swaffield, Gregor Sutherland and Joanne Waterhouse. Team leaders in other countries were: George Bagakis (University of Patras, Greece), Neil Dempster (Griffith University, Brisbane), David Green (Center for Evidence Based Education, Trenton, New Jersey), Lejf Moos (Danish University of Education), Jorunn Möller (University of Oslo), Bradley Portin (University of Washington) and Michael Schratz (University of Innsbruck).
4 Connectors in Gladwell's language means people who are social nodes through which information passes, key people in making networks function. Mavens are those who help to discriminate among various knowledge sources.

References

Abela, J. (2003), 'Beyond childhood depression', *McGill Reporter, 35:1:1*, McGill University Health Centre, Montreal.
Alexander, R. (2003), *Still No Pedagogy? Principle, Pragmatism and Compliance in Primary Education*, University of Cambridge, Cambridge.
Alterman, E. (2004), 'When presidents lie', *The Nation*, October 25.
Berliner, D.C. and Biddle, B.J. (1995), *The Manufactured Crisis: Myths, Fraud and Attack on America's Public Schools*, Perseus Books, Reading, MA.
Bevan, J. (2002), *The Rise and Fall of Marks & Spencer*, Profile Books, London.
Bohm, D. (1983), *Wholeness and the Implicate Order*, Ark Paperbacks, New York, NY.
Bramall, S. and White, J. (2000), *Why Learn Maths?*, Institute of Education, London.
Castells, M. (1996), *The Information Age*, Blackwell, Oxford.
Castells, M. (1999), *The Network Society*, Blackwell, Oxford.
Castells, M. (2000), *End of Millennium*, Blackwell, Oxford.
Collins, J. (2001), *Good to Great: Why Some Companies Make the Leap . . . and Others Don't*, HarperCollins, New York, NY.
Csikszentmihalyi, M. (1990), *FLOW*, Harper Perennial, New York, NY.
Czarniawska, B. (1997), *Narrating the Organization: Dramas of Institutional Identity*, University of Chicago Press, Chicago, IL.
Dewey, J. (1897), 'My pedagogic creed', *The School Journal*, Vol. LIV No. 3, January, pp. 77–80.
Dixon, N. (1994), *On the Psychology of Military Incompetence*, Pimlico, London.
Elmore, R. (2005), *Agency, Reciprocity, and Accountability in Democratic Education*, Consortium for Policy Research in Education, Boston, MA.
Engeström, Y. (1999), 'Activity theory and individual and social transformation', in Engeström, Y., Mietten, R. and Punamäki, R-L. (Eds), *Perspectives on Activity Theory*, Cambridge University Press, Cambridge.
Foucault, M. (1973), *The Order of Things*, Vintage, New York, NY.
Freire, P. (1970), *Pedagogy of the Oppressed*, Seabur, New York, NY.
Frost, D. (2005), 'Resisting the juggernaut: building capacity through teacher leadership in spite of it all', *Leading and Managing*, Vol. 10 No. 2, p. 83.
Galton, M. and MacBeath, J. (2002), *A Life in Teaching?*, National Union of Teachers, London.
Gardner, H. (1999a), *Intelligence Reframed*, Basic Books, New York, NY.
Giroux, H. (1992), *Border Crossings*, Routledge, London.
Gladwell, M. (2000), *The Tipping Point: How Little Things Can Make a Big Difference*, Abacus, London.
Gronn, P. (2003), *The New Work of Educational Leaders: Changing Leadership Practice in an Era of School Reform*, Paul Chapman, London.

Haney, W. (2000), *The Myth of the Texas Miracle in Education*, Education Policy Analysis archives [online- serial 8(41) available at: http://epaa.asu.edu/epaa/v8n41/]

Hargreaves, A. (2004), 'Distinction and disgust: the emotional politics of school failure', *International Journal of Leadership in Education*, Vol. 7 No. 1, pp. 27–41.

Hesselbein, F., Goldsmith, M., Beckard, R. and Drucker, P. (1996), *The Leader of the Future*, Jossey-Bass, San Francisco, CA.

Holt, J. (1969), 'Schools are bad places for children', *Saturday Evening Post*, 8 February.

Inamdar, P. (2004), 'Computer skills development using "hole in the wall" facilities in rural India', *Australasian Journal of Educational Technology*, Vol. 20 No. 3, pp. 337–50.

Levitt, S.D. and Dubner, S.J. (2005), *Freakonomics*, Allen Lane, London.

MacBeath, J. and Galton, M. (2004), *A Life in Secondary Teaching?*, National Union of Teachers, London.

MacBeath, J., Gray, J., Cullen, J., Frost, D., Steward, S. and Swaffield, S. (2006), *Schools on the Edge: Responding to Challenging Circumstances*, Routledge, London.

Mackenzie, R.F. (1965), *Escape from the Classroom*, Collins, Glasgow.

Martin, P.R. (1997), *The Sickening Mind*, Flamingo, London.

Mitchell, C. and Sackney, L. (2000), *Profound Improvement*, Swets and Zeitlinger, Lisse.

Mitra, S. and Rana, V. (2001), 'Children and the internet: experiments with minimally invasive education in India', *The British Journal of Educational Technology*, Vol. 32 No. 2, pp. 221–32.

Moller, J. (2002), 'Democratic leadership in an age of managerial accountability', *Improving Schools*, Vol. 5 No. 2, pp. 11–20.

Moos, L. (2002), 'Cultural isomorphs in theories and practice of school leadership', in Leithwood, K. and Hallinger, P. (Eds), *Second International Handbook of Educational leadership and Administration*, Kluwer Academic Publishers, Dordrecht, pp. 359–94.

Moos, L. and Moller, J. (2003), 'Schools and leadership in transition: the case of Scandinavia', *Cambridge Journal of Education*, Vol. 33 No. 3, pp. 353–71.

Oborne, P. (2005), *The Rise of Political Lying*, Free Press, London.

Perkins, D. (2003), *Making Thinking Visible*, Harvard Graduate School of Education, Cambridge, MA.

Putnam, R. (1999), *Bowling Alone: The Collapse and Revival of American Community*, Touchstone, New York, NY.

Rudduck, J. and Flutter, J. (2004), *How to Improve Your School: Giving Pupils a Voice*, Continuum, London.

Sawyer, M.G. (2001), 'The mental health of young people in Australia: key findings from the child and adolescent component of the national survey of mental health and well-being', *Australia and New Zealand Journal of Psychiatry*, Vol. 35 No. 6, pp. 806–14.

Senge, P. (1990), *The Fifth Discipline: The Art and Practices of the Learning Organisation*, Doubleday, New York, NY.

Sergiovanni, T. (2001), *Leadership: What's in it for Schools?*, Routledge Falmer, London.

SooHoo, S. (1993), 'Students as partners in research and restructuring schools', *The Educational Forum*, Vol. 57, pp. 386–92.

Spillane, J.P., Halverson, R. and Diamond, J.B. (2001), 'Investigating school leadership practice: a distributed perspective', *Educational Researcher*, Vol. 30 No. 3, pp. 23–8.

Starratt, R.J. (1998), 'Grounding moral educational leadership in the morality of teaching and learning', *Leading and Managing*, Vol. 4 No. 4, pp. 243–55.

Tymms, P. (2005), *Measuring Standards in English Primary Schools*, University of Durham, Durham.

Warren-Little, J. (1993), 'Teachers' professional development in a climate of educational reform', *Educational Evaluation and Policy Analysis*, Vol. 15 No. 2, pp. 129–51.

Whitehead, A.N. (1929), *The Aims of Education and Other Essays*, Free Press, London.
Wolf, A. (2002), *Does Education Matter? Myths about Education and Economic Growth*, Penguin, London.

Further reading

Moos, L. (2004), 'Introduction', in MacBeath, J. and Moos, L. (Eds), *Democratic Learning: The Challenge to School Effectiveness*, Routledge Falmer, London.

CHAPTER 12

SHAME TACTICS 'DON'T WORK'

Neil Munro

Originally published in the *TESS*, 6 November, 1998

Schools are not uniformly effective or ineffective, according to the results of one of the most wide-ranging research studies undertaken in Scotland.

The Improving School Effectiveness Project (ISEP), which has attracted £500,000 in Scottish Office funding, concludes that the value added by schools to pupils' progress is complex and subtle.

Peter Mortimore, head of the Institute of Education at the University of London, jointly directed the study with John MacBeath, head of the Quality in Education Centre at Jordanhill.

Both stressed last week, when the findings were unveiled in Edinburgh, that the study underlines the dangers of making simplistic and crude judgments about 'good' and 'bad' schools.

'Naming and shaming doesn't work,' Professor Mortimore said. 'The policy-makers must learn to trust the professionals, which is just as important as establishing trust between pupils and teachers in developing the effective school.'

Professor MacBeath said: 'This research shows that school effects are marked by ebbs and flows, gains and losses.'

The study, which Professor Mortimore said had not been attempted in any other country, conducted detailed investigations into what makes schools tick. It was based on surveys and interviews with 7,100 pupils in 80 primary and secondary schools, 2,540 teachers and 5,400 parents. It tracked the effects of schools by checking attainment in maths and English in primary 4 and secondary 2 in 1995, and following up progress two years later. The S4 group in 1997 also included pupils' average scores from their seven best Standard grade results.

The project reports: 'The pattern of adding value across the curriculum is mixed with a very few schools doing consistently well. Between 25 per cent and 33 per cent of all schools perform significantly well in one outcome and poorly in others.'

A quarter of primary and secondary schools added value in maths, with a smaller proportion doing well for their pupils in English reading. Pupil backgrounds have more influence over performance in reading than in maths.

The research also found that 25 per cent of schools were doing less well than expected in maths. In English reading, 20 per cent of secondaries and 7 per cent of primaries performed 'significantly below expectation'.

Professor MacBeath believes such findings on 'differential achievement' are among the most significant of the ISEP project.

These internal variations suggest that schools which are below par 'may have an unrealised capacity to raise their performance', the projects report states. There also appears to be 'scope for greater consistency of standards within the school'.

CHAPTER 13

STORIES OF COMPLIANCE AND SUBVERSION IN A PRESCRIPTIVE POLICY ENVIRONMENT

Originally published in *Educational Management Administration and Leadership*, BELMAS 2008,Vol. 36, No.1, 123–148

In their commitment to raising standards successive Conservative and Labour governments have moved progressively to tighter prescription of school policy and more far reaching proscription of practices deemed unacceptable. This article examines how 12 headteachers construct the policy environment and how they respond to it in the schools they lead. The evidence base is 12 in-depth interviews with headteachers, in six primary schools and six secondary at the outset of the ESRC research project Learning How to Learn. This subset of headteacher interviews from the total number was selected for this article because these 12 interviews were accompanied by the fullest data set of complementary interviews, questionnaire and observation data which will be the subject of other papers to follow. The interviews provide a baseline picture of how these school leaders were talking about leading learning in their schools and the authority or 'warrant' they referred to in validating their views. Patterns of compliance and subversion are examined with reference to theories of organizational and 'double loop' learning.

KEYWORDS change, culture, inspection, learning, leadership

Twelve school leaders

The 12 English headteachers, six primary, six secondary, whose interviews are the source of this article, had all signed up in 2001 to ESRC The Learning How to Learn Project for the following three years and therefore represent a particular purposive sample of schools. Many had already been involved in a prior project with King's College London on assessment for learning and were therefore predisposed to formative assessment and to reflection on the nature of learning and school-wide learning policies.

The Learning How to Learn – in classrooms, schools and networks Project was a four year development and research project funded by the ESRC from January 2001 to March 2005 as part of Phase II of the Teaching and Learning Research Programme. The full description of project aims are set out in a number of cognate articles (James *et al.*, forthcoming, Pedder *et al.*, 2005). In essence the aim of the project was to advance both understanding and practice of learning how to learn in classrooms, schools and networks and to investigate what characterizes the school in which teachers successfully create and manage the knowledge and skills of learning how to learn. The role of leadership in fostering those conditions was not an explicit focus of the project but the ways in which the 12 headteachers framed the project within their schools emerged as a salient feature of the inquiry. Access to teachers and classrooms was gained through them and in the initial stages at least they worked with the project team on deciding a strategy for introducing project ideas into their school.

Forty-three schools were recruited to the project from five local education authorities and one virtual education action zone. The leading criterion used for selection was the willingness of schools to be involved for the four-year duration, and to contribute actively to the development of thinking and practice. A range of contexts was represented in the overall sample: urban/rural; small/large; mono-ethnic/multi-ethnic, with the proportion of one secondary school to two primary schools (preferably in cluster groups, though this was rarely possible).

Questionnaires administered to teachers and pupils collected data about perceptions of current practice and valued practice, complemented by interviews and observations in classrooms. The project team estimated, initially, that the project would involve approximately 1,580 teachers and over 20,000 students, an estimate that proved to be reasonably accurate. Of the 40 schools remaining at the end of the project 12 schools with the most complete data set were selected for closer analysis.

This article, one of a number which examines these 12 schools, focuses specifically on the initial interviews with 12 headteachers to establish a baseline of how school leaders were thinking about the nature of learning, individual, professional and organizational, at the outset of the project.

Interviews with the headteachers were structured around their learning agenda at pupil, teacher and organizational levels, setting these within the current policy context. Transcriptions from interviews with these 12 heads ran to over 27,000 words, with a mean length of around 18,000 words across all 12 texts.

The key themes addressed in these the interviews provided part of the coding frame developed by the whole project team. In the reading and re-reading of these texts a number of other key themes emerged which referred specifically or obliquely to the policy context in which these schools were located, in particular to current Key Stage Strategies, to Ofsted and to a less definable climate and set of pressures within which their work as leaders and managers was carried out. In examining these transcripts references to external authorities were chosen as a focus for specific analysis, identifying ways in which headteachers located themselves and their schools in relation to those authorities – to DfES and Ofsted as main points of external reference, as well as invited experts' contributions on learning. The following discussion is based on close reading and re-reading of these texts, systematic analysis of key recurring ideas, identifying references to external bodies and the way in which these were contextualized within the narrative. The problematization of policy development or the absence of such critique proved to be salient aspects of these narratives.

Policy environment

In all these 12 narratives an embedded theme is the relationship of school practice to the policy environment in which these heads found themselves.

Light is thrown on government policy but constructed variously among this group of 12 school leaders. Two markedly differing accounts of policy and how it impacts on practice provide the extremes of a continuum, at one end depicted as a positive force for change and highly influential in supporting and improving practice while the polar opposite view describes a government imposing dysfunctional strategies on schools, deskilling and disempowering teachers' practice. These two polar positions, both from primary school headteachers, serve as a frame for the more nuanced or ambivalent narratives which fall between these two extremes.

Policy environment as supportive

The following is a distillation of one headteacher's perception of the policy environment:

> The policy environment is one that has helped to move schools on, to challenge uninformed or simply sloppy practice. It has given teachers something tangible to go on. The Literacy and Numeracy Strategies provide models that work. 'It's the first time we've been given anything to go on'. 'It was brilliant to be told what to do'. The three/four part lesson with starter, input, work, plenary has been most helpful in lending pace and variety to lessons. Good ideas and innovative techniques for teachers have succeeded in engaging pupils more actively in their own learning. Providing teachers with tools to use National Strategies has provided support for weaker teachers. They have encouraged a rigorous approach to teaching and learning. They have focused teachers' attention on outcomes and given an emphasis to targets and target setting. Ofsted too has played its part in making a contribution, affirming good practice, spotlighting areas for development and providing key areas for focus in improving quality and standards.
>
> (Headteacher secondary school B)

Policy environment as oppressive

The following offers an alternative construction of the policy environment.

> The policy dictat is so tight that to survive and do what is important for staff and children one has to be subversive. The policies are both overprescriptive and condescending, deskilling rather than empowering teachers. Richness and creativity are lost by formulaic prescription. The literacy strategy is so superficial we have to take risks in order to free up teachers to take back ownership of teaching and learning. After teachers have gone through the training and jumped through the hoops we help them 'to go wild', while recognising that for their own career promotion needs, in other places they have to be astute in knowing when to toe the line and play the game for inspection purposes. However, 'if people would get off our backs just a little the learning could just rocket because children and people in the schools were doing what they wanted to do and passionately believed in'. We try to help staff to 'fly', to go the way they want rather than having to feel the burden of having a master outside the school.
>
> (Headteacher primary school L)

The contrast between these two depictions of policy may be characterized using Perkins' (2003) notions of 'taming the wild' and 'wilding the tame'. In the first of these narratives the wild is tamed by clear targets, predetermined outcomes and focusing of teachers' attention on templates of good practice. 'Being told what to do', as in the first narrative provides a sense of comfort and security and affirmation by the authority of Ofsted, reassuring staff that practice falls within the bounds of government mandates. Pace and variety in lessons are injected to engage pupils more actively with the task at hand with the formula of the three/four part lesson as a containment, thwarting diversions and offering support and clear direction for weaker teachers. Taken together these routines are seen as providing the rigour that was previously seen to be missing.

'Wilding of the tame' suggests a recognition of domestication and a conscious attempt to loosen the ties that bind teachers to mandated practice. This is explicitly stated in the process of learning to jump through the hoops before 'going wild'. Another metaphor is of shedding the burden so that teachers are able to fly on their own. The term 'empowerment' is used to convey a sense of agency, the rediscovery of richness and creativity in learning and teaching and of reinstatement of professional self-confidence. This is depicted as 'risk' because of its non-compliance with mandated practice but at the same time recognising the nature of the political 'game' which allows teachers to meet the expectations of Ofsted when required. While in the first narrative the locus of change is attributed to external influences, in the second narrative there is explicit reference to leadership (the 'we') in helping teachers to go wild.

The difference between a healthy and an unhealthy organization, argue Senge *et al.* (2004: 32), lies in members' awareness and ability to acknowledge their felt needs to conform and their ability to challenge their habits of seeing and responding to external pressures. How the policy environment is described is as much a reflection of a school's stage of development, of a particular headteacher's construction at a given time, or revealing of a more deep-seated conception of the school policy interface. Nor are these polar positions as crisp and static as these archetypes suggest. As becomes clear through the analysis of the texts, they conceal a deeper struggle for leadership in navigating the path between compliance and subversion.

The implication for leadership is to know what stance is appropriate at a given time and in relation to specific policy movements. Giroux's (1992) counsel is to be alert to the 'omniscient narrator', the authority who speaks on your behalf. There is no grand narrative that can speak for us all, he argues, and therefore professional educators must take responsibility for the knowledge they organize, produce, mediate and translate into practice. If not there is a danger that they come to be seen as simply the technical intervening medium through which knowledge is transmitted to students, erasing themselves in an uncritical reproduction of received wisdom. Rather than internalizing the master narratives, Giroux suggests, the task of leadership is to examine how these narratives become constructed, what they mean, how they regulate our social and moral experience, how they presuppose particular views of the world and how they pre-empt debate as to what is worthy of attention.

Setting the school in context

We are offered a glimpse of how these headteachers view the policy world in their response to the researcher's invitation to set the school in context. How heads choose to describe the salient features of their schools provides a clue as to how they validate their own practice in relation to external pressures. On the one hand their accounts may be constructed predominantly with reference to the external validation of success, or with a more inward focus in which there is validation of the school's own criteria of success. For example, in one transcript a secondary headteacher gives an extended account of his school's success referring exclusively to the school's normative standing in performance tables and the validation of practice by the most recent Ofsted report. By contrast, another secondary head working in a similar urban environment chooses to tell the story in terms of the challenges in putting learning and teaching centre stage and creating a professional development culture. In the course of her lengthy introduction to the school neither Ofsted nor GCSE attainment scores are cited. Validation of the school's progress is by reference to students' and teachers' evaluation of important priorities and through her own efforts as a school leader to create the kind of environment for learning which she values.

These two heads, in common with the ten others in this sample, describe their efforts to put learning centre stage, acknowledging the tensions in trying to accommodate a concern for the 'how' of student learning within a drive for raised achievement. All of them refer to the impact of Key Stage Strategies, to changing lesson structures, to external pressure and accountability. Their approaches to assessment of achievement appear to be broadly similar but it is in the degree of embrace of government policies or a critical distancing from them that differences among these 12 schools begin to emerge most saliently.

Rediscovering learning

Learning, it appears from all of these 12 transcripts, is being rediscovered. There is a sense in which, after a long period of quiescence, learning has reemerged as the essential purpose of schooling. How learning is discussed by these 12 heads is elaborated in response to direct questions by the interviewer as to school policy, but implicit theories also permeate much of the discussion that runs through these interviews. Discussions of learning tend to refer to pupil learning but reference is also made to professional learning and occasionally to organizational, or system, learning. The predominant focus, however, is on a core cluster of ideas that might be said to characterize a Third Millennium view of student learning, reflecting to a high degree a broader policy discourse. That view may be summarized as follows:

Learning is individual. Children learn in different ways. They have their own learning needs, styles or preferences. Learning should be active, interesting and enjoyable. Children should take responsibility, or ownership, for their own learning but this is contingent on development of their self confidence and self esteem. Experience of success and feedback on achievement raises levels of expectation. It is important that children know where they are in their learning and where they need to go, so levels of achievement and goals and targets to aim for are critical. With these as a supportive structure pupils are able to assess their own progress towards those targets and reach, or maximize, their potential. With knowledge of prior attainment and planned outcomes of what children are learning is no longer a matter of guesswork on the part of teachers.

In much of the discussion of learning, as in the above broad summary, there is often a subtle transition from general principles to a specific school form of learning and, more specifically still, a linear conception of progress towards pre-specified targets. While the discourse is generally framed in terms of 'individual needs', targets and levels of achievement circumscribe what is to be learned, and curricular or policy needs appear to assume a higher priority. As illustrative of a new discourse one headteacher says that until he arrived 'nobody ever talked about outcomes'. The persistent reference to 'outcomes' throughout the transcript is generally linked to 'achievement', with the implication that these two things are synonymous. The implication is that under his leadership, with a new discourse on outcomes a concern for achievement is now, for the first time, to the fore. Achievement and outcomes are also bedfellows of 'targets'. These are neither freely chosen by students nor by teachers and although 'negotiated' with students individually, they sit tightly within a National Curriculum/Key Stage mandate.

The 'rigour' of targets appears largely unproblematic, however, an antithesis to a bygone age in which educators were not held to account for leading teachers down the perverse path of child-centredness. Richard Pring (2005) describes a Conservative Secretary of State holding John Dewey and Pring himself collectively responsible for the decline in standards brought about by progressivism and the Left-leaning educational establishment. This is exemplary of a grand narrative which appears to have gained currency even within the teaching profession itself and among school leaders. Referring to the 1970s and 1980s one secondary headteacher claims 'a short period of time ago nobody was interested in achievement in schools'. A primary head makes a similar claim, referring to a previous time when 'teachers took no responsibility for children's learning at all. They had no expectation of them at all'. There is an echo here of Michael Barber's characterization of the 1970s as the decade of 'uninformed professionalism, the 1980s as 'uninformed prescription', the 1990s as 'informed prescription' and the current decade as 'informed professionalism'. Internalization of the grand narrative has, for some of our sample of headteachers at least, not only coloured their view of policy-making but provided a rationale for a more directive form of leadership in accordance with a new orthodoxy. Commenting on the 'Barber quarter' Andy Hargreaves (2004) describes this as governments' tendency to 'denigrate the past in order to justify the present'.

Although these interviews predate 'personalized learning' as a policy (Miliband, 2004), the essential tenets of that are already embedded in the language and reveal inherent tensions between a more directive style of teaching and classroom management on the one hand and a 'personalized' learner-centred agenda on the other. While appealing to more pupil-centred pedagogy there is at the same time a common acceptance that the teacher is firmly in charge of what happens in the classroom. One secondary head spoke of making 'a high profile statement' to teachers that they were in charge of the classroom and that 'whatever happened in the class was their decision'.

Such a view sits uneasily with a common assertion that it is about helping children and young people to take control of their own learning. Where heads speak of pupils 'taking responsibility for their own learning' it is set within the closely defined parameters of National Curriculum and National

Strategies. This is illustrated in the metaphors which heads use in describing students' own target setting. One head, using the metaphor of the 'goalposts', suggests a very clearly defined frame at which learning is aimed. 'I do believe that students need to know what the goalposts are and I do believe that they do need to be told continually what they need to do to improve'. The statement by one secondary head that 'every child is an achiever' is in the 'real world' selfevident, but takes on specialized meaning when interpreted in the context of curriculum targets, levels and key stages.

Within these clearly defined parameters there is a widely shared enthusiasm for a broad canopy of ideas which include learning styles and preferences, thinking skills, emotional intelligence, accelerated learning, multiple intelligences and brain-based learning. As one secondary headteacher puts it, the senior leadership team have 'dripped in things like the visual, the kinaesthetic and a bit of stuff about the brain'.

VAK is the shorthand reference used by a number heads to refer to visual, auditory and kinaesthetic learning styles which are given widespread endorsement by visiting trainers and a substantial body of literature, and tend to be treated as unproblematic. CATs (Cognitive Abilities Test) is cited frequently as a helpful resource in identifying individual biases to one of these three modes and poses teachers and school leader with the challenge of how these can be incorporated sensibly into lesson planning.

Two differing practical applications of learning styles emerge from these discussions. One view sees these constructs as useful for teachers in helping them cater more consciously to individual strengths, while a second (and not necessarily incompatible) view sees awareness of learning styles as helping the teacher widen the repertoire of modes of teacher presentation and modes of student engagement.

Learning journey

The journey is a much used metaphor in relation to learning and progress. It is construed as one undertaken more in expectation than in hope. That is, the destination is clearly understood by the pupil as the next 'level' or the next handhold on the climbing frame.

> I want them to be level three by the end of year on, you know, it's checking that sort of progress and getting them to want to improve the journey together.
>
> (Headteacher primary school J)

There is a broad consensus that students are increasingly internalizing that frame of reference and able to articulate their journey in terms of baselines and targets:

> I think they are able to say, 'this is where I want to be'. 'This is where I think I am. There's where I want to be and this is what I need to get there'. I think they're clever at doing that too. And I suppose the fact that we put letters and number with it merely makes it refined and comprehensible rather than the airy-fairy way I would have of assessing people.
>
> (Headteacher primary school J)

The journey towards agreed targets is from one level to the next, a model that now appears to be deeply embedded in teachers' thinking about learning. The extent to which these permeate practice is illustrated by one secondary head:

> I should be able to go into a classroom, I should be able to ask the child what level they're working at and I should be able to ask what level or what they have to do to improve from that level.
>
> (Headteacher secondary school B)

There is a kind of religious tenor to a statement by one headteacher, referring to 'picking up children who have lapsed', conveying an image of 'backsliding' or losing the faith.

Targets and levels combine to provide the 'road map' and are made explicit and visible on classroom walls, stamped on fronts of books and sometimes on each piece of work, or portrayed on posters on the walls. Targets are often reviewed at the start of lessons, reinforced and highlighted at every opportunity. While the intensity and visibility of targets and levels differ among the 12 schools, in all of them it is a preoccupying concern. Targets have, as one primary head says, 'become a topic of endless discussions'. This appears to reflect a fairly wide agreement that pupils need to know the level they are working at and that parents too should be equally informed and take part in the target setting process.

There is also one dissenting voice among the 12. One primary headteacher argues against this as a form of labelling and as a self-fulfilling prophecy, which she sees as lending itself to a purely instrumental approach to learning.

> I try very hard not to let the children know what their actual level is. I want them to know where they are and what they want to do to improve but I don't want them to get a handle on what level they are because that has lots of baggage with it and they go home to their parents and say, 'I'm a level three' and then, you know, there's the inevitable, the pressure on them that they need to do, you know, they need to be a level four or they want level five so they'll go in the top class of secondary school.
>
> (Headteacher primary school J)

While this head tries to dissuade staff from sharing levels with pupils she is aware that it creates a tension with a policy of openness and transparency and parental partnerships where informed parents are anxious to know their children's stage or level of progress. This headteacher, who has a commitment to assessment for learning as an integral aspect of a Learning How to Learn Project, is aware of the difficulty in recasting parental expectations.

The challenge for leadership is to work with the paradox of a closer collaborative relationship with parents, providing the security of summative assessments while at the same time trying to undo the successful embedding of marks and grades, a commitment to which has over time penetrated deep into the affections of parents.

Nature of the warrant

Much of the discussion of learning refers to and is 'warranted' on the grounds of government strategies. This is not, however, the only source of authority cited for the affirmation of practice. All 12 schools have at some point invited visiting speakers to run sessions on thinking skills, brain-based learning, assessment for learning, or school improvement. One primary head alludes to a 'buzzing around' of ideas about accelerated learning, 'picked up' through other colleagues, from reading, or from people who have returned from courses enthused by what they had heard from inspirational speakers. Reference is made by headteachers to experts, to seminal texts, to research or to school improvement literature. 'I'm a Michael Fullan fan' says one secondary head in the context of her approach to school improvement strategies. Another head cites Shirley Clark's research as 'one of the most influential books I have read I think' and in response to an interviewer probe, 'It's at the heart of our thinking.'

The transition from the 'I' to the 'our' is illustrative of the way on which personal conviction and influence can become embedded in whole school policy. Policies and practice on learning appear in most cases to be driven by a personal conviction of a headteacher whose enthusiasm has been fired by an inspirational authority. These then provide an agreed set of principles of learning which everyone is expected to sign up to.

> There's the general principles of learning within the school are accepted by everybody who works here and they would all work towards and they're quite clear about it. And not only that, but agree with it.
>
> (Headteacher secondary school B)

These various authority sources, empirical evidence or 'warrant' on which these principles rest tend not to be regarded as problematic or open to question. More exception than the rule is the statement by one primary head who says, 'We actually needed to do a lot more thinking about how children learn.'

There is, however, a more commonly shared scepticism of learning as represented by levels attained or test scores.

> If we're only looking at the improvement in children's learning by looking at their SATs I think we could be disappointed, so I'm really quite looking forward to looking at ways in which we can measure the improvement in children's learning and work together to find out how you can measure that.
>
> (Headteacher primary school K)

There is also an explicit recognition that the learning process sits uncomfortably within an assessment 'climbing frame'.

> I think some of the assessments that we discuss as the staff are the tedious bits in giving them the levels for national curriculum. Our own assessments and personal assessments are much wider than that and each teacher assesses for their own individual needs, usually for pushing on and involving the children in their own expectation of what they want to get to.
>
> (Headteacher primary school J)

The ambivalence of being obedient and 'doing what we're told' while at the same time recognizing the need for a more critical appraisal of learning is exemplified by this headteacher.

We've been absolutely bombarded by government initiatives. Some are very good and some are awful, but we've got so caught up in it and we're all very obedient now and we all do as we're told [although] I still think children learn an awful lot of rubbish at school that is totally unnecessary to them as people.

(Headteacher primary school G)

Learning and teaching

There is, running through the conversation, a conflation of the language of learning evidenced in the frequent references to 'teachingandlearning' as one single conjoined concept, particularly when referring to strategy as in 'teaching and learning strategies'. The language of teaching appears at times to be confused with that of learning, and references made in the context of a discussion about learning frequently tend to refer more to what the teacher is doing or to teacher intention rather than to student activity or intention. Occasionally this results in an awkward straddling of two distinct and inherently conflicting ideas.

I think we're aiming to enable every individual student to maximise their potential, to be challenged, to be stimulated, to produce learning outcomes for themselves.

(Headteacher secondary school E)

This is exemplary of a statement that appears on the surface to be about learning but in its language of outcomes betrays a more school-centred frame of reference. It may be nothing more than a child-centred view which, it is felt, needs to be dressed up, ill-fittingly, to conform to a dominant political discourse. The following is a further example of a conceptual slide from a child-centred view to a teaching strategy.

The children are partners in that enterprise [learning] and a whole range of strategies for keeping everybody on task'.

(Headteacher primary school H)

Equally difficult to reconcile is the student taking responsibility while the teacher is 'in control of the learning'.

[Students] taking the responsibility for themselves, the way they manage themselves in the school. So we're not now talking about the teacher being in control of the child in the same way but they [teachers] are still in control of the learning.

(Headteacher secondary school B)

It may be inferred from these comments that headteachers are struggling with a cognitive resolution between a learning-centred or 'personalized' agenda, on the one hand, and a highly prescriptive set of teaching strategies on the other. There is an implicit, and sometimes explicit, recognition that teaching and learning strategies have to be contextualized within a curriculum and assessment framework, the rationale of which is not derived from individual learning needs but from a body of conventional wisdom as to what knowledge is of most worth, and reinforced by strong coalitions of interest in maintaining subject status. Strategies which attempt to be learner-centred have to work from a set of logistical givens about the structure of the school day, week and year, so that references to 'pace', variety, beginnings of lesson, time on task all refer to extracting the maximum learning returns from 'lessons', tightly structured in order to cover the ground with maximal efficiency. There was a time, says ex-HMI David Green,[1] when inspectors understood pace as referring to a rhythm of learning as Whitehead (1929) described it, not to what the teacher was doing to maintain control and attain the predetermined objectives for a whole class.

When it comes to the terminology of teaching, heads seem to be on safer ground and engage more confidently with a greater repertoire of ideas. The elements of good teaching tend to be treated with less ambivalence than when referring to learning and there is a high degree of consensus as to what makes a good lesson. The three- or four-part lesson is mentioned by head-teachers in all the 12 interviews, either explicitly by name or by reference to National Strategies and structuring of teaching episodes. Within this sharper, more highly focused lesson structure teachers work harder, trying to accommodate individual needs and styles while interesting and inspiring students in brisk teacher-directed lessons.

> We're looking at knowing individuals well, having prior information, trying to interest the students and inspire the students in every lesson.
> (Headteacher secondary school E)

'In every lesson' is the sting in the tail of this ambition, a theme taken up by another head who describes his vision of honing lessons to a perfect pitch across the school. To this end he organizes a professional development week in which the focus is on the planning of exemplary lessons. At the same time he acknowledges that the planning and energy required are unsustainable. 'Not every lesson can be delivered with that level of planning, that level of sheer energy in the classroom,' says one secondary headteacher. The language of 'delivery' is highly apposite in a context where the focus shifts from the active construction work on the part of the student to the energetic delivery of the curriculum by the teacher.

Lessons as the unit of instruction appear to have acquired a new status, dating to an earlier era than Key Stage Strategies but given new authority and impetus by those initiatives. In contrast to a previous era, particularly in primary schools, where children were expected to come into the class (or open plan area) and take the initiative to get on with their own project regardless of the teacher, the emphasis in these accounts is on teacher-directed classroom entry, immediate engagement through attention-grabbing warm-up activities, and endings to lessons comprising plenaries or 'carpet time', irrespective of where children are in their learning. Within this teacher-directed framework the filling in the three-part sandwich is student activity, structured to engage them actively in a set task.

> Structurally within every lesson, there is time within every lesson where students are working independently, working in groups, working in pairs where they are actively doing something. They're not listening,

they're not passive. So learning should be active as far as it's possible to do.

(Headteacher primary school L)

This period of 'active learning' sits within what is described by one headteacher as the 'scaffolding' of the learning experienced and provides a theoretical, Vygotskian, justification for the framework within which learning finds expression. 'Active learning' is depicted as an episode within the self contained lesson at the end of which there is assessment of what has been learned, explicitly related to levels of attainment. This is what one primary head talks about as 'upping the ante', ensuring that all staff follow the model of 'making explicit what they [pupils] are to learn, they will learn what we want them to learn, what they're supposed to be learning'. Lessons are framed by objectives at the outset and review of objectives achieved at the lesson's end, and the approach is consistent across the school.

A consistent approach to teaching, all teachers make sure they tell the children the learning objectives for each lesson, all the teachers link to the planning, the planning's linked to assessment. There's a very consistent approach throughout the school, and all staff follow the policy and the ethos of the school.

(Headteacher primary school G)

Consistency is a key word that runs through the pages of these transcripts. 'Enlightened policies are uniformly implemented by all teachers', claims one secondary head while another uses the word 'consistency' 24 times in the course of the interview. Its importance is reiterated with regard to Key Stage Three, with regard to independent learning, study skills, homeworking policy, training areas, 'across colleagues', in the use of LSAs and with reference to parents:

We need to achieve that consistency across all those subjects so a parent would know that a level five in English means the same thing in subject-specific terms, a level five in maths or music or whatever.

(Headteacher secondary school B)

The prevalence of this theme offers a sharp contrast with the absence of terms such as dialogue, dissent, disagreement, or conflict. Conflict is mentioned only in relation to children, or in one case as a management style that heads off potential conflict. Dissent is not in the lexicon of policy and improvement. 'Dialogue' is mentioned in four interviews, in each case referring to an instrumental use – between teacher and pupil in order to set targets, in communication with parents, 'open dialogue' following classroom observation and 'professional dialogue' as integral to appraisal.

While there is a wide scale adoption of a new government discourse, and a generally high level embrace of National Strategies, there is at the same time a critical distancing and accompanying critique. Pace, for example, as dictated by the teacher's agenda is seen as in conflict with the emphasis on thinking, or 'wait' time.

> I don't think we give them enough thinking time either, because of the pace we've been pushed so hard on pace of lessons, that before you know what's happened, you've not given them any thinking time at all.
>
> (Headteacher secondary school A)

A much stronger statement comes from a primary head who, having implemented the Strategies, is highly critical of their effects on learning.

> The literacy came in and it was just unbelievable, the formality of the lessons and I found that . . . well, I just felt that it was obscene, the way we were expected to teach literacy. In fact, it just made literacy die a death in my opinion. The excitement was out of it.
>
> (Headteacher primary school J)

Another critique is of what a head describes as 'the do it by numbers rationale', claiming that it had 'stopped teachers thinking'. Yet another primary head talks of 'the need for a breather to get away from the routine of literacy'. The Literacy and Numeracy Strategies, says another, have encouraged a culture of 'tell me what to do and I'll do it', pushing people too fast, not allowing time to grow or assume ownership.

> [It is] not helpful for teachers' own self-esteem because their teaching styles and their teaching repertoire have been challenged in a way that has not enabled them to feel they have any part in it, they have no ownership of it.
>
> (Headteacher primary school L)

Compliance with Government imperatives has entailed 'ducking and weaving' one's way through the 'narrow' demands of curriculum, striving for the enrichment of the 'wider' curriculum and 'widest' possible opportunities for learning. The vocabulary of 'narrow' and 'wide' is deeply embedded in a discourse of achievement which sets in opposition the pressures for attainment of competitive targets and the more person-centred mission of the school. The words 'passion' and 'excitement', which occur within the learning conversation, sit alongside the embrace of the three/four part lesson and a grateful endorsement of Ofsted, resulting in a curiously ambivalent set of implicit theories.

Ofsted 'warrant'

All heads make unprompted references to Ofsted in the course of the interview. These allusions may be categorized as:

- Affirmation or validation of practice.
- Advice or challenge to practice.
- Use of templates and criteria.
- Critique.

Validation

Validation of practice by Ofsted is highly valued among those heads who made reference to recent inspection.

> You know, with our Ofsted lesson observations we were the highest in [the authority named] with 42% ones and twos and the data I get back as a head which is in the report shows that 66% of our staff got a one or two at some time . . . talking to the inspector I think we have very few unsatisfactory lessons now. You've got to be pleased by that. Obviously I'd like them all to be, you know, ones and twos.
>
> (Headteacher secondary school A)

The importance of Ofsted's affirmation is conveyed in this primary head's ambition for her school to be graded as 'excellent'.

> You know when Ofsted come we don't want good or very good. We want excellent. That's what we're aiming for. So once you reach one plateau you can go to the next can't you?
>
> (Headteacher primary school G)

For another primary head the power of Ofsted endorsement is illustrated in her desire to visit a school given high marks by the inspectorate.

> [I intend] . . . to visit my colleague's school where Ofsted is just gushing about how wonderful they are, you know, now I need to go and have a look at that and see what that looks like.
>
> (Headteacher primary school H)

In one secondary school Ofsted was cited 21 times in the course of the interview, testimony to the extent to which the Ofsted approach to evaluating teaching had been internalized by the school. To an English observer or insider this may be seen as commonplace and unsurprising, so deeply is this now embedded in school and national culture. It is only when seen through the eyes of visitors from other countries that the depth of impact of Ofsted in the lives of schools and headteachers becomes conspicuously apparent.

Advice

Although giving of advice is not strictly speaking within an Ofsted remit, inspectors' pinpointing of weaknesses leads directly into action and appears generally to be seen as helpful and valued.

> Since the Ofsted we've addressed that [independent learning] through the relatively simple aspect of increasing a significant number of computers in the school, the drive at the moment is to try to equip them with the necessary study skills to take on that independent research.
>
> (Headteacher secondary school B)

It is seen in some cases as lending strength to the head's own conviction or desire to move staff to 'a less didactic' style, to more independent learning or to a move away from summative marking to more formative uses of assessment. A primary headteacher, describing the development of an assessment policy in the school, is then asked by the interviewer, 'Who was that for? Who did you have to have a policy for?' and replies, 'Oh, I suspect Ofsted.'

Use of templates

Most of the references to Ofsted were in relation to models or templates that had been adopted by the school. The Ofsted model most often cited was in relation to classroom observation.

> We've done observations, largely based on the Ofsted model of observing teaching quality.
>
> (Headteacher primary school M)

Heads provide examples of a straight adoption of the Ofsted observation scale, a form of self inspection either for internal use or as a prelude to an Ofsted visit.

> When we started and did lesson observations we had a good 10 per cent of lessons that were unsatisfactory and you know, by the time we got to Ofsted we did have three unsatisfactory lessons during Ofsted on five teachers.
>
> (Headteacher secondary school A)

The way in which this way of thinking and talking about teaching is illustrated in the shorthand used by this headteacher, who appears to assume a common linguistic reference point, a 'restricted code' that, it is assumed, will carry the same meaning for the interviewer as it does for the head.

> But the teachers who were struggling have moved quite a long way. I mean several teachers who were teaching six and seven, I mean really sad lessons, are now teaching at four most of the time, sometimes three.
>
> (Headteacher secondary school A)

The internalization of school self inspection is seen in the wholesale adoption of an Ofsted approach in one school.

> You will find that every aspect of Ofsted inspection has been graded by us from the occasional excellent down to the more than occasional but still fairly rare – unsatisfactory. So every aspect of teaching and learning by us. Every dimension covered by Ofsted across everything that Ofsted looks at, has, in a sense been graded now by a senior team.
>
> (Headteacher secondary school B)

The process of self inspection as exemplified here tends to be confused with self-evaluation. Indeed the Ofsted model is essentially a translation of an inspection protocol into a school-led process in which self-evaluation assumes the character of a large scale audit and tends to be undertaken as a prelude to inspection. There is an occasional reflective acknowledgment of an Ofsted way of thinking so powerful that it not only drives a school's development and direction but 'slips into the psyche'.

> [The Ofsted frameworks] drove our thinking in some way. We certainly didn't use them in any way but they've been overshadowing us for long enough and they slip into your psyche really.
>
> (Headteacher primary school M)

Another primary head describes a meticulous application of the Ofsted approach to development planning, but describes it as 'a very strange school development plan' in which the school is measured against '147 statements that are all Ofsted-linked'. Its usefulness she sees primarily in being able to contest Ofsted's judgement because of the school's own thorough preparation. It is further evidence of how seriously inspection is taken and how much energy and time it consumes in a school's life.

Critique

The headteachers' relationship with Ofsted is one replete with paradox. Its endorsement is highly valued and made public. There is an apparently enthusiastic embrace of much that Ofsted has to offer by way of direction and templates and inspectors' observations often serve to strengthen the headteacher's hand. There is also a hint of strategic manoeuvring, as described by this secondary head.

> From a head's point of view, you're wanting obviously to get a good relationship with your Ofsted team because it's actually the essential thing. You learn this, that it is a key thing.
>
> (Headteacher secondary school D)

He adds by way of self-revelation:

> Talking to this guy he said, 'Well, of course, a school like yours, I'm going to give you a real high-powered team.' And I sat down and I said, 'Oh good' where I was really thinking, 'Oh bugger!' You know, can't I have some thick ones who will just do what I tell them.'

There are also frequent allusions to playing the game. Any latitude within the three/four part lesson is set aside for inspection purposes. One primary head talks about the 'tightening up' of the lesson which excludes the normal routine of listening to pupils who come with stories and are eager to relate their experiences. The use of the word 'slippage' is highly significant in signalling the teacher agenda as against a more pupil-centred classroom ethos.

> When Ofsted did come in, the slippage, which they call it, was tightened up because we're all able to do that. It doesn't matter on some occasions. You don't have to teach the minute they [the pupils] come in because sometimes there are desperately important things that they have to tell you.
>
> (Headteacher primary school J)

As this head adds '[human behaviour] that is not allowed. Not during Ofsted week.' Again, resistance to the idea of being 'hide bound' is conveyed in this contrast between what teachers would normally do and what they would do for an inspection team.

> I don't like having it laid down and to be honest, unless it's Ofsted, you're not that hide-bound by it. There is room to put in a bit of interest if you want to and something else. During Ofsted, probably not.
>
> (Headteacher primary school H)

The strength of compliance from headteachers contrasts markedly with the sense of authority and conviction that these heads express in the context of their own schools. In order to stand up for yourself in an Ofsted context appears to require an extra measure of strength and confidence.

> You have to be very strong. You have to be confident enough to say this is where we are, this is where we know we need to go and we will take that in our time and in our own way to advisors and to Ofsted.
>
> (Headteacher secondary school D)

Creating a culture for learning

The term 'culture' has passed seamlessly into the lexicon of schools. In these 12 interviews the concept is used interchangeably with ethos, atmosphere, climate and environment, all of which tend to focus on the learning, or learning and teaching, as lying at the heart of the culture. Heads talk about 'immersion' in the learning culture, keeping teaching and learning 'to the forefront' or 'bombarding' pupils with the singular and ubiquitous message. Heads speak of building culture anew, entailing the assertion of 'good practice' as well as intolerance of certain other practices.

> It was an opportunity for us to actually say, 'This is what we consider to be good practice' and although we needed everybody's agreement, it gave us, I think, that opportunity to share with staff and having visited the school beforehand, there were certain practices which were not going to be acceptable in a new primary school.
>
> (Headteacher primary school K)

There is also a pervasive sense of building a counter culture, one which confronted the previous way of doing things, such as 'a culture of marks and grades' or a 'blame culture', moving to one of mutual support and acknowledgement of vulnerability.

> . . . to move the culture to being a much more achievement one and not blame . . . And I mean one thing I am proud of actually is the fact that we do get a lot of staff, offer a lot of vulnerability and ask for support, expecting us to help them do it better.
>
> (Headteacher secondary school A)

In most cases discussion of culture refers to the professional teacher culture, and concerns are expressed as to how to 'move people' and overcome resistance or cynicism. There is a prevalent theme of new directions, re-ordering of priorities, intolerance of old and ingrained habits, of development and change. It is, in the words of one secondary head, 'a culture of change being expected and change being possible'. A culture of change is seen as a prerequisite for staff taking ownership of new ways of doing things.

> The culture has to change for things to change. The culture will only change if people take ownership.
>
> (Headteacher secondary school C)

One way in which change and ownership happen is through a mutual peer observation, teachers learning from teachers. 'There's a more open door culture, there's people watching each other's teaching,' says one head. This tends not to be seen as something spontaneous or ad hoc but a process that is carefully managed.

> What I do a lot of, when I know someone's got an issue, I think through who's the best person is for them to watch teach and try and go for someone who's better and not daunting because we have got some teachers who would blow the weaker teacher's minds and then they just think, 'Oh, I can't'. It's like a kid. You don't show them an A* when they're an E. So, you know . . . It's been a lot of lesson observation, talking about lessons . . .
>
> (Headteacher secondary school A)

The parallel made between students and teachers suggests that threat, resistance, and sensitivity to peer expectations manifest themselves among mature professionals just as they do among immature students. Confronting expectations of students is seen as running in parallel or in conjunction with the challenge to staff, and as integral to the making of a counter culture. Two heads describe an 'anti-achievement' student culture in which students 'are quite interested but they mustn't show it'. The antidote is 'an atmosphere where students feel secure, where they feel supported in their learning, a culture in which it is safe to learn, in which students are encouraged to play an active role in making the school as a whole a better place in which to learn'. This cannot be effected, it is argued, without teachers too making it a better place to learn and reaching out beyond the school to the parent community.

The counter culture is also characterized as one that challenges the expectations of parents.

> We are trying to counteract a whole culture there and working with parents as well because [of] their expectations that children come to school and sit and learn.
>
> (Headteacher primary school L)

The depiction of ethos and culture in these extracts reveals a strong invisible, or in some cases, highly visible, guiding hand. Culture is not simply something that grows weed-like but is created and nurtured, moulded to a strong vision of school leaders, by those who have, and use, the power to decide.

Leadership and management

While leadership was not explicitly addressed in discussions of culture, nor talked about as a key interview theme, leadership styles and values permeate almost every aspect of the discussion. There is a clear and consistent message that headteachers set the vision and culture of the school and that schools carry the imprint of those personal or professional values. One secondary head reflects this widely held view when he says, 'You wouldn't be a head teacher unless you had a very strong philosophy yourself, unless you had a very strong vision of what a school would be about.' Sometimes the values are alluded to apologetically as having 'a bee in my bonnet', without appeal to evidence or to higher authority.

Most heads make a distinction between what is and isn't negotiable. By virtue of their office heads have the freedom to decide, or impose, ways of working. Ownership of core principles or practices is explicitly seen by one headteacher as lying with the senior team and not the staff.

> So there's a few core things that come from me and senior team that they're not for ownership, they are and if you don't submit to that, it's not really a place to work.
>
> (Headteacher secondary school A)

At its most extreme it takes the form of what Maccoby (2001) terms 'narcissistic leadership' in which self is conspicuously centre stage in the transcript. The following are a few examples from an interview in which the use of 'I', 'me' and 'myself' was the continuous strand in describing policy development within the school.

> This policy has got a lot of me in it. It's largely me.
> That wasn't from the staff. That was from myself.
> It comes from me, an awful lot of it comes from me.
> The policy has got a lot of me in it. It's largely me.
> It was quite brutal. It was tough. It was me.
>
> (Headteacher secondary school D)

The use of words like 'tough' and 'brutal' are one expression of what is widely referred to as 'strong' leadership. It encapsulates ideas of sticking to your own principles, raising the stakes, creating willing followership. One secondary head describes having to 'force' ideas on to his colleagues, involving 'battles' to get people to accept his plans for the school.

This tough stance tends by most heads to be seen as applying in the early stages of headship when the challenge is to get everyone on board and moving in the same direction. The balance of command, consultation and consensus is conceived as one that changes over time as vision and direction are established and key principles become embedded in practice.

> On my arrival here it was the case and I think within the first six months we had a new assessment policy. I think that wasn't something that I consulted on. I was fairly dictatorial on that.
>
> (Headteacher secondary school C)

'Stepping back' from a more directive mode and adopting a lower profile is seen as possible once the school has moved towards a more collegial non-hierarchical culture, one in which people feel empowered to take initiative for themselves, to both lead and follow their colleagues.

> What I'm not trying to do is step back and let different things run. And that does seem to be working. So that's what I see as a learning organization. People take the initiative in a non-hierarchical way, people reflect on what they're doing, they share that practice.
>
> (Headteacher secondary school C)

There is, none the less, a sense of tension among heads between their own driving values and a desire for ownership and empowerment on the part of staff. This ambivalence is explicitly conveyed by a secondary head who talks of empowering people to arrive at the right decisions.

> . . . process is the empowering of people and as you empower them they will then be making that decision, having that input within the school, knowing that they're doing it within what we agreed is important for the school.
>
> (Headteacher primary school K)

In some cases there is a more honest and forthright acknowledgement of this process as manipulation. The word 'forcing' in the following statement is in uneasy juxtaposition with the implied ownership:

> I think teachers have got to feel that they're making decisions but what I suppose I'm forcing them to do is making those decisions.
>
> (Headteacher secondary school D)

As in this case, a 'strong' directive leadership style can be dressed up as consultation, and what makes for genuine consultation among equals becomes hard to discern. One secondary head claims that 'The staff write the policies. I don't write the policy, they're not written by me, they're written by them.' The next statement by this head, however, contains an ambiguity which is picked up by the interviewer:

They [policies] weren't imposed, they were negotiated and people were challenged in their thinking so that they would look to see what it is that we felt were important issues about the school.

Interviewer: Who were 'we' at that point? When you say 'we'. . . .
Head: Well, that would be very much, I think, the management within the school.

> (Headteacher primary school K)

The 'we' is a contentious area in building a genuine learning community and while trying to include, or 'move', all staff toward a common goal there is recognition of the disparate attitudes, values and motivation that comprise a professional body. Schratz (2001) characterizes a school, or perhaps any organization, as containing missionaries, true believers, lip servers, spectators, underground workers, outright opponents and emigrants, distributing themselves along a spectrum, according to the degree to which they 'buy into' the vision and mission of the school, with varying degrees of enthusiasm.

In schools which do encompass a range of motivations the change strategy, as defined by a number of these heads, is to invest efforts at the fertile end of the attitudinal spectrum (the missionaries and true believers) where you can expect high returns for minimal investment. 'You play to your winners,' says one secondary head. The view that 'other people will respond to what they're seeing going on around them' suggests an implicit theory of epidemiological change (Gladwell, 1999; Hargreaves, 2004) in which interesting or 'breakthrough' practice spreads and reaches a tipping point. The strategy includes an encouragement to leave for those who don't fit, or can't adjust to the changing culture, replacing them with carefully selected true believers, in tune with the school's, or perhaps more accurately, the head's, vision.

One head whose school is highly successful in terms of its GCSE results and Ofsted report, ascribes his success to a highly directive style of leadership, aggressive recruiting of quality staff and incentive policies to both attract and retain them.

> I suppose fundamentally I think people make things happen and people are what the school's about and I think I know very quickly when I meet people whether they're people I want here that will make a difference or make it exceptional.
>
> (Headteacher secondary school A)

There are references to 'the thinkers', 'the innovators', the change agents', the 'champions' whom heads rely on and 'use' to foster a climate of change. These people may have no formal status, 'without portfolio', but more commonly they occupy a middle leadership role. In secondary schools departmental heads or departments as a whole are seen as spearheading change. The leading edge departments, or 'those at the sharp end', tend to be seen as those who have been involved most centrally in the National Strategies, offering a core of changed practice and modelling which extends outward to other departments.

In contrast to the departmental focus, and in some cases complementary to it, are cross department groups or working parties devising policies, testing ideas and feeding back to senior leadership. These may take the form of teaching and learning groups, for example, designed to include staff with differing strengths or groups with specific functions, such as professional development, and include members of staff with no formal status, newly qualified teachers for example. While these accounts contain a hint of a welcome for diversity and challenge to the everyday practice the latitude for dissent or radical reappraisal of mainstream orthodoxy remains a more open question.

Conclusion

The clearest message to emerge from these 12 extended interviews is the success of government policies in leaving a depth of imprint on school practice and shaping the discourse which accompanies it. The success of National Strategies is vouchsafed by the compliance of headteachers, for the most part willingly, and by the imprimatur of Ofsted inspection. There is, at the same time, an accompanying critique of the formulaic nature of aspects of the Strategies. There is dissatisfaction with assessment measures such as SATs and a more general depiction of Ofsted inspection as an occasion for strategic conformity. Yet, from an ethnographic perspective, the lack of challenge offered to external authorities is striking and hard to reconcile with the authority and conviction of these heads as powerfully influential within their own schools.

There is a strong sense of a new orthodoxy running through these accounts. It reveals itself in an almost uniform view of learning, bearing the hallmark of brain-based theories of learning styles and multiple intelligences which, while widely endorsed, is contained uncomfortably with highly structured lesson units in which 'delivery' is a predominant metaphor. At the same time there is an almost complete absence of critical reflection on the embrace and advocacy of learning styles (see for example, Coffield *et al.*, 2004; White, 2004) while the all-consuming nature of targets and levels conveys a ruthlessly cumulative image of learning in which any deviation or distraction from the journey to curricular goals is to be eschewed.

All heads agree on the importance of a culture of learning and use every opportunity to reinforce the message. Peer observation, often across subject boundaries, is the mechanism by which the dialogue around learning is fostered, yet the conversations tend to betray a more teaching focused perspective. Use of the Ofsted model focuses observation on what the teacher is doing, and the normative scale to evaluate teaching tends to close down rather than open up a more critical discourse.

The apotheosis of a learning culture is portrayed as a consensual one. Intellectual bonding appears to follow on the heels of social bonding and one has a sense of the individual being buried under the weight of the policy and beneath the pressure for a uniformity of practice. A sense of agency on the part of teachers is hard to detect and even the strong sense of agency among the heads appears to be contingent on policy direction. The apparent lack of room for dissent risks locking schools into what Argyris and Schon (1978) call single loop learning – a continuous loop of defined objectives, planning, implementation and evaluation. The 'double loop', apparent in glimpses in these narratives, is one which provides space to stand back outside of that process, inviting critique, dissent and even subversion of orthodoxy. 'Organizations require a minimal degree of consensus but not so much as to stifle the discussion that is the lifeblood of innovation' write Evans and Genady (1999: 368), arguing that the constant challenge of contrasting ideas is what sustains and renews organizations.

Schools that play safe, driven by external mandates, set tight parameters around what can be said and what can be heard. Such schools are antithetical to the notion of a learning organization which, by definition, is always challenging its own premises and ways of being. For Evans and Genady organizational effectiveness is inherently paradoxical. It is dynamically balanced between control and flexibility, internal and external focus, by the tensions between means and ends. There is freedom to break rules because the culture is resilient enough to learn from it. Their (1999: 369) aphorism 'organize one way and manage another' implies that the greater the external pressure and the tighter the hierarchical constraints the greater the need for flexibility, diversification and agency.

The paradox of agency is that in a context of a top down cascade of government initiatives reaffirmation of teachers' experience is paramount. It is the prime source of knowledge on which a learning organization both rests and moves forward (Senge, 1990, 2005; Boreham and Morgan, 2004). However great the constraints of organizational structures, resource provision and political imperatives, individual agency means that teachers are not only in control of their own practice but able to exert their influence on the very structures which contain them. In Giddens' (1984: 5) terminology it may be described as a dynamic co-construction of change, driven internally by 'a continuing theoretical understanding of the ground of their activity'. Beane and Apple (1999: 7) offer three critical conditions for democratic schools:

- The open flow of ideas, regardless of their popularity, that enables people to be as fully informed as possible.
- Faith in the individual and collective capacity of people to create possibilities for resolving problems.
- The use of critical reflection and analysis to evaluate ideas, problems, and policies.

The 12 schools of this study may be described in Ofsted terminology as 'well led'. The vision and enthusiasm of these senior leaders shine through the transcripts. The words 'passion' and 'excitement' reoccur and there is a prevailing sense of these schools being driven by uncompromising principles. There are elements of heroic and narcissistic leadership, sometimes juxtaposed with an espousal of distributed leadership and a continuing struggle to resolve the tensions between individual and shared leadership, policy dictat and ownership, but needing to be resolved within the school as a unit of improvement in a competitive environment. In a Danish context where schools are beginning to feel the brunt of political pressure, Moos *et al.* (2000) warn that school leaders can easily find themselves blindsided unless they are able to bring a more critical 'reading' to the larger policy context of their leadership activities. In similar vein Frost (2000) describes the process of 'getting colleagues on board' as one which may fall prey to the rhetoric of collaboration 'as a euphemism for strategic manipulation'.

The individual efforts of these heads to improve their schools have to be seen in a context of 'challenging circumstances' which apply not simply to the problematic social context in which they are set but to policy directions which exceed national boundaries. The overriding concern of raising standards and meeting targets is owed in large part to the continuous flow of data from OECD and other sources of international comparison. This is allied to a global trend for self-management at local level and tougher government intervention at national level, combined with higher stakes accountability and external evaluation. These trends, driven primarily by an economic rather than an educational logic, leave headteachers to work out their own salvation within the bounds of their own schools, in a continuous quest to find a marriage of convenience between dutiful compliance and intellectual subversion.

Note

1 Personal conversation in the context of critique of the New Relationship with Schools.

References

Argyris, C., and Schön, D. (1978) Organizational learning: A Theory of Action Perspective. Reading, MA: Addison Wesley.

Beane, J.A. and Apple, M.W. (1999) 'The Case for Democratic Schools', in M.W. Apple and J.A. Beane (eds) Democratic Schools. Lessons from the Chalk Face. Buckingham: Open University Press.

Black, P. and Wiliam, D. (2003) 'In Praise of Educational Research: Formative Assessment', British Educational Research Journal 29(5): 623–37.

Boreham, N. and Morgan, C. (2004) 'A Sociocultural Analysis of Organisational Learning', Oxford Review of Education 30: 307–25.

Coffield, F., Moseley, D., Hall. E. and Ecclestone, K. (2004) Should We be using Learning Styles? What Research has to Say to Practice. London: Learning Skills Research Centre.

Department for Education and Skills, (2004) A National Conversation about Personalised Learning. London: DfES.

Evans, P. and Genady, M. (1999) 'A Diversity-based Perspective for Strategic Human Resource Management', Research in Personnel and Human Resource Management, Supplement 4: 368.

Frost, D. (2000) 'Teacher-led School Improvement: Agency and Strategy', Management in Education 14(4): 21–4 and (5): 17–20.

Giddens, A. (1984) The Constitution of Society: Outline of the Theory of Structuration. Berkeley, CA: University of California Press.

Giroux, H. (1992) Border Crossings. London: Routledge.

Gladwell, M. (2000) The Tipping Point. New York: Little, Brown and Company.

Hargreaves, A. (2004) 'Sustainable Leadership, Sustainable Reform'. Paper delivered at the First World Summit on Educational Leadership, November, Boston.

Hargreaves, D. H. (2003) Education Epidemic. London: DEMOS.

James, M., Black, P., McCormick, R., Pedder, D. and Wiliam, D. (forthcoming) 'How to Learn, in Classrooms, Schools and Networks: Aims, Design and Analysis', Research Papers in Education.

Maccoby, M. (2001) 'The Incredible Pros, the Inevitable Cons', in What Makes a Leader? Boston, MA: Harvard Business School Press.

Miliband (2004) 'Personalised Learning'. North of England Education Conference, 8 January, Belfast.

Moos, L., Møller, J. and Johansson, O. (2000) 'A Scandinavian Perspective on the Culture of Educational Leadership'. Paper presented at AERA in New Orleans, April.

Ornstein, S. (1986) 'Organizational Symbols: A Study of their Meanings and Influences on Perceived Psychological Climate', Organizational Behavior and Human Decision Processes 38: 207–29.

Pedder, D., James, M. and MacBeath, J. (2005) 'How Teachers Value and Practise Professional Learning', Research Papers in Education 20(3).

Perkins, D. (2004) 'Taming the Wild and Wilding the Tame'. Invited lecture to the Faculty of Education, University of Cambridge, June.

Pring, R. (2005) Values in Education and Society, Society for the Study of Comprehensive Schools Conference, Faculty of Education, University of Cambridge, 17 January.

Senge, P. (1990) The Fifth Discipline: The Art and Practices of the Learning Organisation. New York: Doubleday.

Senge, P., Scharmer, O.C., Jaworski, J., Flowers, B.S. (2004) Presence: Human Purpose and the Field of the Future. Cambridge, MA: The Society for Organizational Learning.

White, J. (2004) 'Unpick Woolly Thinking', Times Educational Supplement, 12 November.

Whitehead, A. N. (1929) Aims of Educations and Other Essays. New York: Macmillan Company.

CHAPTER 14

MAGIC MOMENTS HAVE DISAPPEARED, EXPERTS BELIEVE

David Marley

Originally published in the *TES*, 17 October, 2008

New teachers lack creativity and embrace government initiatives like a 'security blanket', a union-funded study out this week has warned.

Too many stick rigidly to the national strategies for maths and literacy, without the ability to adapt to children's needs, according to academics from Cambridge University.

'Schools used to love having new teachers come in because they were creative, but now they have bought into government policy and expect things off the shelf,' said John MacBeath, one of the authors. 'They know nothing about spontaneous moments.'

Professor MacBeath and fellow author Maurice Galton said that teaching had been robbed of 'magic moments' as teachers had to follow government initiatives and strive to meet targets.

Teachers are also under pressure from increased working hours and poorly behaved children, the five-year study, commissioned by the NUT, found. 'What we saw while carrying out the study was a sea change in attitudes,' said Professor Galton. 'Where teachers were unhappy but resilient, they became compliant and did not believe they could change anything.'

Primary teachers are now forced to deal with poor standards of behaviour more normally associated with secondary pupils, according to the report.

Teachers claimed pupils were reluctant to follow instructions and that 'a minority could be extremely confrontational, use foul language and could even be physically aggressive,' the report said.

New teachers blamed the deterioration of pupil behaviour on poor parenting, while longer serving teachers put it down to the pressures of the performance culture in schools, the academics said. Teachers also have to cope with aggressive parents who object to children being disciplined at school.

Elsewhere, the study found that primary teachers' workload had increased in the past five years from just over 54 hours a week to 56 hours, despite workforce reforms designed to cut the working week.

It also criticised the way that children with special educational needs have been integrated into mainstream classes.

Teaching assistants were too often given responsibility for SEN pupils, even though they had inadequate training, said Professor MacBeath.

Christine Blower, NUT general secretary, said that the report was a 'wake up call' for ministers. 'The Government cannot ignore the overwhelming evidence that over-prescription and rigid centralisation are robbing teachers of their creativity,' she said.

A spokeswoman for the Department for Children, Schools and Families said she did not accept the 'negative picture painted by this report'. 'Research shows teachers feel their own professional status is starting to improve after decades of decline,' she said.

CHAPTER 15

MATHEMATICS FOR ALL
The way it spozed to be?

Josephine Gardner

Originally published in the *TES*, 27 February, 1998

It was in my second year of high school that I first put the question to my teacher 'Why do we have to do mathematics, sir?' He replied that if I ever wanted to go to university I would need to 'have it' as one of my subjects. 'Having mathematics' was certainly one way of thinking about the subject and such a perspective did contribute, unhelpfully, to frame our schoolboy attitudes to learning. Not entirely satisfied with that line of reasoning, however, I offered a second proposition: 'What if I don't want to go to university? Or what if I want to study philosophy or French or zoology?' My teacher, who had apparently never been posed with this question in half a lifetime of teaching moved rapidly to a second line of defence to the effect that he did not have to justify his subject, nor for that matter the ancient wisdom of the school curriculum, to a 14-year-old.

A decade or so later reading James Herndon (1968) I was to discover that this was quite simply 'the way it spozed to be'. Herndon's book about the unquestionable rightness of the status quo casts the issue in a different mould, describing the corollary to the quizzical schoolboy's dilemma. His book is about a progressive young teacher in Harlem who tried in vain to encourage his class to think, to challenge their teacher, to ask their own questions, but was persistently met with the stock response 'That ain't the way it spozed to be, Mr Herndon'.

Much later again I was to be reminded powerfully of the strength of people's attachment to the way things are spozed to be. In 1998 I wrote a somewhat tongue-in-cheek piece for the *Observer*, teasing the sacrosanctity of mathematics' place in the core curriculum and reprising my 14-year-old's question. I suggested that children be encouraged to ask 'Why are you teaching me this today?', citing Postman and Weingartner's (1971) famous appeal for pupils to be armed with built-in crap detectors. The flood of responses to the article ranged from the nostalgic through the congratulatory to the outraged. Among them were 20 letters from pupils in a German school in Paederborn. These sixth formers had been set as their homework task a personal response to the article, addressed to its author. The most touching and revealing from a 17-year-old in his final pre-university year of school contained these words:

> It is a very Utopian idea that you have, that people should be encouraged to think for themselves. I do not think it is a good idea because that would be the end of our society as we know it.

It might be argued that there is small cause for celebration of society 'as we know' it or for an educational system which so often betrays itself as hostile to thought. Evidence comes in the starkest form from a source that ought perhaps to 'know' better than a German schoolboy – England's Chief Inspector of Schools. Using the *Observer* piece as a launch pad for his annual invective, Her Majesty's Chief Inspector pronounced my quizzical article high heresy, and the man who perpetrated it, as 'at the heart of the darkness' in British education. It was an awesome reminder of the power of a new orthodoxy, intolerant of thought and unwelcoming of points of view other than its own. It brought to mind the words, attributable as I remember to Peter Medawar, 'a mind so well equipped with the means of refutation that no new idea has the tenacity to seek admittance'.

The article had been spurred by my continuing four-decade-long quest for a well-reasoned answer to my question. Why mathematics for all? Why do we require all young people to continue with mathematics long after it has lost purpose, relevance and interest for them? Have we not learned anything in the last half century? Why do we stick with such tenacity to the inclusion of mathematics in the core curriculum when many other disciplines or areas of study have an equal or more justifiable place? The question has never met, to my satisfaction, with a convincing justification including from informed sources within OFSTED, the QCA, the Standards and Effectiveness Unit of the DfEE. Replies have included the Royal Gambit ('Because it is the Queen of the Sciences'), the MacEnroe Defence ('You can't be serious'), the Cannibal Conjunction ('So that you can become a teacher and teach it to other people'), and the Vocational Prevarication ('It is important for doctors, chemists, architects, accountants, etc.'). The instrumental arguments tend to be the most spurious, while the Platonic arguments, advocating the intrinsic truth and beauty of mathematics are no more than special pleading.

Years, indeed decades after my impertinent, but highly pertinent, question to my mathematics teacher I discovered that I could enjoy mathematical books and puzzles. I read Fermat's Last Theorem and had no difficulty in understanding the obsessional fixation with Fermat's mathematical conundrum. I could sympathize with the discipline of mind that could devote years to the pursuit of a solution, sacrificing personal, social and family life in the search for the combination of numbers that no one before had put into the same sequence. It was intellectually awesome and within its own frame of reference inspiring but, 'out there' in the social world where 99.9 per cent of the population live, it seemed an esoteric and self-indulgent exercise. Could it be seen, in some senses, as a metaphor for school mathematics?

Repacking the curriculum container

Over the years, the curriculum has been unpacked and repacked, more often in the virtual than in the real world. One of the latest examples comes from the Royal Society for the Arts which, in 1999, proposed a quite radical restructuring, suggesting five broad areas of competences: for learning, for citizenship, for relating to people, for managing situations, for managing information. Within this structure there is no place for mathematics as such but a pragmatic case for basic statistical techniques, probability, and concepts of interest and return.

When we engage in this kind of back-to-basic exercise the first step is to empty the curriculum box and scatter its contents around. The task of repacking then starts with Herbert Spencer's question 'What knowledge is of most worth?' Language and literature, of course, because language, written and spoken, is the very stuff of life and without literature our lives would be threadbare indeed. Mathematics, naturally, because it offers other languages – powerful symbolic languages – and, with the invention of a binary code, has given access to a truly transformational technology. Science, imperatively, because it introduces us both to deep outer space and deep inner space, introducing us to methodology and furnishing tools to explore the very origins of our small selves and of the infinite universe.

History, without doubt, because we are what we are, where we are and where we are going because of our past; and because without understanding of the past our present and future are beyond our reach, and without insight we are destined to relive the errors of our past. Religion, self-evidently, because it is concerned with the very meaning of existence. It is the primary driving force of so many people's lives, the source of inspiration and damnation, the single most contentious area of controversy both historically and in contemporary society, the root of wars, holy and unholy, and the underpinnings of much present day charity and intolerance.

Music, for certain, because it is so significant for the very quality of social life; for its healing and exhilarative powers, because it is the most pervasive aspect of modern living, consuming more hours per day of young people's time, and money, than any other single source. Art too, because, together with music it is the oldest most durable form of cultural expression, liberating, challenging, deeply absorbing and immensely accessible to all. Psychology, because it is about understanding ourselves, our emotions, our thinking and behaving, our relationships with other people in social, organizational and industrial contexts where the concepts of psychology have penetrated every level of human discourse. Politics, because it might help us to consider what levels of poverty are tolerable in advanced capitalism, what 'capitalism' is, what 'socialism' was, what these words mean and why they are so fearfully avoided by a Labour government.

Economics, not only because globalization is taking over our lives, but also because, as Margaret Thatcher taught us, there is an important relationship between the micro and macro business of making and moving money. Foreign languages, each with a different claim, mastery of any one providing an escape route from the rigidity and insularity of one's own linguistic culture. Environmental studies, because our future is intimately bound up with the future of the planet and there is scope for knowledgeable and concerned individuals to make a global difference. Philosophy, because it helps us with our most precious human gift, the ability to think, to reason, to wonder, to ask intelligent questions and understand more deeply the paucity of arguments such as 'because that is the way it spozed to be'.

To say nothing of media studies, drama and dance, health and physical education and much more too. Then there is, of course, something that has come to be called information and communication technology (ICT), which is a very small name for a concept so enormous that without it half the population of the world would collapse like puppets whose strings had been snipped.

We might even want to add in 'education', because we might then be able to give our pupils a meta-perspective on themselves and their schools and on the wonder and absurdity of the entity that is called the curriculum.

In the real world of school policy and politics-making where curriculum is king and queen, two items are generally not emptied from the box before the exercise begins. All the pieces have to be squeezed back into it because English and mathematics are already *in situ*. They are seen as the pillars of school education, symbolically representing the twin deities of current government priorities – literacy and numeracy. Yet the logic of this is not self-evident. While English continues to have a fairly close connection with functional literacy, the link between mathematics and functional numeracy becomes increasingly tenuous as children progress through school. Although both disciplines, it might be claimed, help pupils to move progressively deeper and more critically into the 'real world', that is the world in which understanding and intellectual curiosity mature and in which knowledge becomes action – the case for mathematics is precarious.

The case is a precarious one because the arguments for its inclusion appeal to a Socratic age, a Renaissance era or even mid-twentieth-century context and they are no longer sustainable. And the primary reason for this is the very thing that mathematics helped to create – ICT. It has liberated mathematicians and ordinary people from the tedious calculations that were once obstacles to be hurdled *en route* to the desired destination. Programming is a useful metaphor. In the early days of personal computers access to any higher level functioning was through basic programming. Had the technology not advanced so rapidly, we would have been insisting on basic programming for all. However, a decade or so on we no longer need to know about programming and even programmers themselves are offered so many packaged short-cuts that they rarely need to go back to basics. Statisticians need no longer to calculate standard deviations or squares of chi. They simply need to know what they mean and how to use them.

What all of this demonstrates is that the model of the curricular box has outlived its usefulness. It cannot be expanded and its content cannot be reduced into ever-smaller fragments to accommodate everything that the box should contain. We have to think differently about the nature and purpose of what we teach and what we might have to do very differently in the future. We will have factor into the equation what we know about pupils, their social world and their experience of school life and learning.

Pupils' experience of school mathematics tends to be as a series of problems of increasing difficulty and abstraction to which the right answers have to be found. Numbers come to assume some inherent meaning and mystique for them. They are not hypothetical propositions about which you could have a good argument. They are seen as 'facts' (the ultimate defence in any argument – 'just as two and two equal four') but rarely is the mathematics they acquire seen as helping to explain things in their social world. Mathematics exists within the esoteric world of the mathematics classroom and textbook but not in the experiential world of mathematical principles in which snooker balls ricochet lawfully into pockets, footballs curve gracefully behind defensive walls, goalkeepers (with intuitive application of geometry) narrow the angles, while jazz musicians make music according to mathematical formulae.

For pupils the experience of mathematics is generally bereft of deeper understanding or application, not because of the lack of inspiration among teachers, who in a better world might teach mathematics in the snooker hall, on the hockey field or the building site, but because understanding mathematics is a luxury. It is a luxury which time and logistics cannot afford. There is so much to 'cover', increasingly intricate problems to be solved. So pupils learn at a fairly elementary stage to manipulate $x = 1$ and to 'solve' more and more complex constructions built on this basic premise. However, they are typically lost for words when posed with the question 'What does "equal" mean? Does it mean that x is 1 or that x mirrors 1?' or perhaps 'Let us propose for the sake or argument that x be treated as a 1 until we find out otherwise.'

In the minds of children the world of numbers comes to be seen not as a metaphor, not as a set of hypotheses and constructs, but simply the 'way it spozed to be' and in no conceivable system could two and two ever equal five, even if we wanted them to.

This deterministic view of the world is helped along by the logical, ruthlessly cumulative, world of mathematics. However, the tyranny of the logical/mathematical 'intelligence' is not so much a product of mathematics teaching as the space given to it on the timetable, out of all proportion to its relevance, importance and instrumental value; at the same time, paradoxically, serving to diminish its intrinsic value.

Disaffection through compulsion and overexposure is, of course, an argument that could be applied to virtually any subject. The deeper-lying problem is the secondary school curriculum itself, the subject barriers which it erects and the mind barriers it helps to create. As long as mathematics is mathematics is mathematics, and mathematics is what you 'do' and 'get done' and 'cover' and 'pass' and then put away with a massive sigh of relief, the mind set will continue to stay set, and the debate over curriculum priority will remain an endless and ever more fruitless debate.

So, why not provide the option of mathematical specialization alongside a more generalized treatment of what mathematics means and how it applies, taught within a social reference frame, just as we might teach art and music to those who have no pretensions to be artists and musicians; or health and physical education for those who will never be professional sports people or athletes. Or science for those who will not be scientists.

A similar case has been made for science by Morris Shamos (1995) in his book *The Myth of Scientific Literacy*. Shamos, former president of the New York Academy of Sciences, argues for a more practical approach that encourages an appreciation of science, its purposes and history, its potential and limitations, its impact on our own environment, its effects on our personal health and social lives. His views find an echo with many science teachers who are concerned that what children take away from their school science lessons is deeply misleading and does disservice to good science. Roland Meighan, once a mathematics teacher himself writes:

> When I was learning mathematics at school, then teaching it in school myself, and then watching my son learn it, the same heretical thought kept occurring, that surely there are better things we could be doing than this.
> (Meighan, 1998: 30)

Bertrand Russell, hardly a slouch in the mathematics department, was highly critical of the school mathematics 'treadmill' and suggested that there were many more useful things to learn.

It is ironic that a question mark should be placed over the place of mathematics and science at a time when governments around the world are increasingly exercised about their relative performance in the international league tables. The Third International Science and Mathematics Study (TIMMS) has caused much breast beating and soul searching in virtually all countries not placed in the top echelon. The basic assumption is that the mean performance (in more than the statistical sense perhaps) of children at a certain age is an indicator of a country's educational health and, even more tenuously, that it is related to a country's economic performance. Peter Robinson (1998) of the Institute for Public Policy Research has demonstrated the fallacy of this second premise. Drawing on statistics compiled for the World Bank, he finds no correlation whatever between economic growth and school performance in mathematics. He concludes:

> What could be a sober and informed debate about English education is in danger of being drowned out by the simplistic and often shrill rhetoric which seems to dominate policy making in education.
>
> (Robinson, 1998: 60)

If we wish to find a plausible link between the economy and the state of the art in mathematics and science it is obviously to higher education that we should be turning our attention. There we would find that the United States, George Bush's 'Nation at Risk', on account of its mediocre school performance in mathematics/science, is at the leading edge in both these fields at a university and research level.

The challenge for the schools of the year 2000 is to provide secondary age pupils with an array of rich learning resources from which they can derive meaning and benefit, closing as few doors as possible, keeping open the possibility of mathematical adventuring in life after school. Heretical though it might be, we might consider secondary school mathematics as a potentially attractive extra-curricular activity. Just as music has accepted its place in the voluntary twilight zone of lunchtimes, after school, or on Saturday mornings, why not mathematics? Some schools have managed to produce, out of this optional and extra-curricular time, outstanding orchestras, bands, choirs and solo musicians. A school which could boast an equal number of accomplished mathematicians would be an exceptional school.

In fact, the proposition is not so far-fetched or heretical after all. Such voluntary provision does already exist in many schools in the form of mathematics clubs, study support, supplementary classes and residential weekends or summer schools.

'Who ever would have believed I could do mathematics five hours a day during my summer holidays and still come back for more?' said one secondary age pupil who had attended a summer school at Birmingham's University of the First Age. It was engaging and profitable for her, a self-confessed mathematics phobic, because it was built around practical activities in a context where there was time and space to play at mathematics, free from the relentless demands to 'have it' and to give it back.

Perhaps rather than trying to impose the subject in discrete timetabled blocks we should be seeking new imaginative new ways, Third Millennium ways, of keeping mathematics alive by keeping it firmly in its place.

References

Herndon, J. (1968) *The Way It Spozed to Be*, New York, Simon and Schuster.

Meighan, R. (1998) *The Next Learning System: And Why Home-schoolers are Trailblazers*. Nottingham, Educational Heretics Press.

Postman, N. and Weingartner, G. (1971) *Teaching as a Subversive Activity*. Harmondsworth: Penguin Books.

Robinson, P. and Oppenheim, C. (1998) *Social Exclusion Indicators*. London: Institute of Public Policy Research.

Shamos, M. H. (1995) *The Myth of Scientific Literacy*. New Brunswick, NJ: Rutgers University Press.

CHAPTER 16

CHIEF INSPECTOR TARGETS PROFESSORS

TES editorial

Originally published in the *TES*, 27 February, 1998

An outspoken attack launched by Chris Woodhead, chief inspector, on professors of education and teacher-trainers shows just how secure he feels in his position at the heart of Labour's standards crusade, insiders say.

While Mr Woodhead always uses his annual lecture to tease the 'educational establishment', his remarks this time were more personal and directed against colleagues and members of Government task forces. Mr Woodhead, whose contract comes up for renewal in the autumn, appears to enjoy the esteem of the Prime Minister and education ministers, in particular standards minister Stephen Byers. His relations with David Blunkett are a little cooler.

In his speech Mr Woodhead warned that the Government's standards policy would founder unless the reforms addressed 'the real heart of darkness – the trivialisation of culture and erosion of belief in the intellect'. The worst offenders were in university education departments. His attack on Professor Robin Alexander of the University of Warwick, whom he accuses of 'an excess of academic unworldliness' was the most surprising, as they were joint authors of the 1992 Three Wise Men report advocating reform of primary education. Professor Alexander was also recently appointed to the Qualifications and Curriculum Authority. Professor Alexander said afterwards: 'The notion that professors of education are at the heart of some conspiracy to deny children their right to a proper education is plainly ludicrous. It is a novel experience to be pilloried as part of Chris Woodhead's progressive conspiracy. Previously I have been portrayed as a right-wing reactionary.' The chief inspector also accused Professor John MacBeath of Strathclyde University, a member of the standards task force, of 'intellectual shoddiness' and of dismissing with 'contemptuous indifference the idea that education is about teaching the young and ignorant things that they need to know if they are to grow a little wiser'. Professor MacBeath told the *TES*: 'As a member of the task force, I'm obviously committed to standards and I'm all for intellectual clarity. Rhetoric doesn't raise standards.'

Other targets included Professor Tim Brighouse, joint deputy chair of the standards task force with Mr Woodhead; Ted Wragg, Professor of Education at Exeter University and Margaret Hodge, chair of the Commons Education and Employment Select Committee.

After the lecture, Mrs Hodge said: 'He damages what he says because it is not clearly based on evidence. The effectiveness of similar bodies like the Audit Commission comes from the fact that they can always point to the evidence.'

Mr Woodhead warned against giving too much power to local education authorities. 'I am worried by the signs that some LEA officers and members are relishing the prospect of involving themselves in all "their" schools with a great deal of enthusiasm.'

Meanwhile, a book on the history of the inspectorate published this week by John Dunford, former president of the Secondary Heads' Association, criticises Mr Woodhead for failing to keep the chief inspector's office independent of Government policy. He says there was a 'remarkable congruence between the office's findings and the views of . . . the Conservative party'. He said the same situation existed with the Labour Government.

CHAPTER 17

DO SCHOOLS HAVE A FUTURE?

Originally published in T. G. K. Bryce and W. M. Humes (eds),
Scottish Education: Beyond Devolution, 2008, (Edinburgh:
Edinburgh University Press, 2008)

Three decades ago, researchers, educators, pundits and soothsayers specu-
lated on schools of the future, envisaging an age in which schooling as we
know it would no longer exist or be scarcely recognisable in what was then
tomorrow's world. It would be a world so different, we were told, that education and schooling would no longer be synonymous, and schools, if they had
a future, would serve radically different and transformational purposes.

The future never happened, or at least not in any of the ways predicted.
As we move towards the end of the first decade of the third millennium,
schools have in essence changed little. In many cases, the same buildings are
still intact and still in business, high Victorian windows symbolically shielding
learning and learners from the world beyond. Schools, newly constructed,
perpetuate the eggbox structure, thirty pupils with one teacher; the comforting
familiarity of periods, timetable and bells; a disciplinary compartmentalisation of knowledge followed sequentially by testing in barren halls where
knowledge acquired from a set curriculum is reproduced in a time-limited
paper-and-pencil Olympics. Asked about a newly built school in 1963, a
secondary student famously replied: 'It could be all glass and marble, sir, it's
still a bloody school' (Half our Future: the Newson Report, HMSO, 1963).
Schools are schools, no matter how we dress them up!

In many ways, the structure and culture of schooling has regressed rather
than advanced since the heady days of the 1970s when young people believed
they could change the world – and their schools. Youthful aspirations were
fed by a stream of radical literature rejoicing in titles such as Paul Goodman's
Compulsory Miseducation, Everett Reimer's School is Dead and Alan
Graubard's Free the Children and Other Political Prisoners. Those romantic
visions of a brave new world were lent weight by empirical studies which
served to confirm a world of schooling, dividing achievement by class, by
measured 'potential', by parental legacy, by geography, by constructions of
learners as 'academic' and 'non-academic'. In Scotland, Gow and McPherson
documented the world of 'flung aside forgotten children' (Tell Them from
Me, Aberdeen University Press, 1980), one of the first and seminal documents to give voice to the disaffection and alienation of such a large constituency of young people.

In discussing schools of the future, it is important to understand what
happened politically and socially to address the pessimism of forgotten youth
and to nurture the optimism of those who had glimpsed what a learning

society might look like. It would take a much larger treatise than this space allows to disentangle the threads in the complex weave of global trends which tie us so firmly to the present. It took three large volumes by Manuel Castells to tease out the implications of the Information Age and the Network Society (1996, 1997, 2000). His narrative is one which juxtaposes the unforeseen and unimaginable growth of technology with an equally unforeseen implosion of social cohesion. 'Perverse integration' is the term he uses to describe alternative routes for young people into the shadowy economy and the twilight world into which many young people escape from family life and social institutions.

Coincident with this social revolution, we face the paradox that, while the nature of learning has been shown to be more determined by influences that lie outside of schools, teachers have become increasingly more accountable for the performance of their pupils. Comparisons among countries set the stage and provide the script for policy-makers to worry about their place in the international concourse. Comparative data from OECD, TIMSS and the European Commission have provoked a widespread urgency (some might say moral panic) among politicians and their advisers, sending emissaries to Taiwan or, more recently, Finland to bring back the magic bullet of school and classroom practice. A more studied approach and informed analysis would have revealed that the answers do not in fact lie in the classrooms but outside schools, in the social composition of the country, in its history and culture, in the homes and communities from which it draws its pupils, and in complementary forms of learning out of school hours.

The more we learn about the nature and processes of learning that take place out of school, the less we are justified in the pretence that teachers can repair the ruins of the social and economic impact on the lives of families and on children as yet unborn. Year by year, we know more and more about the powerful formative influence of the early years, about the effects of deprivation, about the shaping of children's intelligence, personality and behaviour in those critical intra-uterine years as well as in the formative early years before schooling begins. And, in the years of schooling as children become adolescents and attain adulthood earlier and earlier, now extending into the primary years, we can observe parental and family influence diminishing in proportion to the rise of peers as the significant reference group (Judith Harris's 1998 book The Nurture Assumption is a particularly telling analysis of these issues). As the political imperative grows to make schools more effective, more accountable and more transparent, so the burden falls more squarely on teachers to demonstrate that it is good teaching, not environment, not family, not socio-economics, not culture, not history, that makes the difference.

Scenarios for schools of the future

These insights provide an important frame for any discussion of what schools of the future might look like. With this in mind, what are the most likely and most desirable scenarios for the future based on what we know now and what we have learned from the failures and excesses of the past? In 2001, the OECD posited five possible scenarios: continuation of the bureaucratic system, reschooling (schools as core social centres), schools as focused learning organisations, deschooling, and 'meltdown' due to a teacher exodus from the system (OECD, Schooling for Tomorrow, Paris: Education Policy Analysis, 2001). In many countries, the melt-down scenario would seem to loom largest as one of the likeliest outcomes in a situation where teachers feel less in control of their own teaching, young people are less in control of their own learning, and school leaders are less in control of their own decision-making. The perception of deprofessionalisation and disconnection from fundamental educational values has fuelled a recruitment and retention crisis. Among the 'dissatisfiers' identified in international studies (MacBeath, 2006) were stress, workload, accountability, bureaucracy, personal and domestic concerns, social attitudes, salary and, in sum, 'intensification'.

Addressing this set of inter-connected issues is a precondition for thinking creatively about a different kind of future. The question is: where to start? What is the entry point for radical change? Is it with the macro structures and large-scale reform or with micro initiatives at classroom and school level? Is the centrepiece curriculum? Or assessment? Or does it lie in the social grouping of learners and the structures by which they progress from stage to stage in their educational journey?

In Scotland, a key centrepiece in the change process is A Curriculum for Excellence. Its ambitious title, to which we might add the even more ambitious codicil 'for all', signals the purposes of a 3–18 curriculum designed to 'enable all young people to become successful learners, confident individuals, responsible citizens and effective contributors'. Acknowledging that this takes place in an 'ever-changing new environment for learning', the document characterises future learning as active, challenging and enjoyable, neither fragmented nor overcrowded with content, providing choice tailored to individual interests and needs, extending experiences which blur the boundaries between the 'academic' and 'vocational', attended by forms of assessment that support and enhance learning.

These descriptors might well have been plucked from treatises on the aims of education. They are noble in intent but challenging of the structures which contain them because they confront a set of essential contradictions. Schools as we know them, particularly in the secondary years, simply cannot realise those aspirations within the structural and political constraints that we have locked ourselves into. The essential problem is that policy works, or is obliged to work, in the wrong direction – downwards from school buildings, structures, staffing, conventions, planning and testing to a curriculum which strives for excellence while being denied by the very environment which contains it. In theory, and perhaps in the schools of the future, we may work in the opposite direction, upwards from learning experiences to curriculum, to planning, to staffing, to structures and the design of schools or something similar.

This, however, is too hard and too Utopian. And, one might add, we have been there before. Whatever happened to the alternative schools of the 1970s? Illich's Yellow Pages and convivial tools? Free and freedom schools? Schools without walls and schools without buildings? In Philadelphia, the famous Parkway which runs through the heart of the city became the learning space for a bold experiment in which young people's learning took place in the variety of buildings, spaces and relationships that a city could offer for learning, saving millions on school buildings, textbooks, administration and all the paraphernalia that consumes the lion's share of the education budget.

Parkway (and its many imitators in the United States) inspired a short-lived initiative in the 1970s in two Renfrewshire secondary schools. Two classes of young people enjoyed the experience of learning in the city for the third term of their third secondary-school year. The following is a very brief condensed account of what happened.

We interviewed each youngster individually and in groups, asking them what they would like to learn in the urban and rural world that was their oyster. At first, all they could come up with was English, geography and history (elaborated on as 'kings and queens 'n' that'). After a little more probing and brainstorming on what they would really like to learn, the list included deep-sea diving, marine life, how orchestras work, space exploration, studying the stars, jam-making, milking cows, stuffing tigers, car mechanics, why monkeys are like human beings, hospitals, guns, how a city works and much more.

We then sat down with the Yellow Pages and began phoning hospitals, zoos, museums, astronomy departments in universities, the Scottish National Orchestra, the Royal Navy, the AA, St Andrew's Ambulance service, Robertson's jam factory, Chrysler, car workshops and car markets, manufacturers, gunsmiths, shops and farms. Every student then had an individual, highly varied five-day timetable which met his or her interests, although the taxidermy department in Glasgow museum, clean out of tigers, could only offer the alternative of stuffing penguins. What was both surprising and highly gratifying was the willingness of the Royal Navy, the Scottish National Orchestra, the Glasgow University Observatory, the AA and the ambulance service not only to take on young people but also to help build a coherent educational programme to broaden their horizons. Seminars were arranged with tutors and small student groups in parks and cafés to debrief and share experiences, probing their learning and relating it to a broader educational agenda.

While much of the content learned did not fit easily within a school curricular framework, many of the insights and skills gained exceeded what might have been gained by a third term spent in the classroom. The greatest impact was, however, the enhanced self-esteem of these young people, their new-found sense of agency and re-engagement with learning.

The Learning School

For a host of reasons, this initiative is not replicable on a larger scale; but it does tell us much about the nature of learning and motivation and suggests some principles for the design of educational experiences. The closest contemporary equivalent is the Learning School, now in its eighth successive year. The Learning School is also a school without walls. It exists on a global scale and in its eight years has encompassed Scotland, England, Sweden, Germany, the Czech Republic, South Africa, Hong Kong, Japan, North Korea, Australia and the USA. Each of these countries has, within the last eight years, sent one or two senior students to take part in a year-long research initiative, starting with a six-week induction in the Shetland Islands at Anderson High School before students split into two separate groups in order to visit other schools around the world. These young people spend four to six weeks in each of six or seven schools as visiting researchers, working alongside fellow students and with classroom teachers to research learning. In each location, these young people live with host families, in most contexts without a common first language and, in some cases, with no common linguistic ground at all.

These twenty or so young people keep a diary of their experiences in the ten months they spend with the Learning School. Their depictions of home and school speak personally and sometimes painfully of culture shock and its impact on their sense of self, and entail a large degree of unlearning. While classrooms in Japan and South Africa appeared to these young people surprisingly familiar, they were, with renewed insight, able to penetrate beneath the surface features of classroom life, enjoying the privileged access to students of their own or similar age. Their immersion in the culture through living with host families both complements and problematises research studies which have focused solely on schools and classrooms, confirming that, while schools matter, families and communities matter more. It is from these young people, acolyte researchers, that we are afforded a glimpse into the nature of that home/school relationship. Through their own biographies, we gain new insights about how identities shape and re-form as they travel between home classroom and community and across cultures.

All of the Learning School students have at some time told their stories to academics, teachers, inspectors, civil servants and education ministries in Edinburgh, London and Cambridge and to similar audiences in the other countries, as well as to the International Congress on School Effectiveness and Improvement in Copenhagen and Barcelona. In 2003, students from Learning School cohorts 1 and 2 (LS1–2) wrote eighteen of the twenty-two chapters in the book Self-evaluation in the Global Classroom (edited by MacBeath and Sugimine, London: RoutledgeFalmer, 2002).

As they recount in their book, their identities as learners were re-formed and redefined by three primary contexts – the schools in which they conducted their research, the host families they lived with for a period of four to six weeks, and the peer group in whose close company they travelled, worked and spent their leisure time. All of these three sites were multi-lingual and multi-cultural. As they describe the impact of these new and unfamiliar contexts, they contrast the impact on their learning with their prior school experience: 'I have probably learnt as much in these 10 months as I did in 13 years of school' (Jolene, in MacBeath and Sugimine, p. 38). Another Scottish student takes a retrospective view of the impact of learning beyond school and the test it has offered to his self-awareness and academic identity:

> This year has been a massive education to us all, an almost vertical learning curve. I can see how by watching and feeling another culture from within you cannot help but learn infinite amounts. It is the greatest educational tool ever to have at one's disposal. Teaching things schools will never be able to teach, through first hand experience, feeding a desire to understand the world in which we live. This year has given me a real thirst to continue to test myself academically and to become more aware of different societies, cultures and people, as I am sure it has to everyone who was a part of Learning School 2.
>
> (Colin, in MacBeath and Sugimine, p. 36)

The way in which the sense of self is affected through the transition from one site to the next is striking in its parallels with Weiss and Fine's collection of essays in their edited book Construction Sites (New York: Teachers College Press, 2000), which chronicles how young people construct meaning from their experience in differing situations and through the interplay of the various sites in which they struggle to find meaning and coherence. The narrative of learning for young people growing up in a twenty-first-century environment is how to navigate a hazardous social terrain of inducement and threat. Theirs is a restless dissatisfaction with much of what society offers them, with a far-reaching impact on learning behaviour in and out of school. The perennial challenge for educational leaders is to grasp what it means to grow up in differing social contexts and how to help young people bridge their learning across these disparate construction sites. The more we venture into this tangled territory, the more complex and contested becomes our knowledge of human learning, its social and emotional character and the precarious path that young people have to tread to make sense of what schools promise them.

Once again, the Learning School is simply one singular venture, impossible to replicate on a large scale but nonetheless speaking volumes about the nature of learning 'in the wild' and learning in the captivity of the classroom. 'Back at the ranch' in Anderson High School (remarkably similar to most other secondary schools in Scotland), students are able to reach beyond the containing walls of the school and the perimeters of the island to travel virtually to other places and challenge their own preconceptions and most cherished prejudices. The Global Classroom (progenitor of the Learning School) sees learning as unconstrained by mere geography.

Since 2003, Anderson High School has been sharing aspects of learning and teaching through a range of ground-breaking initiatives by video-conferencing. For example, a group of six Anderson High School students began sharing images of themselves, their school and community with similar groups of students in Scotland and widening the scope of their exchanges, so giving birth to a Global Sharing Images project. Sharing Perspectives was another curricular initiative in which each class group of 12- and 13-year-olds made links with a class group from partner schools. Class groups share ideas, planning and preparations using the Blog/Discussion Forums across subjects based on the following themes:

- To hear ourselves as others hear us – structured around English lessons
- To see ourselves as others see us – structured around Social Subjects
- What is a House and Home? – structured around Art and Design, Technology and Science.

Enterprise Education (in association with schools in the USA) and Virtual Drama are both recent developments. Virtual drama is a collaborative international creation of a drama to be performed at the annual Global Classroom Conference (previously held in Japan, South Africa and Germany as well as in Shetland). The conference brings students together for face-to-face sharing of ideas for a week in which teams of students from each of the six partner schools enact a six-act global drama, each of the acts prepared and constructed by virtual means throughout the year so that the final presentation provides a seamless multi-faceted narrative.

In Highland Region, where schools are separated by hundreds of miles and stretches of water, students are able to download videoed lessons in all school subjects and view them at home or on their i-Pods. On a two-hour bus or ferry journey, a student may review work again or catch up on lessons missed. The development of an online Integrated Learning Community enables teachers to exchange practice and offer collegial support and mentoring to their colleagues in other schools. Videos, podcasts, curriculum and assessment materials and professional-development resources have an even further reach, now in use in the USA, Australia and Yemen, among other countries. For students and their teachers, the off-site availability of increasingly sophisticated and interactive resources raises a challenging question for the future of this scattered community: is your journey really necessary? It is a question that will have much wider applicability for the future.

The more learning crosses spatial boundaries, the more it begins to challenge the physical structures which try to contain and limit it. As the legacy of old buildings and old ways of thinking conspires against new forms of learning, so it implies the dismantling of dividing walls, first in the metaphorical sense, in turn stimulating a re-examination of the physical structures. There is a direct relationship between open spaces in physical architecture and open spaces in thinking, argues the Commission for Architecture and the Built Environment (CABE). It further argues that the ability of school leaders to look to the future and to lead in radically new ways will be hampered not only by the physical and logistical boundaries but also by governments attempting to define what the leaders of tomorrow should know on the basis of what was appropriate for the leaders of yesterday.

Quo vadis?

There are two broad opposing directions in which schools may move in the future. One is to become bigger, more inclusive, more encompassing of a whole community – the new community school writ large. The other direction is to shrink the school in size, so that it becomes more a hub, networked with a range and variety of small, people-friendly, local community sites.

In the first of these two scenarios, we can envisage the educational mall, offering something for everyone and open 24 hours a day for 360 days or so. It is the logical extension of the 'full-service' school: learning on tap for adults as well as children, alive to a 24-hour world economy and information network that never sleeps. Like supermarkets, it accommodates people who work unsocial hours and gives access to libraries, laboratories, Internet, fitness and recreation facilities at times which are people- rather than institutionally orientated. Radical as it may appear, it is essentially a revisiting, like all ideas, of something tried and tested. In the 1930s, Henry Morris, Chief Education Officer for Cambridgeshire, began creating village colleges to realise his vision of learning for all in one cultural learning centre.

> It would take all the various vital but isolated activities in village life – the School, the Village Hall and Reading Room, the Evening Classes, the Agricultural Education Courses, the Women's Institute, the British Legion, Boy Scouts and Girl Guides, the recreation ground, the branch of the County Rural Library, the Athletic and Recreation Clubs – and, bringing them together into relation, create a new institution for the English countryside. It would create out of discrete elements an organic whole; [in which] the whole is greater than the mere sum of the parts. It would be a true social synthesis – it would take existing and live elements and bring them into a new and unique relationship.

The village college, said Morris, would 'provide for the whole man, and abolish the duality of education and ordinary life'.

> It would not only be the training ground for the art of living, but the place in which life is lived, the environment of a genuine corporate life. The dismal dispute of vocational and non-vocational education would not arise in it. It would be a visible demonstration in stone of the continuity and never ceasingness of education. There would be no 'leaving school'! – the child would enter at three and leave the college only in extreme old age.
>
> (Henry Morris, The Village College. Being a Memorandum on the Provision of Educations and Social Facilities for the Countryside, with Special Reference to Cambridgeshire, 1925, section XIV)

The attempt to transfer Morris's rural idyll to a council-house scheme on the fringes of Edinburgh may go down in history as a glorious failure – but the creation of the Wester Hailes Education Centre in the late 1970s was one of the first and most imaginative of attempts in Scotland to transform a school into a learning centre for a whole community. Its essential failing was perhaps in going too far and too fast in trying to realise its transformational vision, failing to meet people's expectations of what a school should look like and what learning should be about. The lesson learned is that you have to take people with you.

We will see over the next few years a revisiting of the educational campus, bringing together special, primary and secondary schools on one site with attendant services and 'one-door' entry for parents, children, nuclear and extended families and others for whom education may become lifelong and lifewide. However, we may also see educational provision emerging on a smaller, more people-friendly scale. The embryos of such a future are already in existence, as the example from Highland local authority shows. Rather than moving libraries, Internet cafés, fitness centres, football pitches, basketball courts and health clinics into new mega-community 'schools', the trend may be to move resources out closer to where people live and play. Internet cafés are an example of one highly accessible user-friendly resource which could be enhanced and developed in new directions, networked with schools and with teachers and education advisers and sited in shop-fronts, supermarkets, high flats, community centres, churches or anywhere that people congregate. Tutorial centres already exist to complement and enrich school-based learning, but they too could offer a broader diet and range of learning pathways. Breakfast clubs, study-support facilities, Saturday and Sunday schools, football clubs and residential centres also complement the limited 9am to 3:30pm school day but might in future also serve as primary sites for learning rather than simply as supplementary, or compensatory, to what is on offer in schools. Small, medium and large businesses, hospitals, museums, parks and zoos already offer placement and work experience on a limited scale but, as the Parkway and the Renfrewshire initiatives illustrate, could potentially play a more explicitly educational role.

Big is not necessarily beautiful, and we have witnessed in many parts of the world attempts to break up large units, to create schools-within-schools, places which are more congenial, convivial and which operate on a more human scale. The rapid growth in home education is a response to the impersonality of mass production and the anti-social effects that come with it. Over a century ago, Dewey wrote:

> Without insight into the psychological structure and activities of the individual, the educative process will, therefore, be haphazard and arbitrary. If it chances to coincide with the child's activity it will get a leverage; if it does not, it will result in friction, or disintegration, or arrest of the child nature.
>
> (Dewey, 'My pedagogic creed', The School Journal, 54 (3), 1897)

A short history of technology

Once upon a time, there was school radio, then the wonders of tape-recording, the huge promise of educational television, the breakthrough with the BBC-B computer, the floppy disk, the palmtop, the memory stick and the interactive whiteboard – each new technological advance offering the promise of a revolution in learning. Yet, alongside the possibility of gaining a PhD simply by Googling around intelligently, the schools of the present have been baffled by how to harness and tame these new technologies. Young people are adept with the new language of blogs, wikis, de.li.cious and podcasts, and are a potential learning resource for their teacher. With each new advance, we make further discoveries as to the incredible potential to store information outside our bodies and how to retrieve it most economically. Yet, school exams in barren halls still require information to be retrieved from inside one's head.

Harvard's David Perkins found that children could be taught with a high degree of reliability to solve problems when they were structured by the teacher and presented to students in the classroom context; thus, with well-designed problem-solving tasks, it was possible to achieve 100 per cent success within the classroom. However, in an unstructured open field outside of school, the success rate may fall to as low as 5 per cent. This, Perkins claimed, was due to three key factors. One, students have to be able to spot the problem. Two, they need to be motivated to want to engage with the problem. Three, they then need to have the ability to select and use the most appropriate tools to solve the problem. In his book The Unschooled Mind (New York: Basic Books, 1991), Howard Gardner reported similar findings with college students. He found that Physics students could not solve the most basic problems if posed in a context slightly dissimilar to the one they first encountered them in. Even successful students responded to problems with the same confusions and misconceptions as young children, reverting to their own implicit theories formed in childhood.

The natural problem-solving ability of children 'in the wild' is exemplified most startlingly in Mitra and Rana's study of children in rural slum villages in India (Mitra and Rana, 2001). In a series of 'hole in the wall' experiments, computers were placed in a wall 'kiosk' in villages. The researchers found that groups of children who had never before seen a computer were able to learn very quickly how to navigate their way through them to produce surprising and creative results. Numerous experiments were conducted to find out how it was that children could learn without being taught, what was termed 'minimally invasive education' (MIE), the borrowing of medical terminology which suggests a form of disruption of the natural rhythm of things. In three Indian villages, 103 children at Grade 8 level were administered the curricular examination for 'Computer Science' for that grade. Results showed that children who had learned at MIE kiosks were able to do well in the exam without having been taught the subject. They scored at nearly the same level as children who had been taught the Computer curriculum in school throughout the school year.

Interviewed by a journalist, one of the authors of the project, Mitra, related the following anecdote.

> One day there was a document file on the desktop of the computer. It was called 'untitled.doc' and it said in big colorful letters, 'I Love India.' I couldn't believe it for the simple reason that there was no keyboard on the computer [only a touch screen]. I asked my main assistant – a young boy, eight years old, the son of a local betel-nut seller – and I asked him, 'How on earth did you do this?' He showed me the character map inside [Microsoft] Word. So he had gotten into the character map inside Word, and dragged and dropped the letters onto the screen, then increased the point size and painted the letters. I was stunned because I didn't know that the character map existed – and I have a PhD.
>
> (Businessweek Online Daily Briefing, 2 March 2000)

The results of this study 'throw new light on pedagogy', concluded the research teams. Some children actually learned better without formal school instruction, and others did appear to need some form of 'scaffolding', while there were others for whom a more structured approach was needed, whether from their peers or from informed adults. But, as the many snapshots and video illustrations showed, learning was highly social. Children learned from and through one another. They distributed intelligence. They networked their knowledge. Experts and leaders emerged while others played the role of 'connectors' who put their peers in touch with the intelligence sources and knew how to access the most expert current knowledge.

While some might conclude that this evidence adds fuel to the deschooling fire, in fact it reveals that there is an apparent need among some learners for scaffolding and for some direct instruction, but also what it reveals is that we have significantly underestimated the capacity of children to learn by self-discovery and through collaborative learning with one's peers. Rather than closeting experts, architects, policy-makers and academics in darkened rooms to devise clever blueprints for the future, we might consider how to create the future as an integral aspect of the present, changing our schools and our thinking about them from within.

However, as Einstein argued, problems cannot be solved by thinking within the framework in which they were created. In its modern, less elegant form, we term this 'thinking outside the box'. When a London-based group of architects decided to involve children in the design of schools of the future, they didn't simply ask them to design a new school constrained by the familiarity of the everyday. They took children out of their schools to visit airports, shopping malls, libraries, art galleries and state-of-the art buildings in order to widen their conceptions of people, spaces and relationships.

The fact is that schools as we know them both solve and create problems. For some, they provide the one and only rescue service from an otherwise impoverished life. For others, they diminish and constrain intellectual and emotional capacity. If schools are to remain with us – and it is hard to envisage any other scenario in the foreseeable future – we will need to rethink how we embed the lessons learned from the various successful and failed initiatives in Scotland and elsewhere over the last half-century. It will prove futile to enjoin schools to become learning and risk-taking organisations if we fail to exemplify what that might mean at a policy level.

References

Castells, M. (1996) The Rise of the Network Society (Volume I), The Information Age: Economy, Society and Culture. Oxford: Blackwell.

Castells, M. (1997) The Power of Identity. Oxford: Blackwell.

Castells, M. (2000) End of Millennium. Oxford: Blackwell.

MacBeath, J. (2006) 'The talent enigma', International Journal of Leadership in Education, 9 (3): 183–204.

Mitra, S. and V. Rana (2001) 'Children and the Internet: experiments with Minimally Invasive Education in India', British Journal of Educational Technology, 32 (2): 221–32.

CHAPTER 18

HELL BENT ON REFORM, BUT WHO CARED ABOUT TEACHER MORALE?

Originally published in the *TES*, 17 September, 2010

Education lay at the heart of New Labour's vision, but ministers were fixated on policy-making and showed little concern about those who actually worked in schools, according to a new book by John Bangs, John MacBeath, and Maurice Galton

Teachers often complain that politicians do not understand the reality of the classroom when they set about trying to reinvent schools. We wanted to discover the extent to which the concerns of teachers had been accommodated in the policy-making of the Blair and Brown governments during 13 years of intensive reform.

Our analysis was based on remarkably frank interviews with teachers, headteachers, leading academics, politicians and policy-makers from across the political spectrum.

Two of our headline findings were:

- Labour's determination to woo middle England led to a souring in its relationship with teachers which, in turn, had deeply damaging effects on its campaign to improve schools.
- In the words of former chief schools inspector Mike Tomlinson: 'There is nothing rational in policy-making.'

Sandy Adamson, a former senior civil servant in the Education Department, tells us that the failure to win teachers' confidence was 'an irretrievable mistake'.

Even Sir Michael Barber, one-time head of the government's school standards unit, admits that the effect on the profession of the government's 'top-down' strategy to raise standards was 'quite negative, and it was much more negative than I might have guessed'. Indeed, he admits that Labour came to power 'without an overview of where we were going with the teaching profession'.

Another senior adviser, Kevan Collins, claims that ministers were too concerned with meeting targets to worry about teacher morale.

'I don't think morale was ever talked about explicitly; we just kept our eyes on the numbers,' he says.

The main reason for the failure to listen to teachers arose from Labour's wish to shed its traditional image. As Estelle Morris, former education secretary – arguably, the one with the greatest understanding of teachers – puts it: 'Labour had to shift in the opposition years from being seen to be the party of the provider . . . to the party of the consumer.'

For her, the government failed to understand the demands of teaching during the first three years in office because 'unless you've done it' it is difficult for anybody to know the pressure in the classroom.

In fact, the government in 1997 did know about the state of teachers' self efficacy and morale, as Lord Puttnam, film director and Labour peer at that time charged with improving teachers' status, recalls.

'What I was asked to do by (then education secretary) David Blunkett was to get out and about in schools and come back to him by December 1997 at the latest. I said: "You probably know this is a devastated workforce".'

Puttnam's solution, the Teaching Awards, almost did not get off the ground.

'My deal with David Blunkett was that we wouldn't go ahead with the awards if we couldn't get a sufficient number of nominees. I got him down to 800 and on the night we closed we had 796. So I sat down with the (awards) chief executive and created eight additional nominations. I went back to David and said, "That was close, 804." He said, "That's good enough." You'll be pleased to know none of our nominations won!'

The prime minister and many of his advisers were more interested in the perceived failure of comprehensives than supporting teachers, it is claimed.

Fiona Millar, former Downing Street adviser and now a campaigner for comprehensive education, says: 'There was a real divide within Number 10 between people they would see as Old Labour like me, Alastair (Campbell, her husband, and Blair's director of communications), (Blair's parliamentary private secretary) Bruce Grocott and to a certain extent (Blair aide) Sally Morgan and the sort of thrusting young middle-England people who allegedly knew what parents wanted. Some of them had just made up their minds that comprehensives were a disaster.'

Indeed, Blair's commitment to education was not initially internalised within his own government. According to Millar: 'Brown made more speeches about education in the Third World than he did about education in this country. Although he was behind Sure Start, I don't think he was focused on education or else he would have been focused on the spending budgets of the time.'

Mick Waters, a former government exams adviser, recalls a meeting with Alan Johnson, then education secretary, who 'went on about teenagers having to read Austen, Hardy and T S Eliot as top of the list of what children should have to do at key stage 3 . . . When the umpteenth youngster was being stabbed in south London.'

In 2001, Alastair Campbell announced 'the end of the bog-standard comprehensive' in an effort to promote specialist schools. In public, Blair condemned the phrase as one he would never use himself. He also rang Lord Puttnam. 'David, I want to apologise. You must be very upset over Alastair's remarks.'

Puttnam replied: 'Yes, upset is right. In one sentence he's just managed to undo six months' work.' Privately, Blair told other advisers that he thought Campbell's comments 'gave us some definition'.

This was not the first time schools had been subjected to such damaging criticism. In the summer of 1997, the entire Education Department ministerial team had decided, with Number 10, to name and shame publicly 14 secondary schools in special measures. It was action which left teachers angry and Ofsted nonplussed. According to Mike Tomlinson, director of Ofsted and subsequently chief inspector of schools:

'The first 14 schools named and shamed were not checked with Ofsted before the announcement ... we didn't think they were the right ones anyway, if we'd been asked. Naming and shaming was essentially a political action designed to give a political message.'

When Blair became interested in market incentives, the mantra of standards, not structures, was abandoned as he promoted academies and trust schools. Researching the book, we found that civil servants had been dismayed as attention shifted from school standards to these new types of schools.

Exams, targets and media

In 2004, Mike Tomlinson thought he had achieved consensus on an overarching diploma for 18-year-olds and that he had convinced Blair that he had preserved the 'gold standard' of A-levels.

Yet his report was scuppered by the agreement that the two opposition leaders should have sight of it in advance. Michael Howard, then Tory leader, made a speech the night before publication saying that he would defend A-levels at all costs. Blair felt he had to say the same even though the Education Department supported the diploma.

Summoned by Blair, head of the Number 10 policy unit David Miliband, who had earlier tried and failed to convince him of the diploma's merits, told Tomlinson he had 'rambled a bit' when asked if A-levels would be safe.

Blair said he could not run an election campaign while the *Daily Mail* was printing stories about his plans to ruin A-levels.

Tomlinson adds: 'We had the wonderful position of a speech being given by the prime minister saying I'm not inclined to get rid of A-levels while his secretary of state and minister were at another event saying this will be implemented in full.

'There is nothing rational about policy-making at all,' he reflects.

The setting of literacy and numeracy targets was not based on evidence. They were at best 'educated guesses', according to Michael Barber.

Judy Sebba, for seven years senior research adviser in the Education Department, says: 'How can a target ever be evidence based? You can say at the moment children make one level or one-and-a-half levels of progress in a year, therefore we will set it at two, but what's the evidence base for challenging targets?'

Sandy Adamson, a senior civil servant who worked on the policy, speaks of 'the stupidity of targets, unobtainable targets simply pulled from the air and then applied to every school in the country'.

'The majority of the reaction was, "this is unachievable" and for a substantial minority it never was achieved,' she says.

A voracious media shaped government decisions. Mick Waters talked to Downing Street advisers soon after he arrived at the Qualifications and Curriculum Authority, predecessor of Ofqual and the QCDA, about the importance of cookery and was told 'No, we don't want to take that on.'

'Then Jamie Oliver did his thing on Turkey Twizzlers and overnight cooking has to be front and centre in the curriculum,' he says.

More seriously, the education reform agenda demanded continued success. The engine for further change had to be based on the need for it. These arguments became a double-edged sword.

Jim Knight, the former schools minister, describes this dichotomy as 'a bit of a rat' in reference to Gerald Ratner, who famously destroyed public confidence in his own company's jewellery products by describing them as 'crap'.

'How do you still sound impatient for improvement while not rubbishing what you've already done?' asks Knight.

Journalists began to ask whether the responsibility for failure lay with government.

What should happen now? Andreas Schleicher of the education directorate at the Organisation for Economic Co-operation and Development points out that Finland and other Nordic countries have strong value-based education systems shared by major parties without 'layers and layers of unfinished and incoherent reforms all on top of each other'.

Our governments need to try harder to achieve consensus on what matters most to teachers, pupils and parents, he says.

'Consensus and coherence are the two very powerful forces for change,' he adds.

'If your goals vary, how do you motivate anyone, be it the teacher of a class or the student, to take learning seriously? If you're a teacher, you know today they're trying this and tomorrow there is something else.'

Our book concludes that many of Labour's achievements were obscured by its poor relationship with the teaching profession. It argues strongly for future governments to have an overview of where they want to go with the teaching profession and to include teachers in that debate – an overview complemented by consistent, coherent and educationally sound policies.

The exams 'market'

Mick Waters, former director of curriculum at the QCA, accuses exam boards of conniving at the dumbing down of school examinations.

'Before I went for this job, I used to think that all this criticism of exams that they were being dumbed down was unfair. You know, the old argument, more people passed than ever before. Since I've been there, I think the system is diseased, almost corrupt. I don't mean QCA or Ofqual or anybody. We've got a set of awarding bodies who are in a market place.

'In previous jobs, I had seen people from awarding bodies talk to headteachers implying that their examinations are easier. Not only that, "We provide the textbook to help you through it".'

He says: Ofqual, the regulator, should 'immediately look at whether the chief examiner should be allowed to write the text with regard to pupils' questions'.

'That's insider dealing.'

Standards and academies

Kevan Collins, who was primary strategy manager at the Department for Education and Employment, describes the collision when Blair became interested in – to use Sir Michael Barber's words – 'market incentives or market-like incentives'.

'Standards not structures was a mantra which created the space for us to work freely across the whole system,' he says.

'We were not interested in structures; we were interested in standards. It meant you could have audiences in rooms up and down the country from Cornwall to Newcastle, have a common language and a common set of priorities that were universal.'

Mr Collins contrasts this with the move to the debate about how to introduce market incentives.

'We moved straight away from the universal language of teaching and learning and began to believe that the solution was in creating certain types of schools . . . the absolute shining example of that was the academies debate.

'It fractured a working alliance between individuals and the common endeavour . . . and it basically segmented the profession.'

Reinventing Schools, Reforming Teaching is published by Routledge.

CHAPTER 19

THREE THINKPIECES

LEARNING FROM THE LEARNING SCHOOL

Originally published in the *TESS*, 17 January, 2003

Self-evaluation by students may be on course to become an integral part of the inspection process, says John MacBeath.

'The most imaginative and ground-breaking initiative in school evaluation in a lifetime.' These words from one of Her Majesty's chief inspectors are no off-the-cuff rhetoric but a sober assessment of an idea, a venture, an adventure, that describes itself as the Learning School.

It is a Scottish initiative, born and nurtured in Britain's northernmost secondary school but global in its reach and impact. It is the brainchild of Stewart Hay, assistant head in Anderson High in Shetland, building on the success of a previously inspired curriculum project known as the Global Classroom.

This is the recipe for the Learning School. Take a group of young people from eight countries. Give them a year out of school to get an education. Provide some intensive training in observation and evaluation then send them off on a world tour of schools, observing in classrooms, shadowing pupils, conducting interviews and administering questionnaires.

Prepare teachers in the schools to get some challenging feedback from them. Help the team to observe astutely, to record faithfully, to feed back sensitively. Keep them in touch through the net with the Anderson home base and with university researchers in Japan and Cambridge. Ensure the receiving schools have host families willing to accommodate someone for four weeks or so, even if there is no common language. Entrust co-ordinators (older students) to blend a disparate collection of individuals into a working group, listening and learning from one another, arguing their corner, compromising and synergising. Grow their confidence to report their findings to critical audiences at universities, government departments and international conferences. Encourage them to write a book and find a major publishing house to print it. Shaken and stirred is what these young people write about their experience in the recently published book Self-evaluation in the Global Classroom (TESS, January 3). Theirs was an emotional roller-coaster ride from Shetland to Korea, via Hong Kong, Japan, the Czech Republic, South Africa, Sweden and Germany.

But that is only part of the story. What they observed and recorded in classrooms is a powerful narrative about learning and its relationship to teaching. Much of their insight is owed to their status as students, talking to their peers and to the repertoire of tools which helped them to dig beneath the surface life of classrooms that so often presents itself to school inspectors.

They can see things unencumbered by habits of seeing. They can know things for the first time without prior knowing. They are also afforded the luxury of time. No 30-minute observation and a summative judgment at the end, but extended visits to classrooms, shadowing a class or a pupil over a week with follow-up interviews to probe the high and low points of learning, reminding us what a school can look and feel like from a pupil perspective. Teachers who bravely volunteered to do their own spot checks found that their estimates of pupils' engagement and interest often rendered wildly differing judgments of the same event. Spot checks often identified consensual high water marks. When a teacher's and a class's judgments did positively coincide it was an indicator of something vital taking place. These small-scale miracles opened up big questions. What is it that engages pupils and sparks their imagination? When does a classroom episode come alive? How much of it is down to the teacher and how much rests with the pupils or peer group themselves?

These questions and the classroom dialogue they provoke lie at the heart of self-evaluation. Self-evaluation remains a topical issue internationally and Scotland can justly claim to be a world leader in the field. The Learning School initiative, however, takes How Good Is Our School? a step change forward. It moves the student from periphery to centre stage.

Archie McGlynn (HMCI at the time), impressed by what he had heard from the Learning School students during a presentation at the then Scottish Office headquarters in Edinburgh's Victoria Quay, immediately composed a memo to colleagues advocating that students be part of an inspection team.

A paradigm shift too far perhaps? But, as he confidently asserts, its time will come.

INSIDE THE THINKING BRAIN

Originally published in the *TESS*, 20 June, 1997

John MacBeath says biology may have much to teach us about the capacity to learn.

The Pacific Rim has an irresistible allure for education policy-makers. So they should pay close attention to what was being said at the Seventh International Conference on Thinking in Singapore this month. The Sunday Times headline after the conference, 'Singapore tries trendy teaching', was characteristically tendentious, but the truth is that Singapore has discovered a deep fault line in traditional teaching. At the conference some of the world's leading thinkers about thinking – Robert Sternberg, Reuven Feuerstein, David Perkins and Howard Gardner – and many of 2,200 delegates from 30 countries, had come to similar conclusions about their own educational systems. They seemed to agree with young people we spoke to in a downtown karaoke bar: 'Your whole school life is memorise, memorise, memorise, but afterwards you remember nothing.'

Goh Chok Tong, the prime minister of Singapore, launched the challenge to inert ideas. In his opening address he promised a cutback in curriculum content and a greater emphasis on skills. He said: 'What is critical is that we fire in our students a passion for learning, instead of them studying for the sake of getting good grades in their examinations. Their knowledge will be fragile, no matter how many A grades they get, unless they have the desire and the aptitude to continue discovering new knowledge well after they leave school. It is the capacity to learn that will define excellence in the future not simply what young people achieve in school.'

The experts at the conference were all quick to admit to being only on the edge of understanding the inner magic of the thinking brain. But they supported radical thinking about education. 'To pretend that we know more than we do is irresponsible. To look to the worn solutions of the past rather than to the possibilities of the future is a form of insanity,' argued Luis Machado, former minister of state for the development of human intelligence in Venezuela. 'Governments that won't listen to this message are either ignorant, stupid or criminal because they are wasting the talents of young people,' said Machado, who argued that there is a Copernican revolution in the making, the science of learnable intelligence.

The Israeli Reuven Feuerstein, whose work has achieved dramatic results with children designated as having special needs, offered proof in the form of case study after case study of children who learnt to be intelligent; children who wildly surpassed the expectations of parents, psychologists and teachers, and exceeded the predictions of testing and the limitations of social background.

Oregon's Robert Sylvester used results of the newest brain scanning technology to reject the analogy of the brain as a computer, inherently logical and systematic. He prefers the metaphor of the brain as jungle, an ecosystem with many layers, and believes that the learning environment of the classroom should be one which invites challenge and discovery across domains.

Schools should be less concerned with 'imposed skills and imposed categorical systems' and promote jungle navigation, encouraging students to seek individual personal solutions to problems. In much of the so-called problem-solving in classrooms, it is the teachers who present the problems, and often also provide a method for solving them. But the vital step, recognising and defining the problem, is left out.

Sternberg, professor of psychology at Yale, despaired of students who arrive bright, well schooled, and examination-smart but are poor jungle navigators, often without what he called the practical, creative and successful intelligences that really matter in life.

Harvard's Howard Gardner revisited his own well-known seven intelligences, and added a further one and a half to the list. He has identified an eighth intelligence which he calls naturalistic (or environmental) intelligence, while the nascent ninth – spiritual or existential intelligence – merits only a half because it has, as yet, no empirical evidence to support it. Despite a growing worldwide acceptance of the idea of multiple intelligences, school practice has, for the most part, ignored this burgeoning field of knowledge. Imagine a school, says Gardner, which really understands and nurtures the unique intelligences profile of each individual child, each with areas of great potential strength and learning difficulties.

Gardner has studied creative, exceptional minds. All of his exceptional minds were singularly deficient in some areas and played to their strengths in one or two others. Many great thinkers and inventors were abysmal failures at school. In the not too far distant future, says Gardner, people will look back on the end of this millennium and laugh at the 'uniform school', which thought it could teach the same things to the all children at the same time and in the same way.

Todd Siler, director of the Foundation for Human Potential in Chicago, called for a curriculum that melted the 'ice cube' compartmentalisation of knowledge so that learning became fluid, real and exploratory, so that physics, when studied through art and music, could provide the stimulus to mathematical problem-solving.

How tragic that art and music become marginal subjects when they are not subjects at all but crucial components of intellectual and emotional life and play such a significant role in the creation of intelligence.

The unsuspecting foetus born with an inherent capacity to speak 3,000 languages knows little yet of the pruning which will take place to fit its prospective cultural and scholastic procrustean bed. At this moment, said Machado, it is midnight in Moscow and a couple are making love. The spermatozoa fighting its way to survival is already thinking: 'When I grow up I am going to be a bullfighter.' Little does she know, yet, that she is living in Moscow.

IN THE VERY THICK OF THINGS

Originally published in the *TESS*, 9 May, 1997

A study of leadership in four countries has revealed a startling difference in emphasis on discipline, writes John MacBeath.

The past six weeks have treated us to a sustained focus on the question of leadership. Leadership has been dissected, analysed, rediscovered and re-invented. We now know that leadership requires to be visionary as well as conservative (with a small 'c'), consistent as well as flexible, conducted with integrity as well as opportunism. The most interesting aspect of the election campaign was the driven desire of all party leaders to meet the expectations of their widely differing constituencies.

These themes find echoes in a study by the Quality in Education Centre, part-funded by the Scottish Office, of school leadership in four countries – Australia, Denmark, England and Scotland. While drawn on a smaller canvas with tighter organisational boundaries, the issues are remarkably similar. The ability to deal with the expectations of the various stakeholder groups that constitute 'a school' proved to be the most acid test of effective leadership.

While careful not to make the assumption that leadership equals head-ship, we started with the office of the head and with the question, 'What makes a good headteacher?' This open-ended question prompted a whole lexicon of personal qualities – fair, caring, humane, humorous, loyal, approachable – interestingly, many of the same adjectives used by heads to describe what they expected of themselves. Recurring themes among professional competences were the ability to motivate and inspire staff, to give direction and purpose, to organise and delegate effectively.

There was a reassuring similarity in the responses across all groups and countries. For everyone, good communication, with an emphasis on listening skills, came at or near the top. Pupils in particular wanted 'someone who cares about your opinion'. Teachers and parents were equally concerned that their voice should be heard and saw headship as being as much about the soft skills of empathy and relationships as about the harder-edged skills of organisational and financial management.

There was an interesting difference in emphasis between the Danish teachers and their peers in the three other countries. The Danes placed higher premium on the arts of leadership skills than on the science of management. They were interested less in firm direction from above and more concerned with collaboration, democratic decision-making and shared leadership. They never mentioned 'strong leadership', a high priority among Scottish and English teachers. Nor did 'firm discipline' figure in their lists of priorities.

The Danish heads, who visited schools in the other participating countries, were bemused by the Scottish love of hierarchy and our national obsession with 'discipline'. A Danish deputy head commented on his English counterpart's approach to monitoring and accountability: 'That is not the Danish way of leading. It wouldn't give a good atmosphere. The Danish way is to have faith and talk. Danish leaders work through trust and not through control.'

The Scottish heads who visited Denmark envied the informality, the laid-back quality of their Danish peers, unencumbered by appraisal, accountability and inspection. At the same time, they warned their Danish colleagues of what one head described as 'blissful disdain' for those things in whose absence 'our own world might be too soft and cosy'.

It was clear both from the data and the exchange visits that English, Scottish and Australian heads are living in a more pressured, competitive and stressful environment. While a Danish head, in jeans and sports shirt, could not easily be picked out from his or her peers, senior management teams in Scottish secondary schools were easy to identify, wearing and walking the aura of management.

Scottish and English heads worked longer hours and experienced a greater sense of distance from teaching staff. While isolation was a common factor in the lives of headteachers, it was the English heads who were most likely to describe their job as 'lonely'. They found it increasingly difficult to share with neighbouring heads and were reluctant to admit to problems and weaknesses which might expose their vulnerabilities to market competitors.

If, at the beginning of the study, we believed we would find the secret ingredients of effective leadership, it became increasingly clear the more we progressed, that leadership is context-sensitive, not only across countries, but within them. Heads accustomed to the status and authority of the Scottish school might flounder in a Danish school, while a democratic Dane could easily run aground in an inner-city Glasgow school. We found that such transferability operates within Scotland itself. A head, successful in one context, was not necessarily successful elsewhere. This point was made forcibly by heads who were in their second or even third headships.

Nonetheless, there were clearly some constant factors of effectiveness and some transferable skills. Fundamental to effective leadership across national boundaries is the ability to read the context, to grasp its phenomenology and understand its internal dynamic. 'Keeping antennae out', 'picking up the vibes', 'following your gut feelings' are not easily dissectable behavioural competences, but they are crucial to effective leadership.

The antennae imagery may prove to be more than metaphor as researchers unravel more and more of the workings of the brain and its ability to tune into different frequencies. Intuition is often described as 'women's intuition', a notion that is less liable to be seen as sexist the more evidence we have that women are better equipped by physiology and nurturance to read social situations than men. Good schools are sailed rather than driven, says David Hopkins, professor of education at Nottingham University, evoking an image of the yacht being steered from the stern, tacking and changing with a reading of wind and current.

The conventional imagery of leadership puts the leader 'in front' or 'on top', but many of the headteachers in our study depicted themselves in their drawing as 'in the thick of things', leading not from the apex of the pyramid but from its central point of gravitation.

Effective leaders, it seems, are more likely to encourage the leadership of others, and have enough self-assurance to be followers and to learn from the most junior members of staff as well as from pupils. While the Danes were for the most part better at this than we were, we could take them to schools in Scotland where the youngest member of staff chaired a working party and where pupils led staff development sessions for teachers.

The 10 Scottish schools which participated in the study (four primary, four secondary, one special school and one independent primary school) found that they did not have to travel far to find challenging and innovative approaches to leadership – they were on our doorstep. They also found that internal networking has proved to be perhaps the most lasting benefit, and that all of us had been involved in a project that could truly be described as collaborative research.

INDEX

Page numbers in bold indicate figures and tables